THE TIRE PAVEMENT INTERFACE

A symposium sponsored by
ASTM Committees E-17 on
Traveled Surface Characteristics
and F-9 on Tires
Columbus, OH, 5–6 June 1985

ASTM SPECIAL TECHNICAL PUBLICATION 929
Marion G. Pottinger, The BFGoodrich Co.,
and Thomas J. Yager, NASA Langley Research
Center, Editors

ASTM Publication Code Number (PCN)
04-929000-27

 1916 Race Street, Philadelphia, PA 19103

Library of Congress Cataloging-in-Publication Data

The Tire pavement interface.

(ASTM special technical publication; 929)
Includes bibliographies and index.
"ASTM publication code number (PCN) 04-929000-27."
1. Tires, Rubber—Traction. 2. Automobiles—
Skidding. 3. Pavements—Skid resistance. I. Pottinger,
Marion G. II. Yager, Thomas J. III. ASTM Committee E-17
on Traveled Surface Characteristics. IV. ASTM
Committee F-9 on Tires. V. Series.
TL295.T57 1986 629.2′482 86-20565
ISBN 0-8031-0497-9

NOTE

The Society is not responsible, as a body,
for the statements and opinions
advanced in this publication.

Printed in Baltimore, MD
1986

£ 50.00

is

2

1

38

Foreword

The symposium, Where Performance Begins: The Tire Pavement Interface, was presented at Columbus, OH, 5–6 June 1985. The symposium was sponsored by Committees E-17 on Traveled Surface Characteristics and F-9 on Tires. Marion G. Pottinger, The BFGoodrich Co., and Thomas J. Yager, NASA Langley Research Center, served as chairmen of the symposium and are editors of the resulting publication.

Related
ASTM Publications

Frictional Interaction of Tire and Pavement, STP 793 (1983), 04-793000-37

Pavement Surface Characteristics and Materials, STP 763 (1982),
04-763000-47

Applied Surface Analysis, STP 699 (1980), 04-699000-39

Tire Reinforcement and Tire Performance, STP 694 (1980), 04-694000-37

Rubber and Related Products: New Methods for Testing and Analyzing,
STP 553 (1974), 04-553000-20

A Note of Appreciation
to Reviewers

The quality of the papers that appear in this publication reflects not only the obvious efforts of the authors but also the unheralded, though essential, work of the reviewers. On behalf of ASTM we acknowledge with appreciation their dedication to high professional standards and their sacrifice of time and effort.

ASTM Committee on Publications

ASTM Editorial Staff

Contents

Overview

Conditions at the tire pavement interface help to prescribe solutions to one of the most economically important sets of boundary value problems in the world. Quite literally the whole modern world turns on this boundary. This boundary is fundamental to current land and air transportation.

The fundamental importance of the tire pavement interface is illustrated by the interest it holds for many groups: highway engineers, tire engineers, automotive engineers, environmentalists, politicians, and so forth. Unfortunately, in this age of specialization each group tends to talk only to itself, thus, reinforcing parochial viewpoints and often preventing synergistic solutions to transportation problems.

The current situation cries out for a systems approach integrating the interests and insights of all groups. The synergism that would occur might produce an improved transportation system at no increase in total cost. Certainly, more creative ideas would be produced.

Based on their belief that better inter-group communication is a necessity to produce a systems approach to tire dependent transportation, the symposium organizers formulated two goals:

1. The papers had to represent many views of various tire pavement interface associated transportation problems.

2. There had to be a balance of both review and research papers so that the needs of both new and experienced workers would be met.

The symposium papers on traction, wear, interfacial mechanics, and tire pavement interaction generated noise and vibration will be discussed in an integrated fashion.

Technical Basics

The tire pavement interface is a variable boundary in which energy is changed from one form to another in response to the kinematics of rolling contact between a flexible thick shell (the tire) and a semi-rigid structure (the pavement). Both the tire and the pavement have surfaces with significant texture. The relationship between the tire and the pavement is directly dependent on the motions of the vehicle on which the tire is mounted and on the demands of the vehicle operator. With all feedbacks considered, this is a very complex dynamic problem, which is also affected by weather, surface chemistry, economics, and a host of other factors.

Texture is a key feature of the tire pavement interface. It influences almost every performance problem.

The pavement has texture of importance to tire pavement interactions covering wavelengths from 10 m to 0.01 mm. The tire has tread pattern (texture) with wavelengths from 2 m to 1 mm. In addition internal irregularities introduced into the tire by manufacturing imprecision (nonuniformities) can make a tire act as if it had an additional texture in the 2 m to 1 mm range.

The textural wavelengths between 10 m and 10 mm contribute to noise and vibration problems as reported by Pottinger [1]. The longer wavelengths can contribute to vehicle control problems if their amplitudes are large enough to generate vibration induced changes in vehicle control forces.

The tread and pavement surface wavelengths between 40 and 1 mm are primary contributors to the drainage of water out of the tire pavement interface. As Henry [2] observes, these wavelengths (macrotexture) are crucial to the design of pavements with good wet traction characteristics.

Veith [3] states that the wavelengths below 1 mm, and particularly those below 0.1 mm (microtexture), are crucial to friction and wear. It is friction that makes the use of tires practical since the tires generate the vehicle control forces from frictional shear stresses induced by the tire's unique kinematic interactions with the pavement. Neglecting lubrication and contamination, friction arises from adhesion to, deformation of, and abrasion of the tire tread compound by the pavement. During this process, viscoelastic behavior of the tread compound excited by the pavement microtexture plays a dominant role [3].

Traction

Traction is the term used to describe the practical generation of vehicle control forces from tire pavement interfacial friction. Traction considers the tire, the pavement, lubrication, contaminants, weather effects, and vehicle control demands.

In this STP the traction papers deal primarily with assessing the traction characteristics of pavements based on standardized tests performed with standard tires, time/seasonal stability of pavement performance, the effect of rubber contamination of the pavement surface on pavement performance, and the effect of footprint shape on hydroplaning velocity. Wet traction was emphasized because of its great importance to safety. About 14% of all fatal automobile accidents occur when roads are wet [2], which is only about 3% of the time.

The three papers directed at assessing pavement effects on available wet traction [2,4,5] conclude that there is a necessity for characterizing both macrotexture and microtexture in order to properly describe a pavement.

The need to characterize both textures in order to properly study wet traction is easily understood in light of Moore's wet traction model [6], which is discussed by Lenke and Graul [5]. In this model the tire pavement interface is divided into three zones. From front to rear of the interface these zones are a sinkage zone where the water drains out from under the tire, a draping (squeeze film) zone where the tire drapes over the major asperities and the minor asperities penetrate the remaining thin film, and a contact zone in which more or less normal dry road contact occurs.

The size of the sinkage zone depends on vehicle speed, tire inflation pressure, and interfacial drainage characteristics. If this zone grows to encompass the whole tire pavement interface zone, the tire hydroplanes and generates no control forces. From the pavement viewpoint macrotexture or grooving is the source of interfacial drainage. Thus, maintaining adequate macrotexture augmented with grooving in crucial locations is the first step in providing a pavement with good traction characteristics. However, when adding macrotexture, tire pavement generated noise and vibration must be kept in mind [1]. If the macrotexture becomes excessive, inordinate noise and vibration will occur in both the vehicle and environment. This is the highway engineers' problem. The tire and vehicle design engineers can not eliminate this noise. Also, longitudinal grooving causes a vibration problem known as "L. A. Wiggle" [1]. This is a tire pavement interaction problem that can be easily solved as long as the tire and highway engineers communicate.

Recognizing that high speeds and low tire tread depths are associated with skidding accidents, the highway community is using the smooth treaded tire as in ASTM Specification for Smooth Tread Standard Tire for Special-Purpose Pavement Skid Resistance Tests (E 524) smooth tire more and more in skid testing [2,4,7]. The ASTM E 524 tire represents the worst case; all the interfacial drainage is due to pavement macrotexture.

By way of contrast, SN_{40}, measured using the ribbed tire as in ASTM Specification for Standard Tire for Pavement Resistance Tests (E 501) is a poor predictor of wet skidding accidents [2]. This is because the E 501 tire provides significant interfacial drainage caused by its grooves. An illustration of this is the fact that the traction of a surface measured with the E 501 tire is almost the same before and after longitudinal grooving, a modification that greatly improves wet traction as measured by the reduction in wet skidding accidents [4].

Based on the work of Horne et al. [7], the measure of skid resistance offered by the E 524 tire might be further improved by testing at light loads. They showed that footprint shape is a very important factor in hydroplaning. A broad, short footprint is adverse. Their work was specifically directed at understanding the source of wet pavement jackknifing accidents occurring with lightly loaded tractor trailers. Horne et al. have also shown that worn truck tires (low tread depth) can hydroplane in spite of high inflation pressures when tire loads are light (the tire footprint is broad and short).

The discussion thus far has centered on the sinkage zone and ways to assure that it is kept small through provision of proper interfacial drainage. This has clarified the importance of macrotexture.

In the remainder of the footprint, the draping and contact zones, microtexture is of paramount importance. In the draping zone the microtexture provides the high local pressures necessary to penetrate the remaining thin water film, thus beginning the development of frictional contact. In the contact zone microtexture excites the tread compound to generate frictional forces as previously discussed. Again, compromise is required because wear is also a function of microtexture [3].

Unfortunately, obtaining good macrotexture and microtexture in a new highway does not insure good traction throughout the life of the pavement. Pavement skid resistance changes with time [2,3,4,8]. Whitehurst and Neuhardt [8] present a comprehensive study of seasonal skid resistance variation for the reference surfaces at the Eastern Field Test Center located at the Ohio Transportation Research Center. These specially constructed surfaces have never been subjected to routine traffic. Yet their skid resistance varies with time in a seasonal manner. This proves that weathering changes pavement skid resistance.

Whitehurst and Neuhardt consider two pavements, PRS1 and PRS2, that can shed light on how to provide longer lasting skid resistance, a major concern of Wambold et al. [4]. PRS1 has exhibited long-term stability with only seasonal variation present. PRS4 has shown both a long-term decrease in skid resistance and a seasonal variation similar in magnitude to the seasonal variation shown by PRS1. The difference between the surfaces is that PRS1 was built of aggregates that do not polish easily and then given a tough, durable epoxy seal coat, which has kept the aggregate in place.

In the whole traction discussion macrotexture and microtexture have been central pavement features. They are crucial. But Lenke and Graul [5], who were concerned with the problem of deciding when to remove rubber buildup from runways in order to improve traction, made an important observation. Using current technology, skid resistance cannot be predicted well enough from texture measurements to eliminate the need for traction tests. There is an obvious need for research to make this prediction accurate enough that optical texture measurements like those mentioned by Wambold et al. can be fully utilized.

Wambold et al. raise a point that is a fitting conclusion to the discussion of traction. The wet skid resistance of accident sites is not different from the wet skid resistance of nearby control sites. They suggest that future research should concentrate on reliably identifying hazardous sites. Since this is the case, plainly more than the pavement skid resistance is involved in making a site hazardous. Can the difference between sites, which cannot be explained by skid resistance, be explained by a difference in traction demand caused by differences in road topography at each site? Could inclusion of vehicle dynamics in a systems approach to traction point out the relative risk at different locations with similar pavement skid numbers?

Wear

Pavement microtexture was just discussed as the pavement initiator of hysteretic and abrasive friction. Microtexture is the predominate pavement influence on tire wear. The symposium papers provide: a review of tire wear from a materials point of view [3], a look at typical stresses at the tire pavement interface [9,10], and an example application of interfacial stresses to the study of uneven tire wear [11]. The papers do not provide a general review of tire footprint mechanics, tire wear testing problems, vehicle influences on wear, or tire structural design effects.

Veith [3] begins his discussion of tire tread compound influences on wear by pointing out that the relationship among the wear rates of various tread compounds depends on pavement surface texture, traction demand (test severity), and how various tread materials interact with roadway materials. Indeed, abrasion is a three body system in which the road surface, road silt, and other contaminants, and the tread compound interact.

Tensile-tear rupture, fatigue, and chemical degradation of the tread compound all play significant parts in tread wear. Veith discusses all of these factors along with the characteristic chemical structure of the tread compound. Included in his discussion are the effect of polymer glass transition temperature, the nature of the reinforcement system (carbon black, and so forth), and the importance of ample amounts of anti-oxidants.

The influence of the factors Veith discusses combined with the nonconstant nature of the road surface [8] can produce great confusion for those testing tire tread wear. For example, it is not possible to study temperature effects using convoy tests without directly measuring microtexture since microtexture is seasonally variable [3,8].

The nonstationary character of the real world has also prevented laboratory abraders (devices for artifically determining the wear resistance of tread compounds) from achieving acceptable correlations to actual tire wear. However, laboratory abrasion experiments can provide a great deal of insight into wear mechanisms.

The kinematics of the rolling tire (a thick shell) on the pavement (a textured, semi-rigid half-space) produces complex three-dimensional stress distributions between the tire and the pavement. These stresses are associated with the abrasion that occurs in the tire pavement interface and can be used in the study of tire tread wear.

The interfacial stresses discussed in this STP were measured with three-dimensional force transducers (load pins) covered with a microtexture of the experimenter's choice [9–11]. For example, Lippmann [9] uses a square tipped transducer with a 5- by 5-mm tip coated with 80 grit abrasive paper.

Lippmann applied his transducer in slow rolling experiments with radial tires. Based on the results, he points out many of the general characteristics of the stress field between the tire and the road for an uncambered tire rolling straight ahead. A careful study of Lippmann's data will produce a good general understanding of the tire pavement interfacial stress field for the experimental conditions used. In examining this data set the reader should keep one point in mind. The shoulder lateral stress distribution discussed in this paper is not universally correct. Depending on tire design factors, the highest lateral and normal stresses may appear at the outside edge of the shoulder rib not at the inside as is the case in Lippmann's paper.

Howell and Perez [10] provide data on aircraft tire footprint forces. These data augment Lippmann's data and are a rare example of footprint force data for an aircraft tire.

Shepherd [11] applies footprint stress measurement to the study of diagonal wear, a particular form of uneven wear. He shows that uneven wear is a true systems problem by demonstrating the effects of small slip and camber angles that originate from suspension alignment. Even when various camber angles, slip angles, and combinations of the two lead to identical footprint shapes the resultant interfacial stresses differ because the combination of mechanisms differs for each slip and camber angle combination. In order to reach definite conclusions about wear Shepherd proposes a wear model denominated in terms of footprint stresses. This is a crucial step in using footprint stress data to study wear. Production of a confirmed and accurate wear model would be of great value to tire engineers.

The direction of the diagonals, high and low areas on the tread developed when diagonal wear occurs, is dependent on the sense of slip angle induced by a particular combination of rotation sense (left or right side of the car) and toe-in. Shepherd demonstrates that vibration of the tire/vehicle system plays a part in the repetition of diagonal wear around the tire. Thus, wear has a relation to tire pavement interaction noise, the final topic in this STP.

Noise and Vibration

Tire pavement interaction generated noise and vibration can originate from pavement texture, tire surface texture (tread pattern), or variations built into the tires. Pottinger et al. [1] provide an extensive review covering the effects of long wavelength pavement texture and macrotexture, tire uniformity, tire dynamics, vehicle dynamic response, human response, and five systems examples for in-the-vehicle noise and vibration. This paper does not cover moving load generated vibrations, environmental interactions, cargo damage, pavement fatigue, vehicle structural fatigue, or feedback paths external to the tire/vehicle system. The authors make the point that the system is paramountly important and should be taken into account by those working on ride and noise

McQuirt and Spangler [12] did extensive work on determination of pavement condition with respect to ride. They correlated jury ride opinions to Mays ride meter results and inertial profilometer results to jury opinions as to the need for nonroutine highway maintenance. The correlation of the Mays meter results with jury ratings varied with pavement type. The correlation of the inertial profilometer results with jury ratings of the need for nonroutine highway maintenance (re-surfacing) varied with road classification. These results are indicative of the variation in types of annoyance rated on different types of pavements, and the fact that human expectations vary in a complex way. This is in agreement with the information summarized in Pottinger et al. The inertial profilometer provides an excellent tool for deciding when nonroutine highway maintenance is required to improve ride.

Concluding Remarks

This STP provides a good general starting place for those interested in traction, wear, and tire pavement generated noise and vibration. Its particular strengths are diversity and a systems emphasis. It would be desirable to organize a follow-up symposium broadened to include the full systems concept envisioned in the beginning of this overview.

References

[1] Pottinger, M. G., Marshall, K. D., Lawther, J. M., and Thrasher, D. B., in *The Tire Pavement Interface, STP 929,* American Society for Testing and Materials, 1986.
[2] Henry, J. J. in *The Tire Pavement Interface, STP 929,* American Society for Testing and Materials, 1986.
[3] Veith, A. G., *The Tire Pavement Interface, STP 929,* American Society for Testing and Materials, 1986.
[4] Wambold, J. C., Henry, J. J., and Hegmon, R. R. in *The Tire Pavement Interface, STP 929,* American Society for Testing Materials, 1986.
[5] Lenke, L. R. and Graul, R. A. in *The Tire Pavement Interface, STP 929,* American Society for Testing and Materials, 1986.
[6] Moore, D. F., "Prediction of Skid-Resistance Gradient and Drainage Characteristics for Pavements," Highway Research Record 131, Highway Research Board, Washington, DC, 1966, pp. 181–203.
[7] Horne, W. B., Yager, T. J., and Ivey, D. L. in *The Tire Pavement Interface, STP 929,* American Society for Testing and Materials, 1986.
[8] Whitehurst, E. A. and Neuhardt, J. B. in *The Tire Pavement Interface, STP 929,* American Society for Testing and Materials, 1986.
[9] Lippmann, S. A. in *The Tire Pavement Interface, STP 929,* American Society for Testing and Materials, 1986.
[10] Howell, W. E. and Perez, S. E. in *The Tire Pavement Interface, STP 929,* American Society for Testing and Materials, 1986.
[11] Shepherd, W. K. in *The Tire Pavement Interface, STP 929,* American Society for Testing and Materials, 1986.
[12] McQuirt, J. E. and Spangler, E. B. in *The Tire Pavement Interface, STP 929,* American Society for Testing and Materials, 1986.

Marion G. Pottinger

BFGoodrich R&D Center, Brecksville, OH 44141; symposium cochairman and coeditor.

Thomas J. Yager

NASA Langley Research Center, Hampton, VA 23665; symposium cochairman and co-editor.

The Traction Connection

John J. Henry[1]

Tire Wet-Pavement Traction Measurement: A State-of-the-Art Review

REFERENCE: Henry, J. J., **"Tire Wet-Pavement Traction Measurement: A-State-of-the-Art Review,"** *The Tire Pavement Interface, ASTM STP 929,* M. G. Pottinger and T. J. Yager, Eds., American Society for Testing and Materials, Philadelphia, 1986, pp. 3–25.

ABSTRACT: In this paper, methods currently in use to measure tire-pavement friction are reviewed. The emphasis is on full-scale measurement systems operated at highway speeds, including systems that measure brake force coefficients (under slip or locked-wheel conditions or both) and side-force coefficients. A comparison is made of the data and information produced by each of these measurement methods. Attempts to relate the data produced by each of these methods are reviewed, and the reasons for their lack of agreement are discussed. In addition to direct traction measurement methods, texture measurements are discussed, and the reliability of texture-friction relationships is reviewed. The influence of texture on each of the full-scale measurement methods is investigated as a means of explaining the lack of agreement of the data produced by these methods.

Tire-pavement traction measurements are used for evaluating pavement safety and for predicting vehicle performance. The procedures for characterizing tire-pavement friction for these two applications usually differ. In the United States, pavements are monitored in annual inventories by a single measurement of skid resistance at a single speed with a standard ribbed test tire. Additional tests at multiple speeds or tests with a blank test tire or both may be conducted at accident sites. In some European countries, side-force coefficients or slip tests, both of which have the advantage of providing continuous measurements, are used to monitor pavement networks. These measurements are generally used in conjunction with a minimum texture depth requirement. A comparison of these approaches with U.S. practice is discussed. In conclusion, the status of consensus standards within ASTM and the International Standards Organization (ISO) is summarized, and recommendations are made for future standards development.

KEY WORDS: tires, pavements, traction, standards

[1]Professor of mechanical engineering and director of the Pennsylvania Transportation Institute, Pennsylvania State University, University Park, PA 16802.

Nomenclature

α	Yaw angle
BPN	British pendulum number
BSN	Brake slip number
F	Friction force
F_s	Side force
MTD	Sand-patch mean texture depth
N	Normal (vertical) load
ω	Angular velocity
PNG	Percent normalized gradient
r	Effective rolling radius
R	Correlation coefficient
rms_{MA}	Root mean square of macrotexture profile
rms_{MI}	Root mean square of microtexture profile
SFC	Side-force coefficient
SN_0	Zero speed skid number intercept
SN_V	Locked-wheel skid number at velocity V
SNG_V	Skid number-speed gradient at velocity V
V	Test speed (velocity)

Introduction

The ability of a tire-pavement combination to provide adequate traction on wet roads is directly related to the safe operation of vehicles by providing shorter braking distances and good road-holding characteristics on curves. The importance of wet-pavement traction to safety is highlighted by the findings of the National Transportation Safety Board, which reported that 13.5% of all fatal accidents in 1976 and 1977 occurred on wet pavements, while the pavements were exposed to precipitation less than 3 to 3.5% of the time [1]. As a result of this observation, research is currently being conducted to develop models to predict, from weather records, the percentage of time that a particular pavement will be wet. Tire wet-pavement traction depends on many factors, which can be assigned to three categories: those related to the tire (rubber compound, tread design and condition, inflation pressure, and operating temperature); those related to the pavement (pavement type, microtexture and macrotexture, and surface temperature), and those related to the substance that interferes with the direct contact between the tire and pavement (the quantity of water and the presence of loose particulate matter and oil contaminants). These interactions are not completely understood, and therefore an empirical approach is required.

The determination of wet-pavement traction is of interest both to members of the highway maintenance community and to proving-ground operators. The former are primarily concerned with obtaining reliable data on the highway systems under their jurisdiction, in order to make rational decisions regarding resurfacing for safety. Proving-ground operations are used to compare tire performance, brake performance, and vehicle handling, and therefore the levels of traction must not vary during the test programs.

When a standard tire and standard test conditions are utilized in a measurement of wet-pavement traction, the results are reported as the skid resistance of the pavement. Skid resistance is therefore a pavement characteristic and is a function of the surface properties, but it may be modified by the presence of contaminants. It is well known that skid resistance is a rather irregular function of time and is difficult to predict at any time other than the time at which it is measured [2].

Systems for measuring skid resistance vary widely but can be classified by three methods:

(1) the locked-wheel method, producing a skid number (SN) as a function of test speed;

(2) the slip method, producing brake slip numbers (BSN) as a function of percent slip and test speed; and

(3) the side-force method, producing side-force coefficients (SFC) as a function of yaw angle and test speed.

Standard test procedures for these methods have been developed, and all are in current use. For wet-pavement traction evaluation, these procedures have supplanted braked-vehicle tests, such as the American Society of Mechanical Engineers (ASME) Stopping Distance Test (E 445) and ASTM Method for Measurement of Skid Resistance on Paved Surfaces Using a Passenger Vehicle Diagonal Braking Technique (E 503) [3]. Although standard procedures for these braked-vehicle methods exist, they are not commonly used for highway evaluation because of the potential interference with traffic and the difficulties of maintaining constant, repeatable, test-vehicle characteristics. The diagonal braking test has seen limited use on runways but has been replaced by slip tests for runway friction. For these reasons, only the three methods, locked-wheel, slip, and side-force, will be discussed below.

Laboratory methods for predicting full-scale friction include low-speed friction methods and surface texture measurements. These procedures can be useful in determining material characteristics and in improving the understanding of the effects of texture on pavement friction. Measurement of surface macrotexture at traffic speeds is now possible [4], and as the equipment becomes available, field texture data will be available to supplement skid-resistance data. It is generally agreed that a single number cannot adequately describe wet-pavement traction, and measurements over a range of test parameters, such as test speed, can provide more significant information than can a friction level at one test speed. While testing at several speeds can be used for proving-ground characterization, it is not practical for the large-scale surveys of a state highway system. Therefore, methods for directly or indirectly measuring pavement texture at the same time that a skid-resistance measurement is made are currently receiving attention, and their use should be encouraged.

Current Methods for Evaluating Wet-Pavement Traction

Table 1 summarizes the current practices in skid-resistance measurement. The information presented in Table 1, which was adapted from a 1981 survey in Ref 5, has been updated and augmented by the author.

TABLE 1—*Skid-resistance measurement systems.*

Locked-Wheel Methods	Test Tire	Water Depth (nominal), mm	Country
Skid resistance trailer (ASTM E 274)	ribbed (ASTM E 501) blank (ASTM E 524)	0.5	United States, Canada, Taiwan
Stuttgarter Reibungsmesser SRM	Phoenix P3 (patterned)	1	Federal Republic of Germany
Remorque de glissance LPC	165-R15 (smooth)	1	France
Skiddometer BV 8	165-R15 (ribbed)	0.5	Switzerland
Cobirt trailer	. . .	. . .	Poland
Kotuki	AICPR (PIARC) 165-R15	. . .	Hungary

Slip Methods	% Slip	Test Tire	Water Depth, mm	Country
Skiddometer BV 11	15	VTI 4.00-8	0.5	Sweden
Skiddometer BV 12	0 to 50	passenger car type	0.5	Sweden (VTI)
Saab Friction Tester (RST)	15	VTI 4.00-8	0.5	Sweden
K. J. Law, Inc.	. . .	under development	. . .	United States
RED Trailer	86	165-R15 (smooth)	0.5	Netherlands

Side Force Methods	Low Angle, degrees	Test Tire	Water Depth (nominal), mm	Country
Side-force coefficient road inventory machine (SCRIM)	20	3.00–20 (smooth)	0.5 to 1	United Kingdom, Australia, Belgium, France, Ireland, Italy, Spain
Mu meter	7.5	special	external	United Kingdom, United States, (FAA), Norway

TABLE 1—*Continued.*

Locked-Wheel Methods		Test Tire	Water Depth (nominal), mm	Country
Stradograph	12	PIARC 165–R15 (smooth)	0.2	Denmark
Finnish	8	Nokia 165 SR15 (smooth)	1.1	Finland

Multifunction Systems	Methods	Country
Stradograph	locked-wheel, slip (0 to 15%), side force (0 to 15°), locked-wheel side force	Belgium, France
Penn State road friction tester	locked-wheel, transient slip (0 to 100%), side force (0 to 12°), locked-wheel side force	United States (Penn State)
Mobile tire traction dynamometer (MTTD)	locked wheel, slip (0 to 100%), side force (0 to 25°)	United States (U.S. DOT)
Skid resistance measuring machine	locked-wheel, slip (0 to 100%), side force (0 to 45°)	Japan
Skiddometer BV 8	locked-wheel, slip (14%)	Switzerland

Locked-Wheel Methods

The locked-wheel methods provide a coefficient of friction for a standard set of test conditions, which is reported either as a coefficient or as a skid number

$$SN_V = F/N \ 100 \qquad (1)$$

where

F = friction force,
N = normal (vertical) load on the test tire, and
V = test speed.

The locked-wheel method for measuring skid resistance is the predominant method used in the United States. ASTM Test Method for Skid Resistance of Paved Surfaces Using a Full-Scale Tire (E 274) [3] and ASTM Method for Testing Tires for Wet Traction in Straight Ahead Braking, Using a Towed Trailer (F 408) [6] are used by the highway community and the tire industry, respectively. The simplicity of the locked-wheel method and the ability to clearly define and control most of the operational variables of the test are clear advantages of the method. The most widely used procedure for pavement evaluation in the United States utilizes the ribbed test tire in accordance with ASTM Specification for Standard Tire for Pavement Skid Resistance

Tests (E 501), with the ASTM E 274 test method, to characterize the pavement by a measurement reported as the skid number at 64 km/h (40 mph) (SN_{40}). The reported skid number is the average of five locked-wheel tests performed along a "uniform" test section. Tests performed in this manner produce a standard deviation of about 2 SN, because of pavement and instrumentation variability. On highways, a significant variation of skid number occurs across the pavement, with the wheel tracks of a worn pavement exhibiting skid-resistance levels as much as 20 skid numbers lower than the skid numbers outside the wheel tracks. In some cases, for example, at proving-ground test pads and accident sites, repeated tests are made at the same location, with the result that the standard deviation is usually reduced to about one skid number since the effects of longitudinal variations in friction are eliminated. In addition, there is usually little variation in proving-ground surfaces across a test section, and lateral placement errors also are less important there.

A significant disadvantage of the locked-wheel method for pavement evaluation is that is does not provide a continuous measurement. When the test wheel is intermittently locked for measurement, low friction areas may be overlooked. There are other disadvantages, however. In some cases the test speed must be reduced; for example, for low radius of curvature, T-intersections, and congested traffic areas. In order to compare these surfaces with tangent surfaces, a correction for speed must be applied. To correct for speed, additional measurements are needed, such as texture, or the test must be performed at several speeds to establish the speed dependence of the friction measurement.

Perhaps the most distressing disadvantage of locked-wheel data, as they are presently being obtained, is that they fail to relate to wet-weather accident data, as demonstrated in Fig. 1 [7]. The poor ability of locked-wheel skid number (SN_{40}) to "predict" accident sites is evidence that the single parameter is not, by itself, a sufficient descriptor of pavement friction for safety purposes. To describe pavements better, the skid number speed gradient (SNG) can be used

$$SNG_V = -\frac{d(SN)}{dV} \tag{2}$$

where

$$V = \text{test speed,}$$
$$SNG_V = \text{skid number speed gradient at speed } V, \text{ and}$$
$$SN = \text{skid number (a function of } V).$$

The percent normalized gradient (PNG) is also used to characterize the speed dependence of the skid number

$$PNG = (SNG_V/SN_V)\,100 = -(100/SN_V)\,(d(SN)/dV) \tag{3}$$

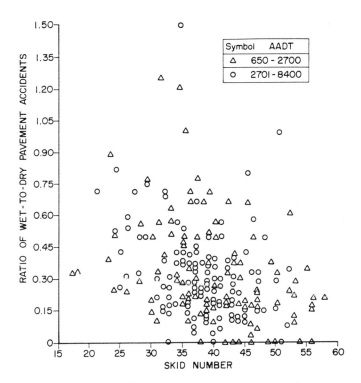

FIG. 1—*Ratio of wet-to-dry pavement accidents versus skid number for a three-year period in Kentucky* [7].

It has been found that PNG is independent of speed [8]. While these parameters, together with the skid number, can be determined by locked-wheel measurements at various speeds, their determination requires that multiple tests be performed at several speeds at each test site. Speed gradient tests have not been implemented on a large scale in pavement surveys, although they are practical for characterizing the friction of proving-ground test pads.

One objection to the locked-wheel method, when the ribbed ASTM E 501 test tire is used, is that the test tire ribs permit water to escape from the interface, even when there is little pavement macrotexture [1].[2] The practice in the Federal Republic of Germany is to use a treaded tire, but with twice as much water (1-mm nominal water depth) delivered to the interface. The procedure with the French LPC uses a smooth-treaded radial test tire, also with 1-mm nominal water depth. The use of the ASTM Specification for Smooth Tread Standard Tire for Special-Purpose Pavement Skid Resistance Tests (E 524) smooth-treaded (blank) tire with the ASTM E 274 test procedure is gaining

[2]Wambold, J. C., Henry, J. J., and Hegmon, R. R., "Skid Resistance of Wet-Weather Accident Sites," in this publication, pp. 4–60.

popularity in the United States, and several states are using the blank-tire skid number (SN_{40}^B) as the preferred measurement for accident studies.

Slip Methods

Slip methods produce brake slip numbers, defined as

$$\text{BSN } (V, \% \text{ slip}) = (F/N) \, 100 \tag{4}$$

where

V = test speed,
F = friction force, and
N = normal (vertical) load on the test tire.

and

$$\% \text{ slip} = [(V - r\omega)/V] \, 100 \tag{4a}$$

where

V = test speed,
r = effective rolling radius of the tire, and
ω = angular velocity of the tire.

Constant-slip devices have the advantage that they can be operated continuously without creating flat spots on the tire. From Table 1, it can be seen that, except for the RED trailer used in the Netherlands and the Skiddometer BV 12 used in Sweden primarily for research, low values of slip from 12 to 15% are preferred. These low levels of slip provide lower test tire wear, while still being above the critical slip value, which corresponds to the peak slide friction. Below the critical slip value, the brake slip number (BSN) increases rapidly with increasing slip, and in this region is subject to significant variability. A practical limitation to continuous operation is the consumption of water, since most systems provide nominal water film thicknesses equivalent to those used in the locked-wheel test (0.5 mm). However, in these devices the test tires are usually narrower, and, therefore, less total water flow is required.

Slip tests, in which the friction forces are recorded during the brake application, from the free-rolling condition to the locked-wheel condition, are used in two ways. The peak friction force during lockup divided by the vertical load on the test tire provides the peak braking force coefficient. The peak braking force coefficient is highly dependent upon the tire characteristics and is therefore useful for evaluating tires and for determining the performance of anti-lock brake systems. The friction force can be measured as the rotational speed of the tire is reduced to zero. It is then evaluated at various levels of slip to provide a brake slip number for those levels of slip. The Penn State Road friction tester is routinely used in this mode with the friction force being evaluated at 25, 50, 75, and 100% (locked-wheel) slip levels.

Side-Force Methods

The side-force coefficient is the ratio of the force perpendicular to the plane of the rotating tire to the vertical load on the tire when the plane of the tire is maintained at a fixed angle with respect to the forward velocity vector

$$SFC(V,\alpha) = (F_s/N)\,100 \tag{5}$$

where

V = test speed,
α = angle between the plane of the tire and the forward velocity vector (yaw angle),
N = normal (vertical) load on the test tire, and
F_s = force perpendicular to the plane of the test tire.

Some systems are capable of operating in a combined slip and side-force mode, but these measurements are usually conducted for research purposes only.

The two most popular side-force measurement systems are the Side-Force Coefficient Road Inventory Machine (SCRIM) and the Mu Meter, both originating in England. Although the Mu Meter has been used for pavement evaluation, most highway agencies have abandoned it, because it was developed for runway friction determination and is inappropriate for highways. Its two test tires are operated at 7.5° yaw angle, with a track width of 1 m (3 ft), so that if one tire operates in the wheel track, the other necessarily be out of the wheel track. It is, however, useful for surveying the friction of airport runways.

The SCRIM was developed for highway evaluation and has achieved popularity in Europe and the British Commonwealth of Nations. Its ability to perform continuous measurements with a narrow (3.00-20) test tire, which requires relatively low water flow, is a particularly attractive feature.

Correlation of Skid-Resistance Data

Although the force transducer and other instrumentation on a friction tester can be calibrated, there is no standard reference surface with which to conduct a system calibration. For this reason, correlation studies of friction testers have been conducted periodically. In 1962, a correlation of locked-wheel testers was conducted at Tappahannock. The results of this study emphasized the need for more rigorous standardization of the systems and test procedures. ASTM Committee E-17 on Traveled Surface Characteristics, founded two years before that study, had already begun the process of standardization. In 1970, a correlation held at The Pennsylvania State University applied the findings of the National Cooperative Highway Research Program (NCHRP) Project 1-12 [2] to improve the correlation between locked-wheel friction testers [9]. These procedures were implemented by the Federal Highway Administration in the establishment, in 1973, of the Central Field Test Center at the Texas Transportation Institute and the Eastern Field Test Center at the Transportation Research Center in Ohio. These centers continue to provide correlation to a reference measurement system for state highway departments on a regular basis. After proper servicing and component calibration, a high degree of correlation can be obtained between a client's locked-wheel friction tester and the reference system.

Correlation between systems using different test methods has also been attempted. In these cases, the correlations are not as reliable as when two systems using the same method are compared. As will be discussed below, the different methods respond differently to different pavement characteristics, and, while good correlation may be exhibited if the testers are operated over a narrow range of pavement types, caution must be exercised in generalizing the results. Excellent correlation was reported in a study in Arizona [10], in which the Mu Meter was compared with two locked-wheel systems and a stopping-distance car (Table 2). The data for the 29 surfaces used in that study were not reported nor were texture measurements made. An attempt to correlate the Norwegian Mu Meter and the BV 11 and Saab RST testers in 1981, in Sweden, was relatively unsuccessful [11]. These tests were performed over 19 surfaces having a very wide range of macrotexture, from a 0.22- to 1.74-mm sand-patch mean texture depth. The results are presented in Table 2 and shown in Figs. 2 and 3.

The Swedish study also included two side-force coefficient systems (the Danish version of the Stradograph and the Finnish side-force coefficient sys-

TABLE 2—*Correlation of mu meter data with other pavement friction testers.*

System	Equation	Correlation Coefficient R	Reference
New Mexico (locked wheel)	$Mu_{40} = 1.21 \, SN_{40} - 14.9$	0.99	*10*
California (locked wheel)	$Mu_{40} = 2.14 \, SN_{40} - 17.8$	0.92	*10*
Arizona stopping distance car	$Mu_{40} = 22.5 + 1.48 \, SDN$	0.98	*10*
BV 11 (50 km/h)	$Mu_{30} = 66.5 + 0.143 \, BSN$	0.36	*11*
SAAB RST (50 km/h)	$Mu_{30} = 52.8 + 0.309 \, BSN$	0.35	*11*
SAAB RST (70 km/h)	$Mu_{40} = 72.7 + 0.039 \, BSN$	0.05	*11*

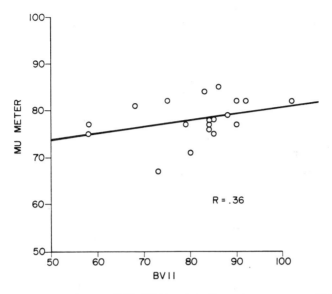

FIG. 2—*Correlation between VTI's BV 11 and the Norwegian mu meter at 50 km/h.*

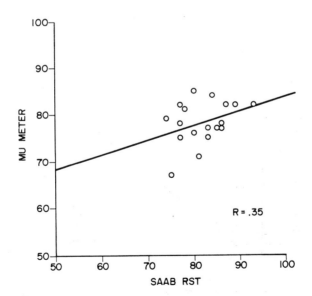

FIG. 3—*Correlation between the Norwegian mu meter and the SAAB RST at 50 km/h.*

tem). These were tested over the same 19 sites, and the results of the correlations with the BV 11 are reported in Table 3 and shown in Figs. 4 and 5.

In a German study, the Stuttgarter Reibungsmesser (SRM) locked-wheel system and the Swiss Skiddometer BV 8, operated in the locked mode, were compared with the SCRIM at 20° yaw [5]. Twenty-four sites were tested at four speeds. The results of the tests at 80 km/h are shown in Table 4 and in Figs. 6 and 7. The results of these correlations were very good.

It would be expected that measurements made by each of the three methods for measuring friction between a wet pavement and a test tire would be affected differently by various levels of pavement texture. The failure to achieve a high degree of correlation between test data for methods measured over a set of surfaces with a wide range of texture, as in the Swedish study, is not surprising.

TABLE 3—*Correlation coefficients R of the BV 11 with the Danish stradograph and the Finnish system.*

Test Speed, km/h	Danish Stradograph, 12° yaw	Finnish System, 8° yaw
20	0.61	0.38
50	0.49	0.56
70	0.81	0.76

SOURCE: Ref *11*.

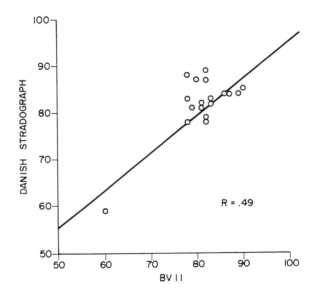

FIG. 4—*Correlation between the Danish stradograph and the BV 11 at 50 km/h.*

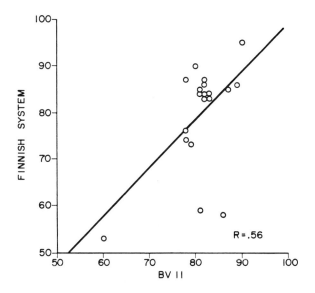

FIG. 5—*Correlation between the Finnish system and the BV 11 at 50 km/h.*

TABLE 4—*Correlation results for the SCRIM with the SRM and Skiddometer BV 8 (test speed = 80 km/h).*

System	Equation	Correlation Coefficient, R
Stuttgarter Reibungsmesser	$SFC(20°) = 0.388\ SN^{1.425}$	0.93
Skiddometer BV 8	$SFC(20°) = 1.52\ SN - 1.40$	. . .

SOURCE: Ref 5.

Brake Slip Numbers and Locked-Wheel Skid Numbers

An expression for the locked-wheel friction as a function of speed can be derived from the observation that the percent normalized gradient (PNG), defined in Eq 3, is independent of speed [12]. Rearranging Eq 3 and integrating from $V = 0$, where the skid number intercept is SN_0, to velocity V results in an expression for the skid number as a function of velocity (see Fig. 8)

$$\int_{SN_0}^{SN_V} \frac{d(SN)}{SN} = -\frac{PNG}{100} \int_0^V dV$$

$$\ln \frac{SN_V}{SN_0} = -\frac{PNG}{100} V \tag{6}$$

$$SN_V = SN_0 e^{-\frac{PNG}{100} V}$$

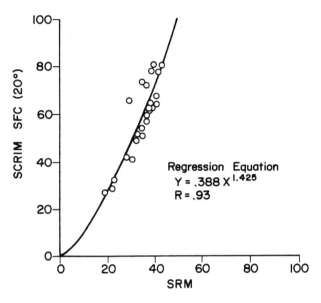

FIG. 6—*Comparison between Stuttgart apparatus SRM and SCRIM at 50 km/h.*

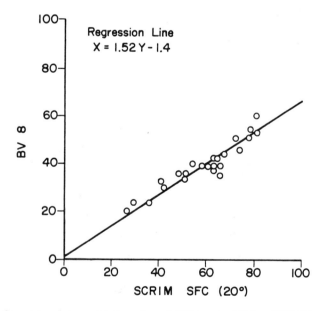

FIG. 7—*Comparison between friction values of Skiddometer BV 8 and SCRIM at 50 km/h.*

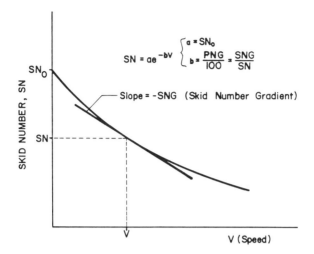

FIG. 8—*Model for skid resistance speed behavior.*

This relationship describes the locked-wheel skid number (SN_V) as a function of speed V in terms of two parameters: the zero speed intercept (SN_0) and the percent normalized gradient (PNG). Measurements at several speeds can be used to determine the values of SN_0 and PNG, and the form of Eq 6 has been shown to fit the observed data extremely well [*12,13*].

It has been reported [*12,14*] that the friction of a tire in longitudinal braking on a wet pavement is solely a function of the velocity of the tire surface relative to the pavement. That is, a brake slip number (BSN) at a given percent slip and specified test speed will be approximated by the locked-wheel skid number (SN) at a speed corresponding to the product of the percent slip times the test speed

$$\text{BSN (\% slip, } V) = \text{SN (\% slip } V) \qquad (7)$$

For example, we can approximate a brake slip number at 25% slip, 64 km/h (40 mph), to a locked-wheel skid number at 16 km/h (10 mph). The approximation is good for tire pavement combinations which have good drainage and where the effects of water film buildup caused by the forward velocity of the tire can be ignored. The ribbed test tires provide adequate drainage on all surfaces at speeds to 128 km/h (80 mph). For the blank tire on smooth pavements the approximation is less reliable. If the lockup rates are slow, transient slip data can be used to estimate the brake slip numbers [*12–14*]. It should be noted that brake slip numbers at low percent slip correspond to relatively low-speed locked-wheel skid numbers.

Side-Force Coefficients and Locked-Wheel Skid Numbers

A simple model has been developed for predicting side-force coefficient (SFC) from longitudinal friction data [*13*]. The result, when combined with Eq 6 above, produces a relationship for SFC at speed *V* and yaw angle α as a function of the parameters SN_0 and PNG

$$SFC = SN_0 \left[3(\rho^2 - \rho^3) + (1 + 3\rho^2 + 2\rho^3)e^{-\frac{PNG}{100}\left(\frac{V \tan \alpha}{2}\right)} \right] \text{ for } \rho > 0 \quad (8)$$

$$SFC = SN_0 e^{-\frac{PNG}{100}\left(\frac{V \tan \alpha}{2}\right)} \text{ for } \rho \leq 0$$

where

$$\rho = 1 - \beta (\tan \alpha / 3SN_0)$$

and

$$\beta = \begin{cases} 1980 \text{ rad}^{-1} \text{ for the ASTM E 501 ribbed test tire} \\ 1500 \text{ rad}^{-1} \text{ for the ASTM E 524 blank test tire} \end{cases}$$

From the form of Eq 8, we can see that this model predicts the side-force coefficient from longitudinal (locked-wheel) friction data at a speed corresponding to $\frac{1}{2} V \tan \alpha$, which for small yaw angles, corresponds to low-speed locked-wheel skid numbers. For example, the prediction of a SCRIM measurement at 64 km/h (40 mph) and a 20° yaw angle would utilize the locked-wheel skid resistance value at 11.7 km/h (7.3 mph).

Skid Resistance and Pavement Texture

Pavement surface texture has been classified into two scales: microtexture and macrotexture, defined by ASTM (E 867) [*3*] as follows:

• *Texture, pavement-micro*—the deviations of a pavement surface from a true planar surface with characteristic dimensions of wavelength and amplitude less than 0.5 mm.
• *Texture, pavement-macro*—the deviations of a pavement surface from a true planar surface with the characteristic dimensions of wavelength and amplitude from 0.5 mm up to those that no longer affect tire-pavement interaction.

The two parameters, SN_0 and PNG, in the model (Eq 6) for skid number as a function of speed, which also were introduced into the model (Eq 8) for side-force coefficient, have been shown to be related to pavement texture [7,13]. The zero speed intercept (SN_0) can be predicted from microtexture parameters such as the root mean square of the microtexture profile height (rms_{MI}) [13] (see Fig. 9)

$$SN_0 = 9.44 \ rms_{MI} - 44.4 \qquad (R = 0.87) \qquad (9)$$

where rms_{MI} is expressed in micrometres ($m \times 10^{-6}$).

Thus, SN_0, which is also an indication of the friction at low speeds, is seen to be a microtexture parameter. Because of the difficulties in obtaining reliable microtexture profile data, the British pendulum number (BPN), measured in accordance with ASTM Method of Measuring Surface Functional

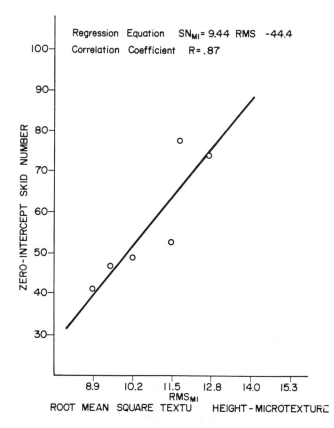

FIG. 9—*Zero intercept skid number versus root mean square microtexture height.*

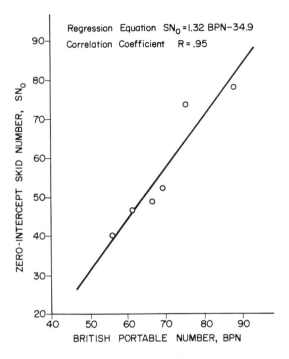

FIG. 10—*Zero intercept skid number versus British pendulum friction tester number.*

Properties Using the British Pendulum Tester (E 303) [3], is frequently used as a surrogate microtexture parameter. BPN is, in fact, a direct measure of low-speed sliding friction. SN_0 also can be related to BPN [13] (Fig. 10)

$$SN_0 = 1.32 \text{ BPN} - 34.9 \qquad (R = 0.95) \qquad (10)$$

The percent normalized gradient (PNG) in Eq 6 determines the rate at which the skid number decreases with speed. The value of PNG has been shown to be related to macrotexture and can be predicted from the root mean square of macrotexture profiles (rms_{MA}) by a nonlinear relationship [13] (Fig. 11)

$$PNG = 0.35 \text{ } rms_{MA}^{-0.52} \qquad (R = 0.92) \qquad (11)$$

where rms_{MA} is expressed in millimetres and PNG is expressed in hours per kilometre. An alternative measure of macrotexture is the sand-patch method, ASTM Test Method for Measuring Surface Macrotexture Depth Using a Sand Volumetric Technique (E 965) [3]. PNG can also be predicted from the sand-patch mean texture depth (MTD) [13] (Fig. 12)

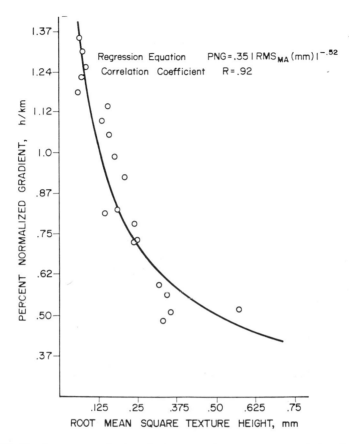

FIG. 11—*Percent normalized gradient versus root mean square macrotexture height.*

$$PNG = 0.45 \, MTD^{-0.47} \qquad (R = 0.96) \qquad (12)$$

where MTD is expressed in millimetres and PNG is expressed in hours per kilometre.

The coefficients in Eqs 9 through 12 are based on a limited number of observations and, unless the pavements are relatively free from contamination, the texture measurements may not adequately account for the effects of contamination in the interface. The general form of these relationships, however, appears to be valid for other data sets as well [15].

Both SN_0 and PNG (or alternatively both microtexture and macrotexture) are needed to predict the skid-resistance data that would be produced by testing in any of the three modes: locked-wheel, slip, or side force. Since two parameters are necessary to predict the skid resistance, a single value (at one speed) of SN, BSN, or SFC is inadequate to characterize the pavement. It is

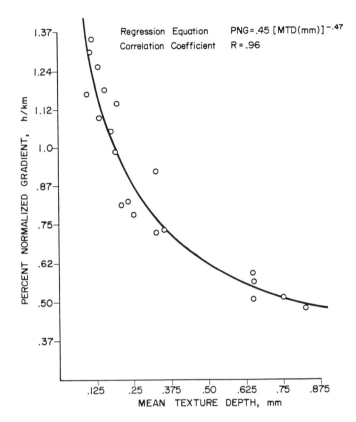

FIG. 12—*Percent normalized gradient versus mean texture depth.*

important that a judicious selection of the pair of descriptors be made. For example, a pavement may be described by its skid resistance at a particular speed and by a texture measurement. To illustrate this, Eqs 7 and 8 show that both brake slip numbers and side-force coefficients are predictable from low-speed locked-wheel friction data. Therefore, they are not very sensitive to macrotexture, and the brake slip number or side-force coefficient should be used in conjunction with an independent measurement of macrotexture. A high side-force coefficient from the SCRIM, together with a high macrotexture depth, would thus indicate a level of skid resistance adequate to ensure safety. In fact, in the United Kingdom, SCRIM data are used in conjunction with a required minimum level of pavement macrotexture: 1.5 mm for newly constructed bituminous concrete pavements,[3] with maintenance required when the macrotexture falls below 1 mm [16].

---

[3]Originally, a minimum level of 2 mm was recommended for newly constructed pavements, but this was later relaxed to 1.5 mm.

The need for two pavement descriptors is further substantiated by another model developed for the prediction of wet-pavement friction of airfield runways [17]. This model uses a macrotexture coefficient C_{MAC} and a microtexture coefficient C_{MIC} to describe the pavement. The model is based on theoretical considerations of hydrodynamic and viscous forces in the interface, and determines the degradation from a measurement of dry-pavement friction to predict wet-pavement friction, and ultimately to predict hydroplaning.

Locked-wheel measurements with the blank test tire are gaining increased attention in the United States [1,18]. It has been recognized that the blank tire is a better indicator of macrotexture than the ribbed tire, in that it relies solely on the pavement to provide relief of hydrodynamic pressures in the interface. Since the two tires respond differently to macrotexture, it has also been proposed to use measurements made with both tires to characterize the pavement. Relationships between the skid numbers produced by testing with the two tires and micro- and macrotexture parameters have produced consistent results with a high degree of correlation. A relationship of texture data and skid resistance data, based on 400 observations, was developed[2]

$$SN_{40}^{B} = 0.745 \text{ BPN} + 15.6 \text{ MTD} - 26.2 \quad (R = 0.93)$$

$$\tag{13}$$

$$SN_{40}^{R} = 0.884 \text{ BPN} + 5.16 \text{ MTD} - 17.8 \quad (R = 0.93)$$

where SN_{40}^{B} and SN_{40}^{R} are skid numbers measured at 64 km/h (40 mph) with the blank ASTM E 524 and ribbed ASTM E 501 test tires, in accordance with ASTM E 274 [3]. Sand-patch mean texture depth (MTD) is expressed in millimetres.

Standards for Skid-Resistance Measurement

For the evaluation of the wet traction of pavements in the United States, ASTM Committee E 17 has developed ASTM E 274 [3]. This standard for the locked-wheel method first appeared in 1965, and has continued, without fundamental revisions, to be the accepted method for pavement evaluation in the United States. A companion standard, developed in 1975 by Committee F-9 on Tires — ASTM Method for Testing Tires for Wet Traction in Straight-Ahead Braking, Using a Towed Trailer (E 408) — is used for evaluating tires by comparison with a control tire [6]. ASTM E 274 provides for reporting data obtained with the locked-wheel method by using either the blank ASTM E 524 or the ribbed ASTM E 501 test tire, and in some agencies the values for both tires are reported. The ASTM F 408 method provides for reporting peak and slide (locked-wheel) coefficients.

In 1984, an International Standards Organization (ISO) working group approved a technical report [19] that attempts to describe current test equipment and procedures for measuring skid resistance by locked-wheel, slip, and side-force methods. While this report is a step towards standardization, more complete standards should be developed for each method.

Conclusions and Recommendations

Skid resistance is currently being measured by three basic methods: locked-wheel, slip, and side-force. Each method has advantages. The locked-wheel method has the advantage of unambiguous simplicity, while slip and side-force methods have the advantage of providing continuous measurement.

A single parameter describing wet-pavement friction is inadequate. To describe a pavement, several alternatives are suggested:

(1) friction data at several test speeds,

(2) a friction measurement in conjunction with a texture measurement, and

(3) friction measurements with both ribbed and smooth tires.

In developing new equipment for measuring wet-pavement traction, consideration should be given to the ability to obtain simultaneously a sufficient set of data to adequately describe the pavement friction. Consideration should also be given to the determination of the lateral variations in skid resistance, and to the provision of continuous longitudinal measurements of friction. Finally, sufficient information to correct for the effects of the environment on friction measurements should be identified and collected.

References

[1] National Transportation Safety Board, "Safety Effectiveness Evaluation: Selected State Highway Skid Resistance Programs," Report NTSB-SEE-80-6, Washington, DC, Sept. 1980.

[2] Saito, K. and Henry, J. J., "Mechanistic Model for Seasonal Variations in Skid Resistance," *Transportation Research Record*, No. 946, Transportation Research Board, Washington, DC, 1983, pp. 29–37.

[3] *1985 Annual Book of ASTM Standards, Road and Paving Materials; Traveled Surface Characteristics,* Vol. 04.03, American Society for Testing and Materials, Philadelphia.

[4] Wambold, J. C. and Henry, J. J., "High-Speed Noncontact Profiling of Pavement Surface Texture and its Significance," presented at ASLE/ASME Tribology Conference, Oct. 1985.

[5] Organization for Economic Co-Operation and Development, *Road Surface Characteristics: Their Interaction and Optimisation*, Paris, 1984.

[6] *1985 Annual Book of ASTM Standards*, Rubber Products, Industrial—Specifications and Related Test Methods; Gaskets; Tires, Vol. 09.02, American Society for Testing and Materials, Philadelphia.

[7] Rizenbergs, R. L., Burchett, J. L., and Warren, L. A., "Relation of Accidents and Pavement Friction on Rural Two Lane Roads," *Transportation Research Record*, No. 633, Transportation Research Board, Washington, DC, 1977, pp. 21–27.

[8] Leu, M. C, and Henry, J. J., "Prediction of Skid Resistance as a Function of Speed from Pavement Texture, *Transportation Research Record*, No. 666, 1978, pp. 7–13.

[9] Meyer, W. E., Hegmon, R. R., and Gillespie, T. D., "Locked-Wheel Pavement Skid Tester Correlation and Calibration Techniques," *NCHRP Report*, No. 151, Transportation Research Board, Washington, DC, 1973.

[10] Burns, J. C. and Peters, R. J., "Surface Friction Study of Arizona Highways," *Highway Research Record*, No. 471, pp. 1-12, 1973.

[11] Arnberg, P. W. and Sjögren, L., "Friction Measuring Vehicles in Scandinavia: A Comparative Study," *VTI Meddelande*, No. 333, Swedish Road and Traffic Research Institute, Linköping, Sweden, 1983.

[12] Shah, V. R. and Henry, J. J., "The Determination of Skid Resistance—Speed Behavior and Side Force Coefficients of Pavements," *Transportation Research Record*, No. 666, Washington, DC, 1978, pp. 13-18.

[13] Henry, J. J. and Meyer, W. E., "The Simulation of Tire Traction on Wet Pavements," *Proceedings of the 18th International Automobile Technical Congress*, Report 369, Hamburg, Germany, 1980, pp. 121-128.

[14] Bradisse, J. L., Ramsey, A. F., and Sacia, S. R., "Mobile Truck Tire Test System," *SAE Paper* 741138, Society of Automotive Engineers, Warrendale, PA, 1974.

[15] Henry, J. J., Saito, K., and Blackburn, R. R., "Predictor Model for Seasonal Variations in Skid Resistance," Report PTI 8217, Pennsylvania Transportation Institute, Pennsylvania State University, University Park, PA, Jan. 1983.

[16] Salt, G. F. "Research on Skid-Resistance at the Transport and Road Research Laboratory (1927-1977)," *Transportation Research Record*, No. 622, Washington, DC, 1976, pp. 26-38.

[17] Permanent International Association of Road Congresses, *Technical Committee Report on Surface Characteristics*, XVII World Road Congress, Sydney, Australia, Oct. 1983.

[18] Henry, J. J., "The Use of Blank and Ribbed Test Tires for Evaluating Pavement Friction," *Transportation Research Record*, No. 788, Washington, DC, 1981, pp. 1-5.

[19] International Standards Organization, *Technical Report: Road Vehicles—Measurement of Road Surface Friction*, prepared by Working Group 3, Subcommittee 9, Technical Committee 22, Geneva, Switzerland, 1984.

Walter B. Horne,[1] Thomas J. Yager,[2] and Don L. Ivey[3]

Recent Studies to Investigate Effects of Tire Footprint Aspect Ratio on Dynamic Hydroplaning Speed

REFERENCE: Horne, W. B., Yager, T. J., and Ivey, D. L., **"Recent Studies to Investigate Effects of Tire Footprint Aspect Ratio on Dynamic Hydroplaning Speed,"** *The Tire Pavement Interface. ASTM STP 929*, M. G. Pottinger and T. J. Yager, Eds., American Society for Testing and Materials, Philadelphia, 1986, pp. 26–46.

ABSTRACT: Previous National Aeronautics and Space Administration (NASA) Langley aircraft tire friction performance investigations indicated the primary parameter influencing dynamic tire hydroplaning was inflation pressure. The empirical equations derived from aircraft tire test data to estimate tire hydroplaning speed were considered applicable to all pneumatic tires. Some recent studies of several tractor-trailer accidents on flooded highway surfaces, however, suggest that in addition to inflation pressure, truck tire footprint aspect ratio (tread contact area width to length) may significantly effect dynamic hydroplaning speed. Although the truck accident data indicated a new equation to predict highway vehicle dynamic tire hydroplaning speed, collection of additional test data was considered necessary. Tests aimed at obtaining this needed data were initiated by researchers at Texas Transportation Institute (TTI) and NASA Langley. Results from these initial tests using a worn truck tire, an ASTM Specification Standard Tire for Pavement Skid Resistance Tests (E 501) and Specification for Smooth Tread Standard Tire for Special-Purpose Pavement Skid Resistance Tests (E 524) tires are discussed in this paper. The status of the work directed towards developing a new dynamic tire hydroplaning speed equation(s) is reviewed. During wet weather, highway vehicle operators are cautioned to be alert to the possibly lower hydroplaning speeds because of the influence of tire footprint aspect ratio effects when their vehicles are lightly loaded.

KEY WORDS: tires, pavements, tire hydroplaning, flooded pavements, tire friction performance, tire footprint aspect ratio

[1]Consultant, 192 Queens Dr., Williamsburg, VA 23185.
[2]Aero-space technologist, NASA Langley Research Center, Mail Stop 497, Hampton, VA 23665.
[3]Associate director, Texas Transportation Institute, College Station, TX.

Previous NASA Langley aircraft tire friction performance investigations indicated that the primary parameter influencing dynamic tire hydroplaning was inflation pressure. The empirical equations derived from aircraft tire test data to estimate tire hydroplaning speed were considered applicable to all pneumatic tires. This relationship predicted that hydroplaning speeds for ground vehicle tires operated at inflation pressures greater than 414 kPa (60 psi) would be well above highway speed limits. Since truck tires are normally inflated to greater pressures than this value, dynamic hydroplaning was not considered likely to occur for these vehicles. Some recent studies of several tractor-trailer accidents on flooded highway surfaces, however, suggest that in addition to inflation pressure, truck tire footprint aspect ratio (tread contact area width to length) may significantly affect dynamic hydroplaning speed. While an automobile tire for a 17.8-kN (4000-lb) vehicle may have a normal load range from 3.6 to 5.3 kN (800 to 1200 lb), a truck tire may be operated with loads varying from 2.7 to 26.7 kN (600 to 6000 lb). With this extremely wide load variation, the truck tire footprint aspect ratio also varies widely, leading to hydroplaning conditions for a lightly loaded, albeit normally inflated, truck tire at speeds common to highway vehicles. Since truck accident data indicated the need for a new equation to predict highway vehicle dynamic tire hydroplaning speed, collection of additional test data was considered necessary. Tests aimed at obtaining this needed data were initiated by researchers at Texas Transportation Institute (TTI) and National Aeronautics and Space Administration (NASA) Langley. Results from these initial tests using a worn truck tire and ASTM Specification Standard Tire for Pavement Skid Resistance Tests (E 501) and Specification for Smooth Tread Standard Tire for Special Purpose Pavement Skid Resistance Tests (E 524) automotive test tires are discussed in this paper. The status of the work directed towards developing a new dynamic tire hydroplaning speed equation(s) is summarized.

Background

Many highway accidents occur when vehicles lose directional control while traversing deep puddles in highway traffic lanes, especially during times of high rainfall rates, strong crosswinds, and when standing water collects on nontangent highway sections. A recent investigation by Horne, reported in Refs 1 and 2, of tractor-trailer truck jack-knifing accidents on wet highways revealed that a wide range of tire loading conditions and footprint aspect ratio values existed for a given tractor-trailer combination. Tables 1 and 2 give truck tire footprint characteristics for two different cases investigated by Horne. It can be seen from these tables that the empty tractor-trailer tires have much higher footprint aspect ratios than loaded tractor-trailer tires for the same inflation pressure. These data suggest that the tire footprint aspect ratio influences the hydroplaning inception speed with higher values found

TABLE 1—*Case 1 tractor-trailer tire footprint characteristics.*

Tire Location and Inflation Pressure P, kPa (psi)	Trailer Load Condition	Load per Tire, kN (lb)	Tire Footprint Measurements		
			Width W, cm (in.)	Length L, cm (in.)	Aspect Ratio, FAR
Tractor front					
steering axle	empty	13.5 (3030)	16.64 (6.55)	19.94 (7.85)	0.834
P = 621 (90)	loaded	20.3 (4570)	20.75 (8.17)	23.11 (9.10)	0.898
Tractor forward					
drive axle	empty	5.2 (1175)	14.30 (5.63)	11.94 (4.70)	1.198
P = 552 (80)	loaded	19.2 (4325)	18.26 (7.19)	21.77 (8.57)	0.839
Tractor rear					
drive axle	empty	5.7 (1280)	13.46 (5.30)	11.02 (4.34)	1.221
P = 552 (80)	loaded	19.2 (4320)	17.78 (7.00)	20.02 (7.88)	0.888
Trailer forward					
axle	empty	2.5 (565)	14.78 (5.82)	11.89 (4.68)	1.244
P = 552 (80)	loaded	17.9 (4020)	19.05 (7.50)	20.57 (8.10)	0.926
Trailer rear					
axle	empty	5.7 (1280)	15.24 (6.00)	17.73 (6.98)	0.860
P = 552 (80)	loaded	22.3 (5010)	18.75 (7.38)	25.91 (10.20)	0.724

TABLE 2—*Case 2 tractor-trailer tire footprint characteristics.*

Tire Location and Inflation Pressure P, kPa (psi)	Trailer Load Condition	Load per Tire, kN (lb)	Tire Footprint Measurements		
			Width W, cm (in.)	Length L, cm (in.)	Aspect Ratio, FAR
Tractor front					
steering axle	empty	19.0 (4270)	17.65 (6.95)	21.34 (8.40)	0.827
P = 690 (100)	loaded	25.4 (5720)	18.03 (7.10)	23.75 (9.35)	0.759
Tractor forward					
drive axle	empty	5.7 (1285)	17.37 (6.84)	11.02 (4.34)	1.576
P = 690 (100)	loaded	19.1 (4285)	18.39 (7.24)	20.88 (8.22)	0.881
Tractor rear					
drive axle	empty	5.0 (1120)	17.17 (6.76)	9.35 (3.68)	1.837
P = 690 (100)	loaded	17.0 (3825)	18.62 (7.33)	17.86 (7.03)	1.043
Trailer forward					
axle	empty	4.8 (1085)	12.27 (4.83)	12.62 (4.97)	0.972
P = 690 (100)	loaded	19.0 (4275)	18.97 (7.47)	20.32 (8.00)	0.934
Trailer rear					
axle	empty	3.7 (840)	14.81 (5.83)	12.55 (4.94)	1.180
P = 690 (100)	loaded	17.7 (3970)	18.49 (7.28)	21.39 (8.42)	0.865

for empty loaded conditions significantly reducing the expected hydroplaning speed. Accident statistics (see Table 3) also indicate that empty tractor-trailers are more prone to jack-knifing accidents on wet highways than loaded tractor-trailers. Reference *1* presents compelling arguments that the minimum truck tire dynamic hydroplaning speed on flooded pavements depends

TABLE 3—*Estimated wet to dry pavement truck accident ratios (data compiled for Texas four lane highways between 1979 to 81).*

Truck Type	Load Status	Wet/Dry Ratio	
		Single-Truck	Collisions
Single-Unit	empty	2.21	0.29
	loaded	0.59	0.19
Van	empty	3.98	0.52
	loaded	1.04	0.33
Flatbed	empty	1.94	0.26
	loaded	0.52	0.16
Tanker	empty	2.50	0.33
	loaded	0.67	0.21
Other	empty	3.07	0.41
	loaded	0.82	0.26

upon the magnitude of both the tire inflation pressure and footprint aspect ratio as shown in Eq 1 from Ref *1*

$$V_p = 7.95 \sqrt{p(\text{FAR})^{-1}} \tag{1}$$

where

V_p = dynamic hydroplaning speed, mph,
p = tire inflation pressure, psi, and
FAR = tire footprint aspect ratio, width divided by length.

Consequently, researchers at the Texas Transportation Institute and NASA Langley Research Center have initiated controlled parameter tests directed towards verifying these findings and better defining tire hydroplaning speed.

Review of Tire Hydroplaning

Tire hydroplaning is defined as the condition that occurs when a pneumatic tire rolling or sliding along a water-covered pavement is lifted away from the pavement surface by the action of water pressures that build up with increasing vehicle speed in the tire-pavement surface contact zone. Thus, when total tire hydroplaning develops, the entire footprint of the tire is riding on a water layer or water film that separates the tire tread from all contact with the pavement surface. Since water is a fluid incapable of generating appreciable shear forces, the friction coefficient developed between the tire and pavement for this hydroplaning condition declines to negligible values, and the tire loses its ability to produce ground forces for vehicle acceleration, deceleration, and directional control. Four manifestations of hydroplaning that are useful in identifying the minimum or inception speed value at which hydroplaning occurs on flooded pavements are detachment of tire footprint from ground, tire spindown, peaking of tire fluid displacement drag, and loss in tire braking/cornering traction. These hydroplaning characteristics were monitored during a variety of aircraft tire tests conducted at the NASA Langley track facility and discussed in Refs 3 to 9. The results from these tests were analyzed to derive an empirical formula for predicting the minimum hydroplaning speed for tires operating on flooded (water depth greater than tread groove depth) pavements. Figure 1 shows the variation in observed hydroplaning speed with tire inflation pressure for some of the aircraft tire sizes and types evaluated during these studies. The curve passing through the data points of this figure represent a remarkably simple formula

$$V_p = 9\sqrt{p}, \text{ knots} \tag{2a}$$

or

$$V_p = 10.35\sqrt{p}, \text{ mph} \tag{2b}$$

where

V_p = the minimum hydroplaning speed and
p = the tire inflation pressure, psi.

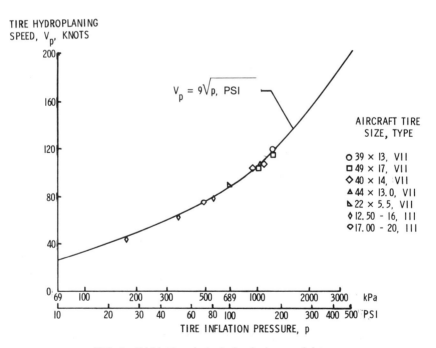

FIG. 1—*NASA aircraft tire hydroplaning speed data.*

Pneumatic Tire Footprint Aspect Ratio

The footprint aspect ratio (FAR) of pneumatic tires is the value derived from dividing the footprint width dimension by its length. This FAR value can vary with tire type, construction, inflation pressure, and vertical loading. Extensive studies of the mechanical properties of a wide range of aircraft tire sizes reported in Ref 6 show that when the vertical deflection of an aircraft tire is increased in magnitude, both the tire footprint width and length increase. This effect is illustrated by the actual aircraft tire footprints shown in Fig. 2. It can be seen that both the footprint length and width change dimension when the vertical load is increased with constant inflation pressure. In general, aircraft tire FAR values are found to remain nearly constant throughout the normal operating load and inflation pressure ranges. Hence, aircraft tire hydroplaning speed can be defined by considering only the inflation pressure parameter as indicated earlier by the data shown in Fig. 1.

Figure 3 illustrates the change in FAR for the ASTM E 524 smooth, bias-ply, G78x15 automotive test tire at constant inflation pressure and two different vertical loads. The footprint width dimension remains constant at 15 cm (5.9 in.) for both load cases, but the length changes considerably with vertical loading. As a consequence, the ASTM automobile tire FAR varies from 1.4

VERTICAL LOAD = 53.9 kN (12120 lb)

FOOTPRINT ASPECT RATIO = 0.79

VERTICAL LOAD = 134 kN (30120 lb)

FOOTPRINT ASPECT RATIO = 0.64

FIG. 2—*Jet transport aircraft main gear tire footprints: 40 × 14, 28 ply-rating, Type VII; inflation pressure, 965 kPa (140 psi).*

VERTICAL LOAD = 2.2 kN (504 lb)
ASPECT RATIO = 1.4

VERTICAL LOAD = 5.2 kN (1160 lb)
ASPECT RATIO = 0.86

FIG. 3—ASTM E 524 test tire footprints: G78 × 15 tire size; inflation pressure, 166 kPa (24 psi).

for the light load to 0.86 for the normal load. Obviously, the automobile tire footprint characteristics differ from that found for aircraft tires, which suggests that the same hydroplaning speed relationship may not be completely applicable to both tire types.

Figure 4 shows 10.00–20 bias ply truck tire footprints obtained at an inflation pressure of 552 kPa (80 psi) with tires mounted on the tractor front drive axle. The variation in vertical loading resulted from using an empty and a loaded trailer. With a vertical load difference of nearly 400% the FAR values varied from 1.2 for the trailer empty case to 0.84 for the trailer loaded case. Figure 5 shows worn 10.00–20 bias ply truck tire footprints obtained by Texas Transportation Institute (TTI) researchers with a vertical load of 4.2 kN (940 lb) and inflation pressures of 138 and 518 kPa (20 and 75 psi). Varying the inflation pressure from 138 to 690 kPa (20 to 100 psi) under constant light vertical load, the FAR values also remained constant at 1.4. It appears from these limited data that truck tire footprint characteristics lie between aircraft tire (constant FAR) and automobile tire (constant footprint width) footprint characteristics.

These observations and measurements indicating the significant differences between aircraft and highway vehicle tire footprint characteristics are related to differing construction techniques, materials, and tread designs used by the tire manufacturers. It is recognized that in addition to footprint aspect ratio and inflation pressure, tire hydroplaning inception speed may be influenced by contact pressure distribution and net/gross footprint contact areas. These two parameters will vary with tire tread design, carcass construction, and pavement surface texture characteristics. As a consequence, a num-

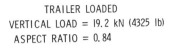

TRAILER LOADED
VERTICAL LOAD = 19.2 kN (4325 lb)
ASPECT RATIO = 0.84

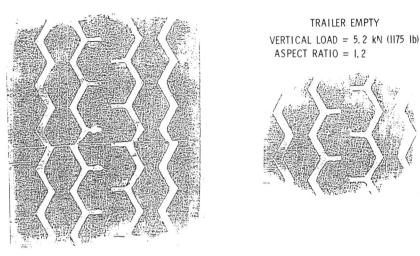

TRAILER EMPTY
VERTICAL LOAD = 5.2 kN (1175 lb)
ASPECT RATIO = 1.2

FIG. 4—*Tractor forward drive axle tire footprints: 10.00 to 20 tire size; inflation pressure, 552 kPa (80 psi).*

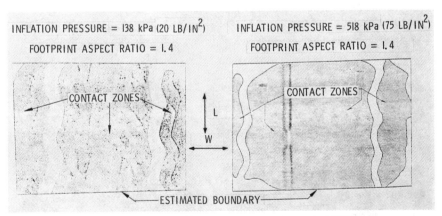

INFLATION PRESSURE = 138 kPa (20 LB/IN^2)
FOOTPRINT ASPECT RATIO = 1.4

INFLATION PRESSURE = 518 kPa (75 LB/IN^2)
FOOTPRINT ASPECT RATIO = 1.4

CONTACT ZONES

CONTACT ZONES

L

W

ESTIMATED BOUNDARY

FIG. 5—*Worn truck tire footprints: vertical load, 4.2 kN (940 lb).*

ber of tire/pavement parameters needs to be measured and monitored during investigations of tire hydroplaning phenomenon.

Worn Truck Tire Tests

Researchers at Texas Transportation Institute (TTI) used the test trailer shown in Figs. 6 and 7 equipped with a worn 10.00-20 bias ply truck tire

FIG. 6—*TTI towing vehicle and tire test trailer.*

FIG. 7—*View of TTI tire test trailer from towing vehicle.*

loaded to 4.2 kN (940 lb) in a series of tests to identify the actual tire hydroplaning speed at different inflation pressures. A photograph of the flooded (average water depth, 6.4 mm [0.25 in.]) test surface is shown in Fig. 8. This surface wetness condition greatly exceeded the average tire tread groove depth of 1.6 mm (0.06 in.). For a given tire load and inflation pressure condition, test runs were conducted at gradually increasing constant speeds until instrumentation on the test tire indicated a reduction of the tire angular velocity (spindown) equivalent to a forward speed reduction of 3 km/h (2 mph) with respect to the towing vehicle speed. Figure 9 indicates the variation in measured tire hydroplaning speed with inflation pressure for these TTI worn truck tire tests. For comparison, the prediction of tire hydroplaning speed based on Eq 2 is also given. At tire inflation pressures above 138 kPa (20 psi), the worn truck tire actual hydroplaning speed is considerably less than that predicted from Eq 2 which was derived primarily from aircraft tire test findings. The best curve fit of the available TTI data indicates the following hydroplaning speed equation

$$V_p = 23.3 \, (p)^{0.21}\left(\frac{1.4}{\text{FAR}}\right)^{0.5} \tag{3}$$

FIG. 8—*TTI flooded test surface.*

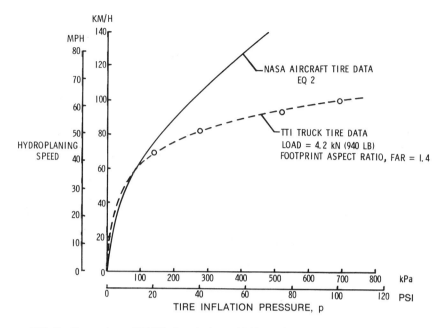

FIG. 9—*Comparison of NASA aircraft tire and TTI truck tire hydroplaning speed data.*

where

V_p = hydroplaning speed, mph,
p = inflation pressure, psi, and
FAR = tire footprint aspect ratio.

Truck Accident Data Findings

For truck accident data to be supportive of the low hydroplaning speed values found in TTI worn truck tire tests, one would expect to find significantly higher ratio of single-truck accidents on wet pavements to those occurring on dry pavements for empty trucks versus loaded trucks. The data base, described in Ref *10*, contained reported truck accidents on 4 or more lane highways in Texas between 1979 and 1981, cross classified by wet or dry pavement conditions, empty or loaded truck, truck type, light condition, and accident type. In order to analyze the proportion of total truck accidents (2588) that were wet weather, single truck accidents, a discrete multi-variate model was used. The purpose of the modeling was to account for the significant effect of truck types and day/night conditions so that the true effect of empty/loaded truck on the proportion of wet weather accidents could be obtained. The model estimation was carried out using a procedure based on the weighted least square principles. The goodness of fit for the resulting model was 17.28 for 12 degrees of freedom, which is considered a good fit.

The estimated model indicates that the ratios of wet to dry pavement truck accidents were significantly influenced by load status (empty/loaded), truck type, accident type (single truck/multi-vehicle), and the interaction between load status and accident type. However, light condition (day/night) was not a significant explanatory variable. Table 3 shows the estimated ratios of wet to dry pavement accidents for all combinations of the significant independent variables. Figures 10a and b are the plots of these ratios for single-truck accidents and for multi-vehicle collisions, respectively. It can be seen that the ratios of wet to dry accidents were consistently higher for empty than for loaded trucks regardless of the accident type or the truck type. However, this difference between empty and loaded trucks was far more pronounced for single-truck accidents than for multi-vehicle collisions. This differential finding was the result of the interaction between load status and accident type. The fact that empty trucks are capable of higher speeds than loaded trucks may also influence these accident statistics.

To illustrate this interaction graphically, Fig. 11 shows a plot of the means of the ratios of wet to dry accidents for single-truck accidents and for collisions that were weighted by appropriate accident cell frequency. If the effect of wet pavements was not particularly pronounced for empty trucks in single-truck accidents, the two lines representing single truck accidents and collisions would be parallel as indicated by the dotted line. Figure 11 indicates

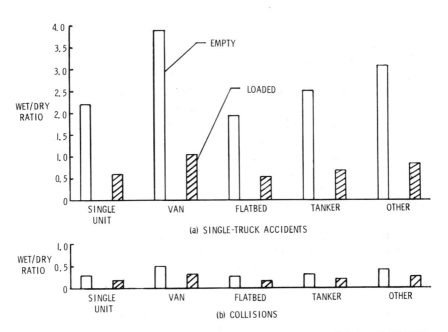

FIG. 10—*Estimated ratio of wet to dry truck accidents in Texas between 1979 through 1981* [10].

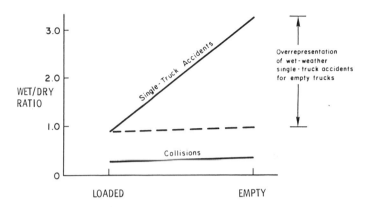

FIG. 11—*Means of wet to dry pavement ratios for singe truck accidents and collisions.*

that the ratio of wet accidents to dry accidents for empty trucks on four or more lane highways in Texas was on the average about three times higher than expected, when collisions involving at least one heavy truck were used as a control group. This immediately suggests a very strong influence of wet pavements on single-truck accidents for empty trucks that was not observed for loaded trucks.

ASTM Tire Tests

NASA Langley Research Center personnel conducted a large number of flooded runway surface tests using the instrumented tire test vehicle shown in Fig. 12. Tests were performed at speeds up to 113 km/h (70 mph) with both the ASTM grooved E 501 and smooth E 524 automotive, G78x15 test tires. This specially designed test truck has an instrumented tire test fixture mounted in the rear (see Fig. 13) to measure the loads developed on the tire during test runs. Continuous time histories of the instrumentation output are recorded on an analog tape recorder mounted in the vehicle cab compartment. In addition to the test tire loads, wheel speed is also measured and test truck speed and distance traveled is recorded from sensors mounted on the trailing fifth wheel. References *11* and *12* provide a more detailed description of the various features of this unique test vehicle. The test run matrix included 0° and 4° yawed rolling runs on the flooded ungrooved concrete surface A and grooved concrete surface B shown in Fig. 14. The average surface water depth was measured and maintained at 12 mm (0.5 in.), which was more than twice the average tread groove depth of ASTM E 501 test tire. Figure 15 shows the two test surfaces in this flooded condition with the grooved concrete surface B in the foreground. Rubber belt dams were used around the perimeter of a 2- by 57-m (6- by 188-ft) strip to contain the proper amount of water.

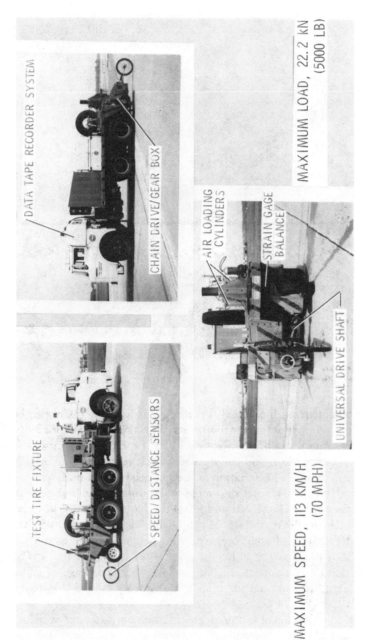

FIG. 12—*Instrumented tire test vehicle.*

FIG. 13—*ASTM E 524 on NASA test vehicle fixture.*

Before commencing the actual test run series with the instrumented tire test vehicle, a number of test tire footprints were taken at three different inflation pressures and five different verticle loads. For each tire footprint condition, the footprint width and length dimensions were measured and the aspect ratio calculated. The variation in tire footprint aspect ratio with vertical load and inflation pressures is shown in Fig. 16. No significant difference was found between the ASTM E 501 and E 524 tire footprint data. The data indicated that the tire footprint aspect ratio decreased with increasing vertical load and decreasing inflation pressure. An average footprint aspect ratio of approximately one was found for the normal load range of the ASTM test tires, but there was a variation from 0.4 to 1.8 for the range of loads and pressures used. The normal inflation pressure for these ASTM automotive test tires is 166 kPa (24 psi).

For each combination of test tire type, inflation pressure, and vertical load, a series of test runs at different constant speeds was conducted through the flooded concrete surfaces with the test truck. Some of the results from these

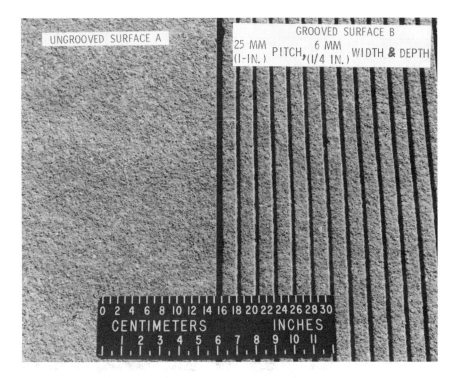

FIG. 14—*Concrete test surfaces on Runway 4/22 at NASA Wallops Flight Facility.*

tests are given in Figs. 17 through 19 for the flooded ungrooved concrete surface. One key parameter used to identify the hydroplaning speed for each set of tire test conditions was test tire speed values less than the truck test run speed. Under hydroplaning conditions, tire rolling resistance and side force friction coefficient should also decrease to near zero values as indicated in Refs 3 to 5. The side force and rolling friction data shown in Figs. 17 to 18 for the ASTM E 501 and E 524 tires indicate an increasing hydroplaning speed with increasing inflation pressure. When the inflation pressure is held constant, the tire friction data shown in Fig. 19 indicate that hydroplaning speed increases with increasing vertical load.

Figure 20 shows the variation in demonstrated hydroplaning speed for the ASTM automotive tire (NASA tests) and truck tire (TTI tests) with tire footprint aspect ratio for three inflation pressures. The solid symbols depicting the worn truck tire data at the three inflation pressures used in the ASTM tire tests were obtained from the data curve given in Fig. 9. The agreement between the two different data sets is considered good. The data in Fig. 20 indi-

FIG. 15—*Flooded test surface condition at NASA Wallops Flight Facility.*

cate that increasing tire footprint aspect ratio produces lower hydroplaning speed. If a least squares curve fit is applied to this limited data base and tire inflation pressure and footprint aspect ratio are treated as the two independent variables influencing hydroplaning speed, the following relationship is identified

$$V_p = 51.80 - 17.15 \text{ FAR} + 0.72p \qquad (4)$$

for tire footprint aspect ratios between 0.4 and 1.4 where

V_p = hydroplaning speed, mph,
p = inflation pressure, psi, and
FAR = footprint aspect ratio.

Although additional test data with a variety of automobile, truck, and bus tires are needed to substantiate this new tire hydroplaning speed relationship

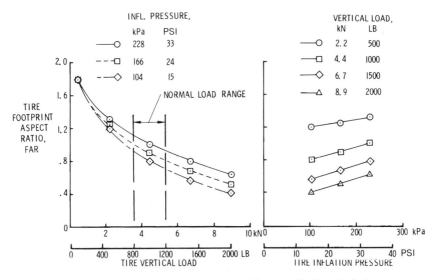

FIG. 16—*Variation of tire footprint aspect ratio with vertical load and inflation pressure ASTM E 501 and E 524 test tires.*

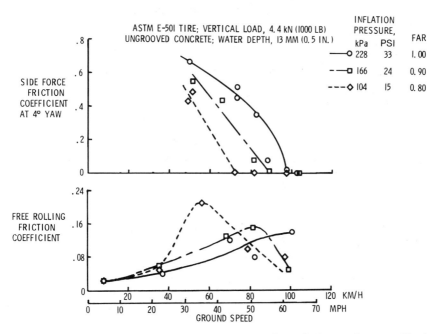

FIG. 17—*Effect of ASTM E 501 tire inflation pressure on hydroplaning speed at normal load.*

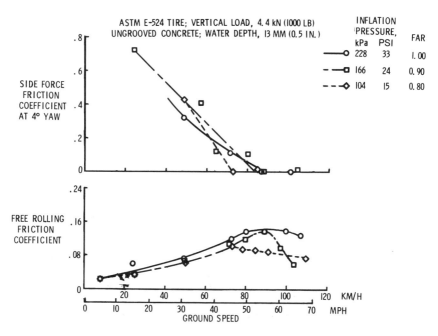

FIG. 18—*Effect of ASTM E 524 tire inflation pressure on hydroplaning speed at normal load.*

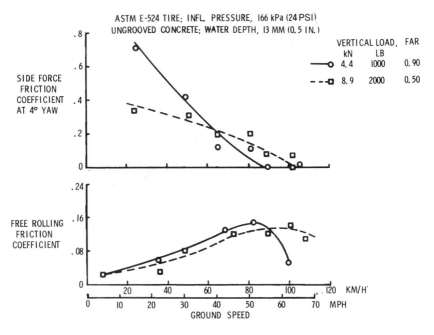

FIG. 19—*Effect of ASTM E 524 tire loading on hydroplaning speed at normal inflation pressure.*

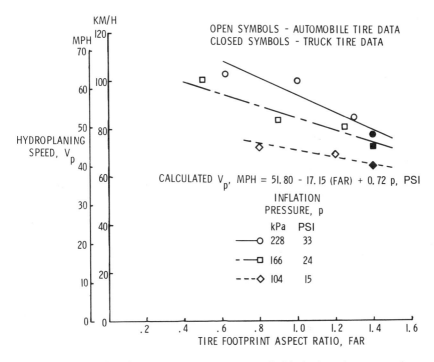

FIG. 20—*Variation of dynamic hydroplaning speed with tire footprint aspect ratio.*

for ground vehicle pneumatic tires, sufficient data have been collected by NASA and TTI researchers to indicate that tire footprint aspect ratio does play a significant role.

Concluding Remarks

Limited results from Texas Transportation Institute truck tire tests and NASA Langley ASTM tire tests show the influence of tire footprint aspect ratio on dynamic hydroplaning speed. A new dynamic hydroplaning speed equation has been formulated based on these limited test results for use with ground vehicle pneumatic tires that exhibit a large range of tire footprint aspect ratio values for different inflation pressure and vertical load values. The aircraft tire hydroplaning speed relationship of nine times the square root of the tire inflation pressure appears to be valid since aircraft tire footprint aspect ratios remain nearly constant through the operating load and inflation pressure range. Future NASA Langley studies of new aircraft tire designs will include consideration of tire footprint aspect ratio in evaluating flooded pavement performance. It is also recognized that additional ground vehicle tire tests are required to refine and substantiate the pneumatic tire hydroplaning speed relationship identified from the limited data base collected in the NASA and TTI studies.

References

[1] Horne, W. B., "Predicting the Minimum Dynamic Hydroplaning Speed for Aircraft, Bus, Truck, and Automobile Tires Rolling on Flooded Pavements," presented at ASTM E-17 Committee meeting, College Station, TX, 4-6 June 1984.

[2] Horne, W. B., "Tractor-Trailer Jack-Knifing on Flooded Pavements," presented at Transportation Research Board Committee A2B07 meeting, Washington, DC, Jan. 1985.

[3] Horne, W. B. and Dreher, R. C., "Phenomena of Pneumatic Tire Hydroplaning," NASA TN D-2056, Hampton, VA, Nov. 1963.

[4] Horne, W. B., Yager, T. J., and Taylor, G. R., "Review of Causes and Alleviation of Low Tire Traction Wet Runways," NASA TN D-4406, Hampton, VA, 1968.

[5] Horne, W. B. and Joyner, U. T., "Pneumatic Tire Hydroplaning and Some Effects on Vehicle Performance," SAE International Automotive Engineering Congress, SAE 970C, Detroit, MI, 11-15 Jan. 1965.

[6] Smiley, R. F. and Horne, W. B., "Mechanical Properties of Pneumatic Tires With Special Reference to Modern Aircraft Tires," NASA TR R-64, 1960, supersedes NASA TN 4110.

[7] Horne, W. B. and Leland, T. J. W., "Influence of Tire Tread Pattern and Runway Surface Condition on Braking Friction and Rolling Resistance of a Modern Aircraft Tire," NASA TN D-1376, Hampton, VA, 1962.

[8] Leland, T. J. W. and Taylor, G. R., "As Investigation of the Influence of Aircraft Tire-Tread Wear on Wet-Runway Braking," NASA TN D-2770, Hampton, VA, April 1965.

[9] Horne, W. B. and Buhlmann, F., "A Method for Rating the Skid Resistance and Micro/Macrotexture Characteristics of Wet Pavements," *Frictional Interaction of Tire and Pavement, STP 793*, W. E. Meyer and J. D. Walter, Eds., American Society for Testing and Materials, Philadelphia, 1983, pp. 191-218.

[10] Chira-Chavala, T., "Problems of Trucks on Wet Pavements: An Accident Analysis," Texas Transportation Institute, College Station, TX, paper presented at the Jan. 1986 Transportation Research Board annual meeting, Washington, DC.

[11] McCarty, J. L., Yager, T. J., and Riccitiello, S. R., "Wear, Friction, and Temperature Characteristics of an Aircraft Tire Undergoing Braking and Cornering," NASA TP 1959, Hampton, VA, 1979.

[12] Yager, T. J. and Horne, W. B., "Friction Evaluation of Unpaved, Gypsum-Surface Runways at Northrup Strip, White Sands Missile Range, in Support of Space Shuttle Orbiter Landing and Retrieval Operations," NASA TM 81811, Hampton, VA, June 1980.

James C. Wambold,[1] *John J. Henry,*[1] *and*
Rudolph R. Hegmon[2]

Skid Resistance of Wet-Weather Accident Sites

REFERENCE: Wambold, J. C., Henry, J. J., and Hegmon, R. R., **"Skid Resistance of Wet-Weather Accident Sites,"** *The Tire Pavement Interface, ASTM STP 929,* M. G. Pottinger and T. J. Yager, Eds., American Society for Testing and Materials, Philadelphia, 1986, pp. 47–60.

ABSTRACT: A small-scale, wet-weather accident study was conducted in the years 1981 to 1983 as part of a wider study on pavement texture. The researchers were notified of wet-weather accident occurrences, and the skid resistance was measured as soon as possible after the accident, usually within one day, but never more than two days. During the study period, 79 such sites were tested, 21 of which had multiple accidents. All sites were tested with the ribbed and blank test tires. Similar tests were made on control sections within 1.6 km (1 mile) of the accident sites. These were selected to have geometric and traffic characteristics similar to those of the accident sites. As it turned out, the data base was too small to warrant definitive conclusions. Uncertainties about accident causation were reflected in the fact that the data from the control sites were not significantly different from those of the accident sites. The results, however, show a trend consistent with findings by other researchers. Skid resistance measured with the blank tire is not only lower than that measured with the ribbed tire, but is also better as a predictor of skidding accident potential. Wet-weather accident data from Florida were also analyzed, and the results reinforced this conclusion. The use of data from both the blank and the ribbed tire for pavement evaluation is recommended for future study.

KEY WORDS: tires, wet-weather accidents, skid resistance, blank tire, ribbed tire, microtexture, macrotexture

In a global study of wet-weather accidents, the National Transportation Safety Board [1] found that the frequency of wet-road accidents is about four times the frequency of dry-road accidents. However, not all wet-road accidents result from skidding. It is much more difficult to determine the extent

---

[1]Professor of mechanical engineering and director of vehicle/surface interaction and professor of mechanical engineering and director of the Pennsylvania Transportation Institute, respectively, Pennsylvania State University, Research Building B, University Park, PA 16802.

[2]Research mechanical engineer, Federal Highway Administration, 6300 Georgetown Pike, McLean, VA 22101.

of skidding accidents. Plotting wet-weather accidents against skid resistance shows a preponderance of sites with low skid resistance. Based on the experience from many states, it is generally agreed that a skid number of 35 or greater (as measured according to ASTM Test Method for Skid Resistance of Paved Surfaces Using a Full-Scale Tire [E 274] [2]) gives adequate skid resistance under most conditions. Skidding accidents have occurred on pavements with adequate skid resistance according to the above criterion. This has raised the question of the adequacy of this measurement. For instance, grooving of pavements has resulted in significant reduction in wet-weather accidents without a corresponding increase in the skid resistance measured with a ribbed test tire. As a result, some researchers have taken skid-resistance measurements with a blank test tire and have concluded that these may be better predictors of skidding potential.

It has been recognized that skid resistance is a function of both microtexture and macrotexture. These have been defined as follows by ASTM Definitions of Terms Relating to Traveled Surface Characteristics (E 867) [2]:

- *Texture, pavement-macro*—the deviations of a pavement surface from a true planar surface with the characteristic dimensions of wavelength and amplitude from 0.5 mm up to those that no longer affect tire-pavement interaction.
- *Texture, pavement-micro*—the deviations of a pavement surface from a true planar surface with characteristic dimensions of wavelength and amplitude less than 0.5 mm.

The primary function of macrotexture is to provide drainage; the primary function of microtexture is to penetrate the remaining thin water film. The ribbed tire provides drainage through its grooves and is therefore less sensitive to the presence or absence of adequate macrotexture.

In a study of the relationship between 5 variables and 500 wet-weather accidents, Hankins et al. [3] came to the following conclusions:

1. The pavement at the accident site had low macrotexture.
2. The tread depths of the vehicle involved were small.
3. The friction value of the pavement at the accident site was low.
4. The speed of the vehicle immediately before the accident was high.
5. The tire pressures of the accident vehicle were high.

Thus, inadequate texture and tread depth are major contributors to wet-weather accidents. All states have some minimum requirement for tread depth; therefore, a skid-resistance measurement with the blank tire represents the extreme condition of worn tires. Nevertheless, since a majority of the vehicles in Hankins' accident study has small tread depths, the blank tire skid numbers may represent a conservative rating, that is, most tires in use would experience somewhat better frictional resistance. Several states (Connecticut, Florida, Illinois, and Maine) have investigated the use of the blank tire in accident studies and research programs, but as yet none has adopted it for survey testing. One of the reasons is that skid-resistance surveys have been discontinued by many states; testing is done on a sampling basis and is concentrated on experimental pavements and suspected hazardous or known accident locations.

For a better characterization of the frictional performance of pavements, the current skid-resistance measurement would have to be augmented to provide additional information. But, unless this can be done at very little additional cost, the chances for adoption by state highway agencies are slim. In any case, the following three combinations of measurements could provide better data than a single skid-resistance measurement.

(1) macrotexture and microtexture (profiles or average values),
(2) macrotexture and ribbed-tire skid resistance, or
(3) blank and ribbed-tire skid resistance.

The first combination includes microtexture. There is currently no measuring method that would not interfere with traffic. Thus, such a combination may be useful in special or research studies only. Macrotexture can now be measured at traffic speeds with a recently developed vehicle-mounted video system. (The prototype is currently being evaluated by several state highway agencies.) Such a system in conjunction with a skid-resistance measurement could be a practical alternative and provide better data on the safety of wet pavements. The third combination, skid resistance with ribbed and blank tires, was used in the study reported here, together with related data from some state highway agencies.

Skid Resistance at Wet-Weather Accident Sites

Recently, the use of the ASTM Specification for Standard Tire for Pavement Skid Resistance Tests (E 501) for evaluating wet-pavement safety has been questioned [4–10]. Pavement grooving is widely accepted as an effective means of reducing wet-pavement skidding accidents. It has been noted, however, that the skid number measured with the ribbed tire is not significantly improved by grooving [5]. Wet-pavement accidents decreased dramatically in the grooved areas, which showed only a slight increase in skid resistance when measured with the ribbed tire, but a large increase when the blank tire was used. Since the presence or absence of grooves on pavements does not affect the ribbed-tire skid number, it is apparent that sufficient drainage is provided by the grooves of the tire. Because these grooves provide escape channels for the water, the ribbed tire, when used for measurements on dense-graded (fine-textured) pavements, may not predict the low friction that a car with worn tires might encounter on the pavement with water films, even at the thickness of the film applied during the test.

For this study, data were collected using locked-wheel skid trailer measurements in accordance with ASTM Method E 274 [2], with both blank ASTM Specification for Smooth Tread Standard Tire for Special-Purpose Pavement Skid Resistance Tests (E 524) and ribbed ASTM E 501 test tires. The test road sections where wet-weather accidents occurred included both asphalt and concrete pavements. Skid resistance tests were conducted on all 79 sections between 1981 and 1983; 21 sections were sites with multiple wet-weather accidents and the remaining 58 were sites on which only a single accident was reported in wet weather during the period of the study. The tests were performed as soon as possible after the accident.

Measurements were also taken at control sites that had pavement and traffic characteristics similar to those of the accident sites and were within 1.6 km (1 mile) of those sites. Also, 6 of the 12 sites with multiple accidents were compared with the control sites. Skid numbers obtained from measurements with the two types of tires are given in Ref 9 for the single-accident sites, the control sites, and for multiple-accident sites. Also recorded were descriptions of the test sites as well as information about accidents that had occurred at those sites.

Figure 1 is derived from a previous study conducted in Virginia and published in a paper by Henry [5]. Texture classification was based on qualitative observation. Blank-tire data (SN_{40}^{B}) and ribbed-tire data (SN_{40}^{R}) are compared

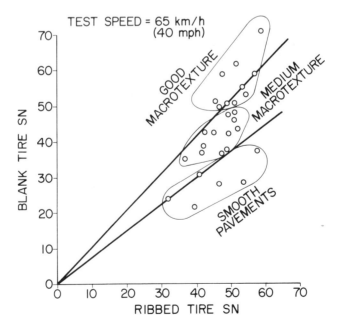

FIG. 1—*Relationship between skid numbers measured with the ribbed tire and the blank tire on pavements in Virginia* [5].

for the accident sites and the control sites in Figs. 2 and 3, respectively. Most of the accident sites and the control sites have skid-resistance values that are contained within the region below 30 for the blank tire and below 40 for the ribbed tire. The line dividing smooth and medium macrotexture established in Fig. 1 indicates that most of the accident and control site data of Figs. 2 and 3 would be classified as smooth textures. No texture data were obtained for the accident or control sites in this study. However, the skid test operators noted on the data sheets of six sites the qualitative observation that four sites were particularly coarse (Sites 34, 45, 48, and 56), and two of the sites appeared to be heavily polished (Sites 36 and 37). These sites are marked on Fig. 2 with the symbol C for the four coarse pavements and the symbol P for the two polished pavements. Qualitatively, therefore, these observations appear to be consistent with the previous study, and the line separating good, medium, and smooth microtexture sites is shown in Figs. 2 and 3 as well.

It is tempting, when observing plots of the data, such as those in Figs. 2 and 3, to try a linear regression in order to predict blank-tire data from ribbed-tire data. The significance of such an exercise would be to characterize the relationships between the two skid numbers for average or typical pavement textures. In fact, it is the deviation from such a prediction that is of interest here. Pavements exhibiting an unusually high blank-tire skid number are expected to have medium or high macrotexture. On the other hand, pavements with high ribbed-tire skid numbers but low blank-tire skid numbers would be ex-

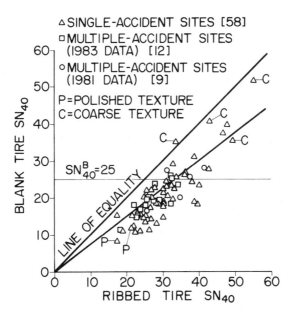

FIG. 2—*Relationship between skid numbers measured with the ribbed tire and the blank tire at the accident sites.*

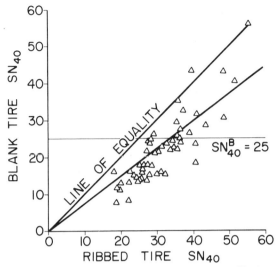

FIG. 3—*Relationship between skid numbers measured with the ribbed tire and the blank tire at the control sites.*

pected to have low macrotexture and good microtexture. Pavements in which both numbers are low are deficient in both macrotexture and microtexture. In Maine, in fact, Madden [10] concluded: "Large variations in the percent of frictional reduction from the use of smooth tires existed within all of the specific pavement types. Therefore, predicting frictional levels for either the smooth or ribbed tires based upon values obtained with the other cannot be considered valid."

It has been suggested [7] that when the blank-tire skid number is in the low twenties or below, the wet-weather accident frequency is high. It can be seen in Fig. 2 that most of the multiple-accident-site data fall below a blank-tire skid number of 25. It should be noted, however, that the criterion for a multiple-accident site in this study was established as a site where more than one accident occurred and thus does not necessarily imply a very high accident frequency. The Florida data (Fig. 4) discussed later supports the observations in Connecticut [7] as well as the observations here.

The frequency of skid numbers obtained with the two test tires on the wet-pavement accident sites is plotted in Fig. 5. The histograms representing the frequency of skid numbers are clearly skewed to the left, where the skid numbers are smaller, but the range of the skid numbers and the frequency for each skid number class are significantly different for the two test tires. What is their theoretical probability distribution and is there any essential distinction between the blank-tire skid numbers and the ribbed-tire skid numbers? The chi-square test can be used to answer these questions by evaluating the goodness of fit of the distributions.

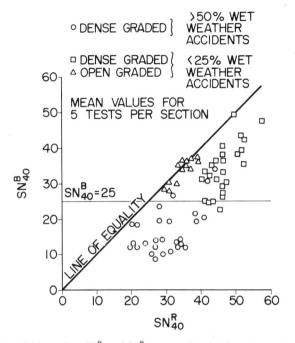

FIG. 4—*Skid numbers SN_{40}^R and SN_{40}^B measured at accident sites in Florida.*

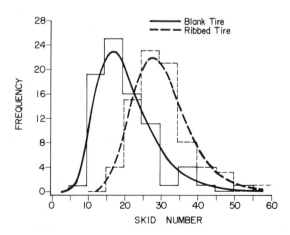

FIG. 5—*Histogram of skid numbers at all accident sites for the two tires.*

According to the shape of the histrogram, an attempt was made to fit the data to a specific model. It was assumed that the skid numbers were distributed in a log-normal distribution. The probability density function of the log-normal distribution is defined as

$$f_y(y) = \frac{1}{y\sigma_{lny}\sqrt{2\pi}} \exp\left[-\frac{1}{2\sigma_{lny}^2} ln^2\left(\frac{y}{\Theta_y}\right)\right] \qquad y \geq 0 \qquad (1)$$

$$= 0 \qquad\qquad\qquad\qquad\qquad y < 0$$

where

y = measured skid number,

m_y = mean of the measured skid number,

σ_y = standard deviation of the measured skid number,

σ_{lny} = standard deviation of the natural logarithm of the measured skid number, and

$\Theta_y = e^{m_{lny}}$ where m_{lny} is the mean of the natural logarithm of the measured skid numbers.

The mean and the standard deviation are given by

$$m_y = \Theta_y \exp\left(\frac{\sigma_{lny}^2}{2}\right) \qquad\qquad (2)$$

$$\sigma_y^2 = m_y^2 \left[\exp(\sigma_{lny}^2) - 1\right] \qquad\qquad (3)$$

For the given data the following values were obtained

$$m_y = 20.54 \qquad \sigma_y^2 = \overline{7.97}^2$$

$$\Theta_y = 19.15 \qquad \sigma_{lny} = 0.374$$

where y_i is the upper limit of each interval.

The value of chi-square is calculated to be 0.874. The critical value of chi-square for two degrees of freedom at the 5% level of probability is 5.991. The value of chi-square is less than the critical value, and therefore the actual skid number distribution may be represented by the log-normal distribution; in other words, the log-normal hypothesis is accepted at the 5% level. Figure 6 indicates that the log-normal distribution is a better distribution to fit the blank-tire data than is the gamma distribution, despite the fact that the gamma distribution hypothesis can be accepted at the 5% level.

The results of the chi-square test applied to the ribbed-tire data are plotted

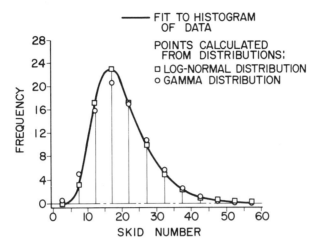

FIG. 6—*Comparison of log-normal and gamma distributions of blank-tire data.*

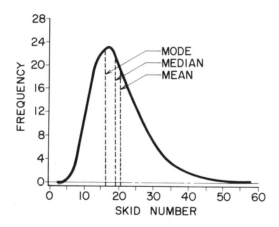

FIG. 7—*Distribution of skid numbers obtained with the blank tire at accident sites.*

in Fig. 7. The distribution is similar to that of the blank-tire data and can be represented by a log-normal distribution.

Similar analyses were conducted for the control sites; the skid numbers for these sites also are distributed according to the log-normal distribution [9]. The means of the skid numbers for the accident sites were two numbers lower than those for the control sites for both tires. It must be concluded that the skid resistance of the control sites was not significantly different from that of the accident sites.

Comparison of the Skid Number Distribution Between the Two Test Tires

As already mentioned, the blank-tire data (SN_{40}^B) from the wet-pavement accident sites can be assumed to fit a log-normal distribution. The mode, median, and mean were calculated as follows

$$\text{mode} = \Theta_y / \exp(\sigma_{\ln y}^2) = 16.65 \tag{4}$$

$$\text{median} = \Theta_y = 19.15 \tag{5}$$

$$\text{mean} = \Theta_y \exp(\sigma_{\ln y}^2/2) = 20.54 \tag{6}$$

Figure 7 shows that 96% of all skid numbers will lie within ± 2 standard deviation points from the mean value; this means that SN_{40}^B will range approximately from 4.6 to 36.5, that is, $20.54 \pm 2 (7.97)$.

For the ribbed-tire data (SN_{40}^R)

$$\text{mode} = 27.68$$
$$\text{median} = 29.39$$
$$\text{mean} = 30.28$$

Figure 8 shows that 96% of all SN_{40}^R values will lie within the range from 15.2 to 45.4, that is, $30.28 \pm 2 (7.55)$.

It is possible to compare the actual skid number frequency with the theoretical frequency from Figs. 7 and 8. In Fig. 8, the actual frequency is larger

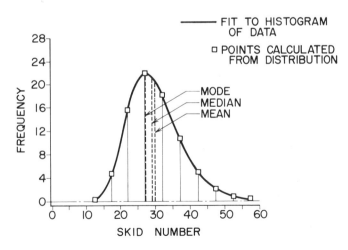

FIG. 8—*Distribution of skid numbers obtained with the ribbed tire at accident sites.*

than the theoretical frequency within the SN range of 10 to 20. The probability is about 51% of the distribution. The range of SN_{40}^B from 10 to 20 can be considered sensitive to wet-pavement accidents. With the ribbed-tire (SN_{40}^R) data, a log-normal distribution gives a smaller frequency of SN_{40}^R in the range of 25 to 35 skid numbers. This sensitivity to wet accidents is 51% of the total distribution (see Fig. 8).

The plots in Figs. 9 and 10 show cumulative frequency versus SN_{40}^B and SN_{40}^R, respectively. The figures indicate that 95% of the skid numbers obtained with the blank-tire data are less than 35, whereas the corresponding figure is less than 45 for the ribbed-tire data. Generally, the ribbed-tire skid numbers are larger than the blank-tire data by 10 units.

Figures 5 and 11 show that the bias of the skid number distribution for the

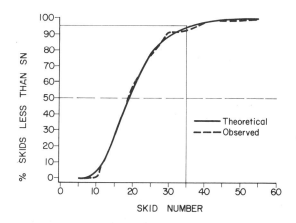

FIG. 9—*Cumulative distribution of blank-tire skid numbers.*

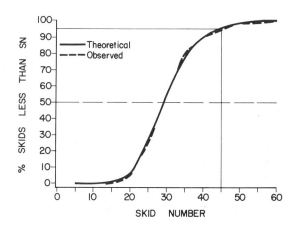

FIG. 10—*Cumulative distribution of ribbed-tire skid numbers.*

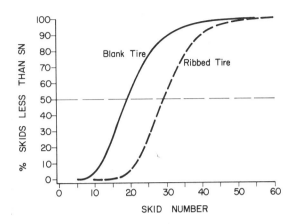

FIG. 11—*Comparison of skid number distribution for the two tires.*

TABLE 1—*Results obtained from Eq 7.*

Tire	Coefficient of Skewness	Proportion Less Than the Mean
Blank tire	1.22	0.574
Ribbed tire	0.76	0.549

two tires is somewhat different. The coefficient of skewness of the log-normal distribution is calculated from the following equation

$$\gamma(y) = \eta^3 + 3\eta \tag{7}$$

where $\eta = \sqrt{\exp(\sigma^2_{\ln y})} - 1$. Applying this equation gives the results shown in Table 1.

These results illustrate that the probability density function of the blank-tire data is more skewed towards lower values than is that of the ribbed-tire data. Since these sites are samples from a population of accident sites, the measure that relates better to skidding accidents would be expected to show greater skewness to the low skid-resistance values. This result shows up more clearly in the Florida accident data (Figs. 4 and 12). The histogram (Fig. 12) of the Florida data (Fig. 4) clearly shows the difference in the distribution of the data for the two tires with a second mode for the blank tire at "low skid number."

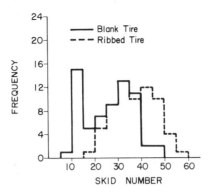

FIG. 12—*Histogram of skid number frequency from Florida data.*

Summary and Conclusion

A limited study was conducted for relating wet-weather accidents to skid resistance, and particularly to two somewhat different measures of skid resistance. Both measurements are identical except for the test tires. The test method is the ASTM Method E 274. A ribbed (ASTM E 501) and a blank (ASTM E 524) tire were used on all test sites. The experience of many other accident research studies was confirmed in this study. However, it is very difficult to come to definitive conclusions for several reasons.

Accidents are statistically rare events and, when stratified by selected causes, such as skidding accidents, the number shrinks further. Also, few accidents have a single cause and sometimes cause and effect are difficult to separate. Did skidding occur because of panic or did skidding cause the panic? Such uncertainties were borne out by the fact that the control sites were not significantly different from the accident sites.

Nevertheless, some trends based on data in this study and data from some states were reinforced. Skid numbers measured with the blank tire are somewhat better predictors of skidding accident potential. However, further data collection is needed to show that they are statistically more significant. Ideally, two measures should be taken, which would provide information as to why the skid resistance is low and also allow the skid resistance-speed gradient to be computed. These could be by the use of (1) both tires, (2) one tire and a macrotexture measurement, or (3) a macrotexture and a microtexture measurement. However, if the cost of data collection is increased significantly, it would be impractical to implement such recommendations.

However, one clear conclusion can be drawn. Accident studies to provide sufficient and reliable data are too costly, both in time and in money. We can accept the fact that the accident potential is greater on slippery pavements than on high friction pavements. No single number can define this potential; it depends on the frictional demand associated with driving maneuvers, such as braking, cornering, and overtaking. Future research should concentrate on methods for providing better and lasting skid resistance and methods for reliably identifying hazardous sites.

References

[1] "Fatal Highway Accidents on Wet Pavements, the Magnitude, Location, and Characteristics," NTSB-HSS-80-1, National Transportation Safety Board, Washington, DC.

[2] *1983 Annual Book of ASTM Standards, Road and Paving Materials; Traveled Surface Characteristics*, Volume 04.03, American Society for Testing and Materials, Philadelphia, 1983.

[3] Hankins, K. D., Morgan, R. B., Ashkar, B., and Tutt, P. R., "The Degree of Influence of Certain Factors Pertaining to the Vehicle and the Pavement on Traffic Accidents Under Wet Conditions," Research Report 133-3F, Texas Highway Department, Austin, TX, 1970.

[4] Wambold, J. C. and Henry, J. J., "Pavement Surface Texture—Significance and Measurement," Report FHWA/RD-84/091 and 092 (PTI 8312), Federal Highway Administration, Washington, DC, 1984.

[5] Henry, J. J., "The Use of Blank and Ribbed Test Tires for Evaluating Wet Pavement Friction," Transportation Research Record 788, Washington, DC, 1981, pp. 1-5.

[6] "Safety Effectiveness Evaluations: Selected State Highway Skid Resistance Programs," Report NTSB-SEE-80-6, National Transportation Safety Board, 1980.

[7] Ganung, G. A. and Kos, F. J., "Wet-Weather, High-Hazard Locations: Identification and Evaluation," Report FHWA-CT-RD-403-F-79-4, Connecticut Department of Transportation, Wethersfield, 1979.

[8] Dierstein, P. G., "Treaded Tire Versus Smooth Tire Friction on Various Portland Cement Concrete and Bituminous Surface Textures in Illinois," paper presented at the 1979 Research Review Conference, Federally Coordinated Program of Highway Research and Development, Williamsburg, VA, Dec. 1979.

[9] Henry, J. J., Wambold, J. C., and Huihua, X., "Evaluation of Pavement Texture," final report FHWA/RD-84-016 (PTI 8321), Federal Highway Administration, Washington, DC, 1984.

[10] Madden, D. A., "Frictional Resistance of Pavements—Smooth Versus Ribbed Tires," Technical Paper 83-3, Maine Department of Transportation, Bureau of Highways, Materials and Research Division, Bangor, May 1983.

Eldridge A. Whitehurst[1] and John B. Neuhardt[2]

Time-History Performance of Reference Surfaces

REFERENCE: Whitehurst, E. A. and Neuhardt, J. B., **"Time-History Performance of Reference Surfaces,"** *The Tire Pavement Interface, ASTM STP 929*, M. G. Pottinger and T. J. Yager, Eds., American Society for Testing and Materials, Philadelphia, 1986, pp. 61–71.

ABSTRACT: The paper describes briefly the construction of reference surfaces for use in skid trailer correlation at the Field Test and Evaluation Center for Eastern States and discusses in detail the performance of two of these surfaces over a nine-year period. The seasonal variation in skid number widely reported for pavement surfaces in service is clearly observed in these surfaces subjected to only test traffic. One of the surfaces having an epoxy cement overspray applied at the time of construction has retained essentially the same level of skid resistance throughout the nine years; the other, without the overspray, has experienced a continuing decrease in skid resistance. It is concluded that overspraying a surface with a wear-resistant membrane, which inhibits both loss and polishing of the surface aggregate, may result in a test pad, which will maintain its original skid number for a long period of time.

KEY WORDS: reference surfaces, pavements, construction, skid resistance testing

In the early 1970s the Federal Highway Administration undertook a program for the development of three centers in the United States to which individual states or other governmental agencies could transport their skid trailers for complete calibration, some repairs or modifications to improve compliance with ASTM Test Method for Skid Resistance of Paved Surfaces Using a Full-Scale Tire (E 274), and correlation against a "standard" system to be known at each center as the area reference skid measurement system (ARSMS). Correlations were to be conducted at each center on a series of test surfaces, referred to as primary reference surfaces (PRS), to be built as nearly alike at the three centers as possible.

[1]Professor of civil engineering, The Ohio State University, 2070 Neil Ave., Columbus, OH 43210; and director, Field Test and Evaluation Center for Eastern States, Transportation Research Center of Ohio.

[2]Professor of systems and industrial engineering and professor of statistics, The Ohio State University, 1971 Neil Ave., Columbus, OH 43210.

The surfaces were constructed at the three centers during the summer of 1974. The ARSMS became available in the spring of 1976. The Western center operated only during 1975, resulting in the production of too little data to be of use in evaluating PRS performance.

Caused primarily by procedural changes during the past ten years, and in part by the fact that one PRS was found to have an impractically high skid number, not all of the surfaces have been used continually throughout the period. At the Eastern Field Test Center (EFTC) located at the Transportation Research Center of Ohio, however, PRS 1 and PRS 4 have been in continual use.

The following describes the construction of the reference surfaces, the results of nine years of testing on two of the surfaces at EFTC, and a limited comparison of the performance of those surfaces at EFTC with that of presumably identical surfaces at the Central/Western Field Test Center (C/W FTC) at College Station, TX. The testing at EFTC involves approximately 12 000 individual skid tests on each surface.

The test results show clearly that the same seasonal variations in skid number (SN), which are widely reported for highways in service, have occurred in the reference surfaces that are exposed to no traffic except test traffic. They also show a significant difference in performance, in terms of long-term stability of SN level between two surfaces constructed by somewhat different techniques. This difference may suggest a procedure for building test surfaces that will maintain the same general level of SN over a period of years.

Reference Surface Construction

Before construction of the PRSs, considerable attention was directed at determining what was desired of such surfaces and how they might best be constructed to achieve those objectives. It was agreed that the PRSs should

(1) provide a wide range of SN values for use in skid trailer correlations,
(2) be durable, requiring little repair over an extensive period of time, and
(3) exhibit as small a change in SN value with time as possible.

It was agreed that these objectives might best be met through the construction of epoxy seal coats. A single contractor, Adhesives Engineering Company of San Carlos, CA, was selected to construct the surfaces at all three Centers.

Adhesives Engineering first shipped its equipment to the Central Field Test Center (CFTC) at the Texas Transportation Institute, College Station, TX, and constructed a number of small test sections in the spring of 1974. Evaluation of these test sections resulted in the selection of aggregates and aggregate gradations to be used in the PRSs.

Five PRSs were constructed at each center. The aggregates and gradations

TABLE 1—*Aggregates and gradations for PRSs.*

PRS	Aggregate	Gradation
1	finely graded silica sand	No. 10 to No. 16
2	crushed river gravel	$3/8$ in.
3	finely graded silica sand	No. 20 to No. 30
4	finely graded silica sand	No. 4 to No. 8
5	crushed expanded shale	$3/8$ in.

for these are shown in Table 1. The epoxy adhesive used was identified as Concresive AEX1042, a two component epoxy cement. It was formulated for application at pavement base temperatures between 10 and 49°C (50 and 120°F). Appropriate quantities of the two components were shipped to each Center in 208-L (55-gal) drums and combined in a pressure distributor immediately before application.

The finely graded silica sands used on PRS 1, 3, and 4 were materials used as fracture sands in the oil recovery industry. Adequate quantities of each were shipped to each Center in 45-kg (100-lb) sealed double paper bags. The crushed river gravel and crushed expanded shale were shipped to each Center in 208-L (55-gal) drums.

After all materials had been distributed, Adhesives Engineering transported its pressure distributor, aggregate distributor, and crew to EFTC, in East Liberty, OH, and constructed the PRSs at that site in July 1974. Each PRS is 159 m (520 ft) long and 5 m (15 ft) wide. The contractor's equipment was capable of covering a strip 2.3 m (7½ ft) wide on each pass; hence, each PRS was constructed in two passes. Great care was taken to assure that the longitudinal joint between the two passes was tight and that no overlap occurred between the two passes.

For each PRS, the pressure distributor applied the epoxy adhesive over a 2.3-m (7½-ft) wide strip at the rate of 1.63×10^{-3} m³/m² (0.36 gal/yd²). It was followed immediately by the aggregate distributor, which was driven just outside the epoxy covered strip and dropped the aggregate onto the strip through a cantilevered boom and worm gear feed. The aggregate was applied at a rate sufficient to drop at least twice the amount of aggregate, which might be expected to be held by the adhesive. After this first strip had thoroughly set, the loose aggregate was swept back from the edge, which would become the centerline joint, the bonded material carefully covered with roofing paper, and a second adjacent strip constructed. Approximately 24 h after construction of the second strip, the surface of the pad was swept clean; all surplus aggregate being removed.

The above process completed construction of PRS 3, 4, and 5. For PRS 1 and 2, an overspray of 1.118×10^{-3} m³/m² (0.26 gal/yd²), of the epoxy cement was applied to the swept surfaces. No further aggregate was applied.

Reference Surface Performance

Changes in operational procedures and other considerations at centers have resulted in broad differences in usage of the various PRSs, both at a single center and between centers. For example, PRS 5 was found to have a highly abrasive surface with a very high SN, resulting in tremendous tire wear and occasional blowouts. Its use was discontinued after 1975. As previously noted, the Western Field Test Center operated only during 1975, and too few data are available for meaningful analysis.

At EFTC two of the five original surfaces have been in continual use since late 1974, PRS 1 and PRS 4. The following evaluation of service performance is based largely on the record of those surfaces.

Before considering long-term performance, it is interesting to look at how well the PRSs have met the original objectives specified for them.

With regard to the first objective, the five surfaces did at each center provide a wide range of skid numbers. The skid number of each surface was, however, about 10 SN higher than had been anticipated, resulting in the very high SN of PRS 5 and no surface with a very low skid number. This resulted in the abandonment of PRS 5 and the construction of a low skid number surface. At EFTC, this took the form of a Jennite surface on an existing base.

With respect to the second objective, all of the PRSs constructed at EFTC have proved to be very durable. A few construction joints from the underlying base have come through as surface cracks, and there has been some loss of aggregate from PRS 4. No surface has received any maintenance other than periodic cleaning, and all are still quite serviceable. The surfaces constructed at C/W FTC have not proved to be as durable. Considerable surface distress, apparently associated with some failure of the epoxy binder, has occurred in several. It has been speculated that the epoxy binder used may be more compatible with the weather exposure in Ohio than with that in Texas.

With respect to the third objective, data collected over a period of nine years on PRS 1 and PRS 4 at EFTC have been analyzed to evaluate skid number constancy. Although the surfaces were placed in service in late 1974, only a few tests were performed that year and these have not been included in the evaluation. All tests performed during 1975 were made with a Law skid trailer, which was used at EFTC until the area reference skid measurement system (ARSMS) became available in early 1976. At that time a correlation was conducted between the Law unit and the ARSMS, and the 1975 data reported herein have been adjusted on the basis of that correlation. All data reported for 1976 and subsequent years were collected with an ARSMS.

Data analyzed are reported as "average skid numbers," or tests. Each value is the average of all tests made at 32, 64, and 97 km/h (20, 40, and 60 mile/h) by the ARSMS on a single day during a correlation with a state system. Through June 1978, this involved the average of 48 individual skids, 16 at each of the test speeds. Since that time, each average value has been based on 36 skids, 12 at each speed. During the nine years for which data are

TABLE 2—*Month and frequency of data collection.*

Year	Months of Data Collection	Number of Tests in Month, Respectively	Total Tests
1975	4,5,6,7,8	3,4,2,4,2	15
1976	4,5,6,7,8,9,10,11	1,7,7,9,8,3,8,3	46
1977	3,4,5,6,7,8,9,10,11	6,4,8,7,9,3,7,1,1	46
1978	3,4,5,6,7,8,9,10	6,8,7,8,3,8,7,2	49
1979	3,4,5,6,7,8,9,10	2,6,5,6,4,6,4,2	35
1980	4,5,6,7,8,9,10	3,2,2,4,4,4,2	21
1981	3,4,5,6,7,9,10	3,3,5,6,4,4,2	27
1982	3,4,5,6,7,8	1,3,9,4,1,2	20
1983	3,4,5,6[a]	2,7,3,7	19
		Total	278

[a]Data available through June only.

reported, 278 such series of tests were performed on each of the surfaces. Chronological distribution of the tests, by month and by years, is shown in Table 2.

Initially, two relationships were investigated for relating SN values to day of year. One was a sinusoidal functions, as used by Burchett [1] taking the form

$$SN = A - B \cos [360° (YRDAY - D_1)/365]$$

where

SN = predicted average SN over speeds of 32, 64, and 97 km/h (20, 40, 60 mph) at same day in the year,
$YRDAY$ = day of year, that is, 1, 2, ... 365; 1 = Jan. 1,
A = "centerline" SN about which SN varies during the year,
B = largest deviation during the year of SN about the value A, and
D_1 = day at which SN is lowest.

The other was a "folded" exponential, taking the form

$$SN = Ce [-S (YRDAY - 30)], 0 < YRDAY < D_1$$

$$SN = Ce [-S (395 - YRDAY)], D_1 < YRDAY < 365$$

where

C = highest value of SN for the year and
S = a constant related to the rate of SN change.

In using the exponential function, days were measured from 30 since in no case were data collected before Feb. 1. Preliminary runs using this function and varying values of D_1 in ten-day increments resulted in best least squares fits with $D_1 = 210$, approximately Aug. 1. This value was used in all subsequent analyses. (It is interesting to note that Burchett [1] obtained a median value of 243 days, based on measurements of many sections of highways having individual values ranging from 190 to 315).

The 278 daily average SN values of each PRS were analyzed by years, allowing the values of A, B, C, and S to vary each year. Statistical tests showed that B and S could be held constant across some or all of the nine years involved.

Table 3 shows values of the coefficient of determination R^2, resulting from the use of four different models in analyzing the data. It may be seen that for each reference surface differences in R^2 are small, regardless of the model used in the analysis. Since the sinusoidal model with the value of B held constant was convenient to portray graphically, it was used in all comparative analyses.

Figure 1 provides an example of the fit of observed average SN values about a curve of predicted values using the above model for one surface and one year (PRS 4, 1979).

Figure 2 shows the family of yearly curves for PRS 1 at EFTC from 1975 to 1983. If values of A are taken to occur at YRDAY 120 (about May 1), it is apparent that such values have ranged from about 36½ to about 41½ SN over the nine-year period. Importantly, no chronologically systematic sequence to this variation can be observed.

Figure 3 shows a similar family of yearly curves for PRS 4 from 1975 to 1983. Two differences between Fig. 2 and Fig. 3 are immediately noticeable. The range of values of A for PRS 4, from about 46 to 63½ SN, is much larger than the range of such values for PRS 1. Chronologically, the change in value of A for PRS 4 has been quite systematic, the value falling almost without exception in each successive year.

The data shown in Figs. 2 and 3 are summarized in Figs. 4 and 5, respectively. In this case, the daily average SN values for each month have been totalled and averaged, providing a monthly average SN for each PRS. The monthly average SN values have been plotted for the nine-year period and the

TABLE 3—*Coefficients of determination for four models.*

Model	Restrictions	R^2 PRS 1	R^2 PRS 4
Sinusoidal	A, B different for all years	0.68	0.84
Sinusoidal	A different all years B constant	0.62	0.82
Exponential	C, D different for all years	0.65	0.85
Exponential	C different all years		
	D different in 1982 (PRS 1)	0.63	
	D different in 1981, 1982 (PRS 4)		0.74

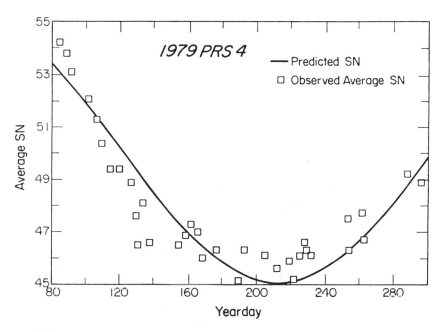

FIG. 1—*Example of the fit of observed SN values about a curve of predicted values.*

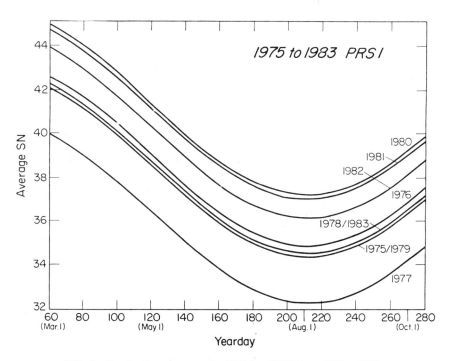

FIG. 2—*Family of yearly curves for PRS 1 at EFTC from 1975 to 1983.*

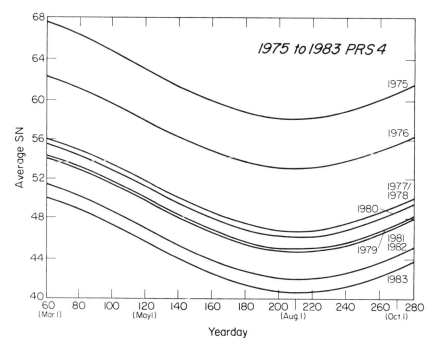

FIG. 3—*Family of yearly curves for PRS 4 from 1975 to 1983.*

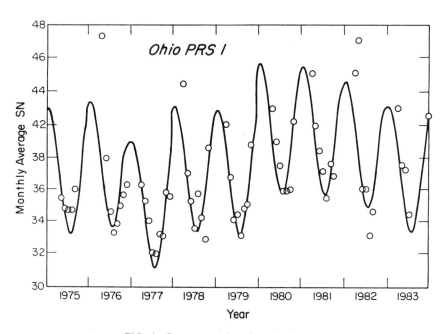

FIG. 4—*Summary of data shown in Fig. 4.*

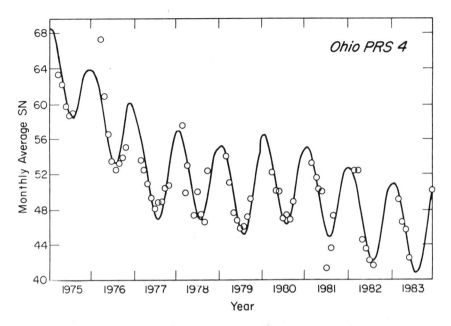

FIG. 5—*Summary of data shown in Fig. 5.*

nine yearly prediction curves have been overlayed. The difference in the performance of the two surfaces over the nine-year period is clearly apparent.

Thus, it may be concluded that ARS 1 met reasonably well the objective of providing long-term stability of SN value, subject to a yearly seasonal variation of about ±5 SN, while PRS 4 failed to meet this objective.

Comparison of PRSs at Two Centers

It was previously stated that not all PRSs have had the same use history at EFTC and at C/W FTC. PRS 1 and PRS 4 were used at C/W FTC from 1976 through 1979. During that period, the surfaces at EFTC were tested with ARSMS 3 and those at C/W FTC with ARSMS 1. Before attempting to compare the performances of the surfaces, therefore, it is appropriate to compare the performances of the two ARSMSs.

The construction of the ARSMSs was completed in March 1976. The systems were correlated at EFTC in April 1976 and have been subsequently correlated at C/W FTC in the early spring of 1977, 1978, 1979, and 1980. Throughout these correlations, ARSMS 1 and ARSMS 3 have been found to perform in very similar manners when both are properly calibrated. ARSMS 3 had regularly reported skid number values that were on the average 1 to 1¹/₂ SN higher than those reported by ARSMS 1.

The data for four years (1976 through 1979) for PRS 1 and PRS 4 at C/W

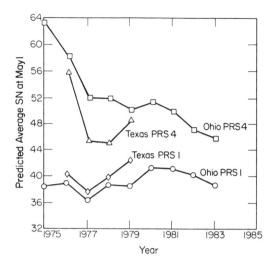

FIG. 6—*Data for PRS 1 and PRS 4 at C/W FTC (1976–1979).*

FTC were subjected to the same analyses as described above for the surfaces at EFTC. After prediction equations had been developed, SN values for YR-DAY 120 (about May 1) were calculated. These represent the *A* value for each year, or the value about which SN experienced its yearly variation. These values are plotted for nine years for the surfaces at EFTC and for four years for the surfaces at C/W FTC in Fig. 6.

The data shown in Fig. 6 indicate that the surfaces constructed in Ohio and in Texas were at least similar. The Texas PRS 1 showed values of SN about 1¹/₂ SN higher than did the Ohio PRS 1 during three years and a value about 4 SN higher during the fourth. If the difference in performance of the two ARSMSs is taken into account, the differences between the surfaces would be about 3 to 5¹/₂ SN. The Texas PRS 4 showed values of SN about 2 to 2¹/₂ SN lower than did the Ohio PRS 4 during two years and values about 7 to 7¹/₂ lower during two years. If the differences in test unit performance are again taken into account, the differences between the surfaces would be about ¹/₂ to 6 SN.

Conclusions

The data reported herein suggest that it may be possible to construct test surfaces that will perform, with respect to surface friction, in at least a similar manner when reproduced at locations far apart. Great care must be exercised in the selection of materials for the surfaces and in their construction. The type of construction required may be quite different from that of usual pavement surfaces.

The data also show the fallacy of specifying that tests be performed on a surface having a fixed, finite skid number. The surfaces discussed herein have been subjected to no traffic except test traffic. They have, nonetheless, exhibited a variation in skid number about some annual mean value of approximately ±5 SN. It would seem that any specification requiring testing against a specified level of surface friction must take such variation into account or provide a technique for continually treating the surface in some manner to prevent the variation from occurring.

Finally, the performance of these surfaces suggests an approach to a technique for the construction of skid pads that will retain a relatively unchanged mean SN (the SN value about which seasonal variation occurs) over a long period of time. Two major causes of reduction in pavement SN with time and traffic exposure are loss of aggregate from the pavement surface and polishing of the aggregate that remains. PRS 4 has suffered loss of aggregate, and it is almost certain that the remaining aggregate has been polished. The mean SN of this surface fell from about 63 to about 46 over a nine year period. The epoxy cover coat on PRS 1 is still fully intact. There has, therefore, been no loss of aggregate from the surface and no aggregate polishing. The mean SN has changed little over the nine-year period. The epoxy cover coat cannot have polished much; its original SN is very low indeed.

It thus appears that if a surface is built with sufficient texture to provide a somewhat higher than desired SN and covered with a tough, durable cover coat such as epoxy (which will somewhat reduce the texture and the initial SN), the probability is high that the mean SN of the resulting surface will remain essentially constant for a long period of time.

Acknowledgments

The authors wish to acknowledge the support of the Federal Highway Administration in funding the Centers from their establishment in 1971–1972 until 1979. The views expressed in this paper, however, are those of the authors and do not necessarily reflect the official views or policies of the Federal Highway Administration, Department of Transportation. This paper does not constitute a standard, specification, or regulation.

The authors wish also to express their appreciation to the Texas Transportation Institute, particularly in the person of A. J. Stocker, for the high level of cooperation, which has facilitated the successful operation of the Centers almost as a joint operation for so many years, and for providing the data on the Texas surfaces included herein.

Reference

[1] Burchett, J. L., "Seasonal Variations in The Skid Resistance of Pavements in Kentucky," Research Report 499, Division of Research, Kentucky Department of Transportation, 1978.

Lary R. Lenke[1] *and Richard A. Graul*[1]

Development of Runway Rubber Removal Specifications Using Friction Measurements and Surface Texture for Control

REFERENCE: Lenke, L. R. and Graul, R. A., **"Development of Runway Rubber Removal Specifications Using Friction Measurements and Surface Texture for Control,"** *The Tire Pavement Interface, ASTM STP 929*, M. G. Pottinger and T. J. Yager, Eds., American Society for Testing and Materials, Philadelphia, 1986, pp. 72–88.

ABSTRACT: The phenomenon of runway touchdown zone rubber buildup is a potentially hazardous problem. Rubber buildup covers the runway surface and occludes the surface texture. This results in a reduced wet friction coefficient between the runway pavement and the aircraft tires. Methods and equipment are available for evaluating the wet friction coefficient; however, these methods are expensive and require highly trained personnel. Therefore, most airport and airbase managers rely exclusively on visual impressions of rubber buildup in lieu of quantitative friction measurements. Nonetheless, quantitative evaluation techniques are desirable for evaluating rubber buildup. A field evaluation experiment was developed to ascertain which of five selected texture measurement techniques are indicative of Mu-Meter friction values in pavement areas with rubber buildup. The five texture measurement techniques included two volumetric techniques for determining average texture depth, ASTM Test Method for Measuring Surface Macrotexture Depth Using a Sand Volumetric Technique (E 965) (sand patch) and the silicone putty test, two methods of rating the pavement microtexture, the Penn State (PTI) drag tester and the chalk wear tester, and stereophotography. This field experiment was designed to provide quantitative methods for ascertaining rubber buildup and removal requirements. Predictive models were established for estimating friction levels using texture measurements but were found to be too variable for specification implementation. Therefore, Mu-Meter friction was used in developing contract specifications for runway rubber removal.

KEY WORDS: friction, hydroplaning, microtexture, macrotexture, runway rubber removal, specification, Mu-Meter

[1]Senior research engineer and research engineer, respectively, Engineering Materials and Civil Systems Division, New Mexico Engineering Research Institute, P.O. Box 25, University of New Mexico, Albuquerque, NM 87131.

The operating velocities of modern aircraft require high shear forces generated at the tire-pavement interface for safe operation. These shear forces are dependent solely upon the available tire-pavement friction. Because of the chemical and physical characteristics of the rubber and mechanical properties of the tire, dry friction between the tire and pavement is not a problem. However, a serious loss of friction can occur once a lubricant, most commonly water from rainfall, is introduced at this interface. On a damp pavement friction loss can be slight, requiring the operator to reduce speed during maneuvering to maintain directional control. In the case of hydroplaning, where directional control of the aircraft is lost, the results can be disastrous.

A separation of the roles played by the tire and the pavement is not appropriate because both components of the tire-pavement system interact to produce tractive or shear forces. However, knowledge of the physics and empirical modeling of the phenomena occurring at the tire-pavement interface will enable the pavement engineer to increase the friction level and the safety of the pavement.

When a contaminant other than a lubricant is placed upon a pavement, the physical and chemical characteristics of the pavement change. On a runway, rubber deposits formed by landing aircraft can dramatically reduce wet friction values. Currently, both the U.S. Air Force (USAF) and the Federal Aviation Administration (FAA) periodically recommend removal of these rubber deposits. At the present time, the airport pavement engineer must rely heavily upon limited visual impressions or experience or both to determine when rubber removal is required and when it has been adequately conducted. Test results obtained by the USAF [1] indicate that this method of inspecting rubber buildup does not correlate well with the results obtained by Mu-Meter friction testing. Therefore, development of a more efficient rubber removal program requires a quantitative evaluation of runway frictional levels.

Current methods of monitoring levels of friction are expensive, require highly trained personnel, and are unavailable at many air facilities. The New Mexico Engineering Research Institute (NMERI) was contracted by the Air Force Engineering and Services Center and the FAA Airport Technology Program to develop a procedure to quantify rubber buildup and its effect on runway friction. An extensive literature search suggested the use of the textural properties of a given pavement to measure its friction level. This paper presents the current empirical theories for determining friction levels from texture measurements, the design of an experiment to correlate the use of texture measurements to friction levels measured by a Mu-Meter, the results of this experiment, and the development of a rubber removal specification.

Current Textural Theories

Pavement engineers have attempted to use the measurement of the pavement's textural characteristics to determine friction levels. Pavement texture is divided into two relative size groups. The smaller asperities are called microtexture. This is the fine texture or grittiness of a pavement. The larger asperities are termed macrotexture. According to Moore [2] typical wavelengths associated with macrotexture are 6 to 20 mm (0.25 to 0.80 in) and for microtexture are 10 to 100 μm (0.0004 to 0.004 in).

Moore [3] models the wet tire-pavement interface as a combination of three zones, and describes these zones, as shown in Fig. 1 as follows:

Zone A: Sinkage, or Squeeze-Film Zone

Under wet conditions, the forward part of what would normally be considered the contact area under dry conditions floats on a thin film of water, the thickness of which decreases progressively as individual tread elements traverse the contact area. Since the tire, water film, and road surface have virtually no relative motion in the contact area, the tread elements in effect attempt to squeeze out the water between rubber and pavement.

Zone B: Draping or Transition Zone

The draping zone begins when the tire elements, having penetrated the squeeze film, commence to drape over the major asperities of the surface and to make contact with the lesser asperities.

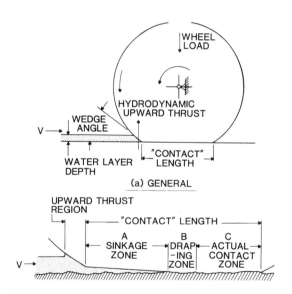

FIG. 1—Wet tire footprint model [3].

Zone C: Actual Contact, or Tractive Zone

This is the region where the tire elements, after draping, have attained an equilibrium position vertically on the surface. The length of this region depends on vehicle velocity; it occupies the rear portion of the overall contact area. Tractive effort is developed here.

This conceptual tire model and the observed linearity in Mu-Meter wet friction speed plots (Fig. 2) have led researchers to the following hypothesis:

1. The intercept of a wet-friction speed plot is the maximum friction value obtainable since the full tire should be in Zone C.
2. The decrease in wet friction caused by increasing speed, or the gradient of the wet-friction speed plot is indicative of the migration of water into Zone C, thereby forming Zones A and B.
3. The extent of water migration can be related to water drainage times.

From Fig. 2, slope M and intercept B can be determined. The intercept B is believed to be dependent upon the pavement's microtexture. The pavement microtexture is believed to determine the adhesional friction of a specific pavement. This adhesional friction is hypothesized as a combination of microhysteresis caused by both geometry and equivalent electrical roughness as proposed by Kummer [4]. Slope M is dependent upon the drainage properties of the pavement macrotexture and tire tread design. For the case of a blank test tire, as used with the Mu-Meter, the pavement's macrotexture controls the drainage characteristics and water removal rate. Since the water removal rate is related to macrotexture, deeper macrotexture ensures efficient and fast bulk water removal.

An alternate method was proposed by Horne and Buhlmann [5]. This method describes the water removal rate in Zone A and Zone B of the tire footprint model. The relative drainage times from both zones are expressed in

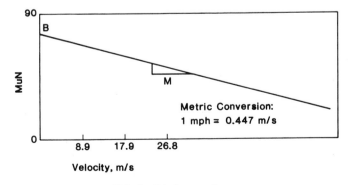

FIG. 2—*Friction speed curve.*

terms of pavement drainage coefficients C_{mac} and C_{mic}. C_{mac} determines the percentage of the tire footprint that is in Zone A. Since in this area dynamic effects of water predominate, the removal rate is dependent upon bulk channel flow, which is determined by the amount of pavement macrotexture for the case of a blank test tire. C_{mic} also determines a percentage of the tire footprint; namely, the relative size of Zone B. Unlike Zone A, fluid viscous forces prevail in this region. Since high localized contact pressures are required to penetrate and break this viscous film, this coefficient is dependent upon the pavement microtexture.

These two pavement drainage coefficients are combined to yield a peak obtainable friction in the following form

$$Y_R = 1 - \left[C_{mac} \left(\frac{p_1}{p}\right)_u + C_{mic} \left(\frac{p_2}{p}\right)_u \right] \tag{1}$$

where

$$
\begin{aligned}
Y_R &= \text{friction ratio of actual friction divided by the maximum} \\
&\quad \text{obtainable friction,} \\
C_{mac}, C_{mic} &= \text{the previously defined pavement drainage coefficients,} \\
p_1 &= \text{hydrodynamic fluid pressure,} \\
p_2 &= \text{viscous fluid pressure,} \\
p &= \text{tire inflation pressure,} \\
C_{mac}(p_1/p)_u &= \text{percentage of tire in Zone A, and} \\
C_{mic}(p_2/p)_u &= \text{percentage of tire in Zone B.}
\end{aligned}
$$

Thus the available tire friction at any speed, according to Eq 1, is determined by the percentage of the contact area still in the dry contact zone.

Since both of these modeling systems attempt to generate a wet-friction speed curve using pavement micro- and macrotexture measurements, a combination of these measurements can be used to predict the friction for any given speed.

Task Constraints and Experimental Philosophy

Because this experiment was the result of an applied research project, various constraints were inherent in the design. The buildup of rubber deposits on the touchdown zones of a runway decrease the wet friction characteristics of a runway. Therefore, a method to determine when this rubber requires removal and when rubber removal has effectively increased the friction level of the runway is desirable. Currently the USAF and the FAA use the Mu-Meter to measure tire-pavement friction and have developed tentative standards by which a runway is rated. These standards are based upon a critical Mu number (MuN) describing the likelihood of an aircraft tire hydroplaning. These guidelines are shown in Table 1.

TABLE 1—*Hydroplaning potential* [1].

MuN at 17.9 m/s (40 mph)	Aircraft Braking Response	Hydroplaning Response
>50	good	no hydroplaning expected
40 to 50	fair	transitional (not well defined)
25 to 41	marginal	potential for hydroplaning
<25	unacceptable	hydroplaning probability high

However, since measuring tire-pavement friction by the Mu-Meter is expensive, requires highly trained personnel, and is unavailable to many airfields, a more economical method is desired. This method is subject to the following constraints. It must be

(1) economical, costing less than $10 000 to implement;
(2) simple, the tests and techniques must be readily understandable and usable by typical airport personnel;
(3) reliable, the method must be able to predict friction levels and differences in friction levels due to rubber removal; and
(4) readily accepted, the method must be based on tests that are currently available and do not require large amounts of research and development to substantiate.

An extensive literature review conducted by the authors [6] evaluated current theories and test methodology used to predict tire-pavement friction. As a result of this study, measurements of the pavement's microtexture and macrotexture characteristics were deemed an economical method for predicting tire-pavement friction. Since the selected measurement techniques were to be simple, economical, and readily accepted, the following field candidate procedures were selected. Two volumetric methods of determining average texture depth to measure macrotexture were used; one method was in accordance with the ASTM Test for Measuring Surface Macrotexture Using a Sand Volumetric Technique (E 965), the other was the silicone putty method.

Two distinct methods, a rubber slider device (the Penn State [PTI] drag tester), and a chalk abrasion device (the chalk wear tester, developed by the authors) were used to quantify microtexture. The last method was stereophotography, which is known to be useful in classifying the pavement's micro- and macrotexture characteristics. No further reference to this stereophotographic method will be made during this paper since analysis of the data is still pending at this writing. All of these procedures are discussed in detail in a previous report [6].

The field test plan was designed to statistically show that measurements of the pavement's macrotexture or microtexture or both are indicative of wet pavement friction levels as obtained with a Mu-Meter. This test plan required collection of Mu-Meter friction values, both wet and dry, at 8.9, 17.9, and 26.8 m/s (20, 40, and 60 mph) along with texture evaluation using the five candidate procedures.[2] As the Mu-Meter provided an analog output of friction levels, the MuN were determined at set locations so that a point by point comparison of these values with the candidate procedures could be made. These tests were conducted before and after rubber removal in touchdown zones where rubber buildup is of concern. In addition, measurements were collected in a centerline nonrubber section and a pavement edge nonrubber section. As rubber removal is not always 100% effective, these last two sections were used as control sections that should determine the maximum obtainable friction on any runway surface. Thus, since a limiting value is known, a comparison can be made showing relative levels of improvement for each runway.

Each test section was approximately 146 m (480 ft) in length with three test locations placed at the quarter points of the section. A general layout of a given runway is shown in Fig. 3. Care was taken to ensure control sections were of the same pavement type and textural finish as the touchdown zone. The statistical approach described was limited to the collection of two replica-

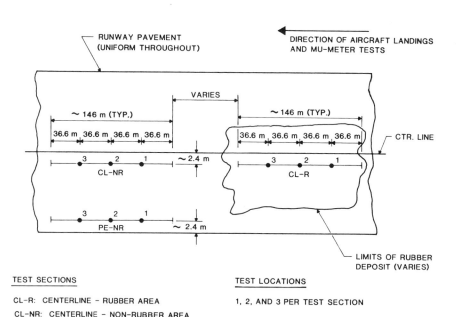

TEST SECTIONS

CL–R: CENTERLINE – RUBBER AREA
CL–NR: CENTERLINE – NON–RUBBER AREA
PE–NR: PAVEMENT EDGE – NON–RUBBER AREA

TEST LOCATIONS

1, 2, AND 3 PER TEST SECTION

METRIC CONVERSION: 1 FT. = 0.3048 m

FIG. 3—*Runway layout* [6].

[2]All experimental data were obtained in English units of measurements.

tions at each location. The number of samples per location was restricted because of limited operational time on each runway.

Test Sites

The experiment required testing of rubber buildup areas on runways before and after rubber removal operations. A total of 18 runways was investigated. To evaluate a wide range of operating conditions, military and commercial air facilities were included.

Typically, military runways use portland cement concrete pavements in the touchdown zones of the runway. This design prevents premature damage to the runway caused by fuel spillage, jet burn during takeoff, and static standing loads. However, since the majority of these runways were designed and constructed during the age of the turboprop, the higher landing speeds and consequent higher frictional demands were either not considered, or the pavement texturing had worn off with age. Thus military runways had lower texture values and MuN as measured by the Mu-Meter. The nine military sites surveyed consisted of the following pavement types: two macro portland cement concrete pavements, which were older concrete runways where the larger stones protruded above the concrete matrix; five micro portland cement concrete pavements, which were concrete runways where only the finer sand particles were visible; one burlap-dragged portland cement concrete runway where relatively deep grooves existed in the pavement surface caused by heavy longitudinal dragging of the surface while the concrete was still plastic; and one porous friction surface, which was a uniform graded asphalt concrete overlay allowing drainage from both the surface and through the thin overlay.

The commercial runways surveyed were more recently constructed and their design included texturing techniques to ensure fast and efficient bulk water removal. These nine runways were either grooved or porous friction overlays. Seven runways were grooved; of these, five were saw cut portland cement concrete, one was a wire-tined portland cement concrete, and one was a saw cut dense-mix asphalt concrete pavement. All saw cut groove dimensions were 6 by 6 mm (0.25 by 0.25 in.) uniformly spaced at 38 mm (1.5 in.). The last two runways were porous friction surfaces as described earlier.

Results

The purpose of this research was to devise a rubber removal specification based upon frictional characteristics of the pavement. This section discusses the findings of the Mu-Meter friction survey, the development of a specification using the Mu-Meter, empirical modeling of Mu-Meter friction levels using texture measurements, and the possibility of using texture measurements for a specification.

Because the data collected were grouped by base, section, location, and repetition, an analysis of variance (ANOVA) procedure was used to determine the largest possible groupings. It was determined that no statistically significant difference existed between the three locations in a given section; thus, a section was considered a representative population. The Mu-Meter data within any section was first checked for precision. It was determined that the repeatability of this data was in agreement with the precision and bias statement of the ASTM Test for Side Force Friction on Paved Surfaces Using the Mu-Meter (E 670).

Next, an ANOVA procedure was performed upon section groupings. The four sections, centerline rubber before, centerline rubber after, centerline nonrubber, and pavement edge nonrubber, had increasing means of 51.9, 54.9, 64.3, 66.0 MuN, respectively. This ordering is consistent with aggregate polishing and rubber buildup mechanisms present upon a runway. However, the differences between the before and after values in the rubber-contaminated area are slight. Also, the overall frictional levels in these areas are above

TABLE 2—*Mean runway friction levels.*

		Mu Values of Control and Before and After Rubber Removal (MuN)			
FACTYPE	PVMTYPE	Pavement Edge Control	Before	After	Improvement[d]
AFB	PCC	39.2[a]	38.8	48.8	yes
AFB	PCC	52.5	33.7	48.5	yes
NAS	PCC	53.5	39.8	40.0	no
AFB	PCC	57.3	56.5	52.8	no
AFB	PCC	58.2	34.8	44.0	yes
NAS	PCC	59.8	44.2	48.8	yes
AFB	PCC	62.2	34.7	37.7	yes
CAF	GPCC[b]	62.5	46.2	43.2	no
CAF	GPCC	65.3	55.3	51.2	no
CAF	GPCC	69.3	49.0	48.5	no
CAF	PFS	71.5	48.2	56.2	yes
CAF	GPCC	72.3	71.0	69.5	no
CAF	PFS	74.5	66.0	67.2	no
AFB	PFS	75.3	59.7	66.7	yes
CAF	GAC	75.5	67.5	69.2	no
AFB	GPCC[c]	78.2	63.5	68.8	yes
CAF	GPCC	79.8	44.2	54.0	yes
CAF	GPCC	83.5	76.7	75.0	no

[a]Control section not representative of centerline pavement.
[b]Wire-tined portland cement concrete.
[c]Heavy burlap drag portland cement concrete.
[d]Improvement indicates a significant increase of 3 MuN after removal.
NOTES: FACTYPE = facility type. PVMTYPE = pavement type. AFB = Air Force Base. NAS = Naval Air Station. CAF = commercial air facility. PCC = portland cement concrete. GPCC = grooved portland cement concrete. PFS = porous friction surfaces. GAC = grooved asphaltic concrete.

the minimum of 50 MuN suggesting that rubber removal is being done needlessly. This confirms the need for a specification or guidelines or both to improve the cost effectiveness of the rubber removal program.

The ANOVA between the 18 runways demonstrated that pavement texturing is an important determinate of overall friction levels. Table 2 demonstrates this dependence of surface on friction levels and rubber removal effectiveness. Table 2 is ranked by increasing MuN of the pavement edge control section. The use of the pavement edge versus the centerline nonrubber section for control was deemed necessary for two reasons. First, many of the military runways had different pavement types in the centerline nonrubber section than in the rubber buildup section making comparisons impossible. Second, a number of runways had appreciable rubber contamination over the centerline length of the runway.

Some obvious inferences may be made from Table 2. First, the ungrooved portland cement concrete pavements do not reach as high a friction level as the grooved portland cement concrete or porous friction surfaces. Second, approximately one half of the runways investigated had friction values above the critical 50 MuN before rubber removal, thus reinforcing the idea that rubber removal is being done before it is necessary, or in some cases where it is not required at all. Third, the increase of friction on any runway after rubber removal is limited by the frictional value of a clean section of the same runway surface. These observations led to the development of a removal specification using the Mu-Meter.

Specification Development

To devise a specification for rubber removal based upon friction criteria, three questions should be addressed:

1. Is the friction level on the runway critical, that is, is the friction level low enough for hydroplaning to be a potential problem?
2. Can removal of rubber improve friction levels to a point where hydroplaning will be unlikely?
3. Has removal of rubber effectively improved the frictional level of the runway?

Earlier research has developed tentative standards for determining when the frictional level of any runway is critical. The results of this research, summarized in Table 1, relate friction levels measured by the Mu-Meter with the potential for aircraft hydroplaning. Since a MuN greater than 50 ensures minimal hydroplaning potential, both the USAF and FAA acknowledge this value as a minimum frictional level required for safe operation. Therefore the critical runway friction level was taken as 50 MuN.

Once a runway's friction level has deteriorated below 50 MuN, remedial action should be taken. Removal of touchdown zone rubber has been determined as one possible solution to increase touchdown zone friction levels [7]. However, since the friction level of any runway surface is limited by its textural characteristics, the friction level after rubber removal cannot exceed the friction level of a clean section of the same runway where rubber deposits have not reduced its textural properties. Therefore, rubber removal will only be effective when the potential increase of friction level is great enough for improvement to occur. Table 3 ranks the evaluated pavements in order of increasing difference between a clean pavement edge control section and a rubber-contaminated section. As seen in Table 3, an improvement in friction does not occur until the potential increase in friction is greater than 10 MuN. Therefore, rubber removal can be considered for improving runway friction, if the friction in the rubber-contaminated zone is more than 10 MuN below the MuN of a clean pavement edge control section. Below this level of potential improvement ($<$10 MuN), improvement in friction by rubber removal is unlikely.

The question of rubber removal and effective improvement of the frictional level of the runway is determined by a ratio of improvement. Since on any given runway the contractor cannot remove 100% of the rubber deposits with-

TABLE 3—*Ranking of rubber removal potential.*

FACTYPE	Δ Control- Before	Δ After- Before	Improvement Ratio	Removal Effective
AFB[a]	0.3	10.0	30.00	yes
AFB	0.8	−3.7	−4.40	no
CAF	1.3	−1.5	−1.13	no
CAF	6.8	−1.7	−0.24	no
CAF	8.0	1.7	0.21	no
CAF	8.5	1.2	0.14	no
CAF	10.0	−4.2	−0.42	no
NAS	13.7	0.2	0.01	no
AFB	14.7	5.3	0.36	yes
AFB	15.7	7.0	0.45	yes
NAS	15.7	4.7	0.30	yes
CAF	16.3	−3.0	−0.18	no
AFB	18.8	14.8	0.79	yes
CAF	20.3	−0.5	−0.02	no
AFB	23.3	9.2	0.39	yes
CAF	23.3	8.0	0.34	yes
AFB	27.5	3.0	0.11	no
CAF	35.7	9.8	0.28	no

[a]Control section not representative of centerline pavement.

NOTES: ΔControl-before = difference in MuN between control and rubber section before removal. ΔAfter-before = difference in MuN between after and before rubber removal. Improvement ratio = ratio of Δafter-before to Δcontrol-before. Removal effective = indication of ratio of improvement greater than 0.3. FACTYPE = facility type. CAF = commercial air facility. AFB = Air Force Base. NAS = Naval Air Station.

out damaging the pavement and requiring a set value of frictional improvement is not valid because of the disparity of improvement potential, the measure of effectiveness was decided by a ratio of actual improvement to potential improvement. The combined use of both Table 3 and field observations suggested that an improvement ratio of 30% was a reasonable and achievable friction increase.

In summary, three criteria determine whether or not rubber removal is a viable solution to increase the reduced touchdown zone friction levels. First, runway friction levels must be either critical or approaching the critical level of 50 MuN. Second, a potential of frictional increase of at least 10 MuN must exist for removal to be effective. Finally, an improvement of 30% of the potential difference is indicative of an effective removal process. Therefore, if a combination of critical runway friction coupled with a small potential of increase exists at any runway, remedial action other than rubber removal should be considered.

Modeling Using Texture

The second phase of data analysis consisted of analyzing various theories using texture measurements to develop a predictive model for the direct tire-pavement friction measurement or Mu-Meter value. After an extensive review of the literature [6] three models were deemed probable for use in predicting direct tire-pavement friction by use of texture measurements. These were

(1) using texture measurements to predict slope and intercept of friction speed curves,
(2) using texture measurements to predict pavement drainage coefficients C_{mic} and C_{mac} [5], and
(3) using texture measurements to predict the 17.9-m/s (40-mph) wet MuN.

In the first method, as friction speed plots are linear above a finite velocity, two characteristics of these plots can be computed, namely, slope and intercept. The tire footprint hydroplaning theory discussed previously suggests that the slope of these plots can be shown as a function of the time required to drain both Zone A and Zone B of the tire footprint (Zone A being the drainage of bulk water and Zone B being the drainage of the thin viscous film). Therefore the slope can be related to macrotexture, which indicates depths of bulk water channel flow (greater channel depth—faster water dissipation), and microtexture, which indicates depths of viscous water channel flow. The first assumption of this theory, that the slope can be related by the macrotexture, is upheld by regression Eq 2

$$M = -2.23 + 1.23 \text{ SAP} \qquad (2)$$

with a correlation coefficient R and root mean square error $\sqrt{MSE}$ of 0.81 and 0.394 MuN/m/s, respectively. In the above equation SAP is the sand patch texture depth expressed in millimetres and M has units of MuN/m/s. The $\sqrt{MSE}$ has the same units as M. The inclusion of a microtexture term does little to explain further variance of the slope

$$M = -2.48 + 0.0049 \text{ DTN} + 1.23 \text{ SAP} \tag{3}$$

with

$$R = 0.82 \text{ and } \sqrt{MSE} = 0.394 \text{ MuN/m/s}$$

or

$$M = -2.33 + 0.123 \text{ CT} + 1.14 \text{ SAP} \tag{4}$$

with

$$R = 0.82 \text{ and } \sqrt{MSE} = 0.394 \text{ MuN/m/s}$$

In Eqs 3 and 4, DTN is the drag tester number as determined using the PTI drag tester, and CT is the chalk wear tester coefficient in units of millimetres of chalk wear per metre of travel (mm/m).

According to this theory, the intercept is the friction value obtained when the complete tire footprint is in the dry tractive zone. Predicting this limiting value is much more difficult because of the strong presence of adhesional effects as shown in the following equation

$$B = 52.8 + 0.559 \text{ DTN} - 6.69 \text{ SAP} \tag{5}$$

where B is the intercept value in MuN, and DTN and SAP are as previously defined. The degree of correlation is poor with $R = 0.53$ and $\sqrt{MSE} = 7.60$ MuN. Once the above models for M and B are combined, the expected variance at a 17.9-m/s (40-mph) test speed is too large for use in any frictional predictive scheme.

The second correlation scheme used the pavement drainage coefficients as proposed by Horne and Buhlmann [5]. Values of the pavement drainage coefficients C_{mic} and C_{mac} were computed by Eqs 6 and 7 as derived from their approach

$$C_{mic} = 1.153 - 1.153b + 0.297 |m| \tag{6}$$

$$C_{mac} = -0.155 + 0.155b + 0.725 |m| \tag{7}$$

where

C_{mic} = the microtexture drainage coefficient,
C_{mac} = the macrotexture drainage coefficient,
b = the intercept of the transformed friction velocity curves, and
$|m|$ = the absolute value of the slope of the transformed friction velocity curves.

The transformation of the friction velocity curves is accomplished by dividing the friction axis by an ultimate friction value and dividing the velocity axis by a critical hydroplaning velocity. For the Mu-Meter the ultimate friction was taken as 92 MuN and the critical hydroplaning speed was taken as 14.64 m/s (32.75 mph). These values are consistent with the suggested guidelines of Ref 5 for a Mu-Meter tire pressure of 69 kPa (10 psi).

Correlating these values with texture measurements yielded the following results. The macrotexture drainage coefficient C_{mac} can be estimated by the equation

$$C_{mac} = 0.243 - 0.146 \text{ SAP} \qquad (8)$$

with $R = 0.78$ and $\sqrt{MSE} = 0.052$ and the microtexture drainage coefficient C_{mic} can be estimated by the equation

$$C_{mic} = 0.333 - 0.144 \text{ CTT} \qquad (9)$$

with $R = 0.47$ and $\sqrt{MSE} = 0.093$. In Eq 9, CTT is the chalk wear coefficient as measured in the transverse direction on the runway.

Once again, by combining the two models and back calculating the 17.9 m/s (40 mph) wet Mu value, the expected variance of friction is too large to use in any predictive scheme. Since neither of the above methods predicted friction values to the close tolerance required for development of specifications, direct modeling of Mu-Meter values by texture measurements was tried.

A summary of these regression models, Eqs 10 to 12, is shown in Table 4. Table 4 identifies pavement sections and provides the statistical models developed for each. Figure 4 shows the relationship between the measured 17.9-m/s (40-mph) MuN values and the MuN predicted by regression Eq 10. This plot shows a strong relationship between MuN as predicted by texture measurements and measured MuN, yet is not refined enough for accurate predictions. Similar plots were generated for the other regression equations but are not included here for brevity.

TABLE 4—*Regression models for MuN.*

Equation Number	Section	Model	n	R	$\sqrt{MSE}$
10	before	MW40 = 42.7 + 36.9 LSAP + 14.4 CTT + 9.6 CTL	103	0.88	6.43
11	after	MW40 = 48.2 + 32.5 LSAP + 10.9 CTT + 5.3 CTL	104	0.82	6.76
12	control[a]	MW40 = 69.2 + 38.6 LSAP + 6.7 CTT − 5.9 CTL	104	0.84	6.24

[a]Pavement edge control section.

NOTES: (1) MW40 = Mu*N* predicted for a 17.9 m/s (40 mph) wet test. (2) LSAP = common log of average texture depth (expressed in mm). (3) CTT = transverse chalk wear coefficient (expressed in mm/m). (4) CTL = longitudinal chalk wear coefficient (expressed in mm/m). (5) n = number of observations. (6) R = regression correlation coefficient. (7) $\sqrt{MSE}$ = root mean square error (standard error of prediction).

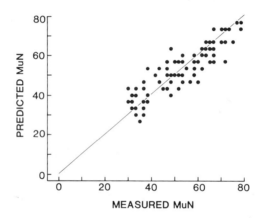

FIG. 4—*Comparison plot of predicted versus actual values for Eq 10.*

Conclusions

First, texture measurements can be used to approximate tire-pavement friction as measured by the Mu-Meter. Standard errors of prediction are as low as 6.5 Mu*N*. This low error is comparable to other published literature. For example, when correlating one Mu-Meter with another, the expected error would be around 3 Mu*N*. While correlation of the Mu-Meter with the SAAB friction metre yielded standard errors ranging from 3 to 8 Mu*N* [8]. However, improvements in friction caused by rubber removal cannot be determined by texture measurements since friction improvements caused by rubber removal are slight compared to model error.

Second, the Mu-Meter was found to be repeatable within the limits of the precision and bias statement of ASTM Method E 670.

Third, specifications for determining need, potential improvement, and satisfactory completion of rubber removal operations were devised by using a Mu-Meter. These are

(1) if the friction level in the rubber deposit area is less than 50 MuN, rubber removal should be considered;

(2) if the difference between friction levels of a clean pavement edge control section and the rubber contaminated section is greater than 10 MuN, rubber removal can be effective in improving friction levels; and

(3) if rubber removal increases friction 30% of the difference of the friction levels between the clean control zone and the rubber deposit zone, rubber removal is effectively accomplished.

Fourth, rubber removal will not cure all friction problems. If the friction level of a clean section of runway is low enough to be critical (< 50 MuN), no amount of rubber removal will cure this problem. Other types of surface treatments must be investigated to increase the friction level on such surfaces. In addition, if the 30% improvement does not produce friction levels above the minimal requirement, then alternative methods should be evaluated for improving the textural and frictional levels of such runways.

Recommendations

Since many airfields remove rubber unnecessarily, use of a standardized specification will save these airfield managers money and possibly ensure longer pavement life. The Mu-Meter can be used to provide the airport manager with information that indicates when rubber removal is required and cost effective. Because not every airfield can afford a Mu-Meter, texture measurements can be used to track the decline in touchdown zone friction. When values approach a critical value, they can be checked against Mu-Meter values to determine whether rubber removal is warranted. Thus, a continuous log of texture measurements can become part of a pavement friction management system.

The military bases tested in this study predominantly use concrete touchdown zones; consequently, the measured friction values were considerably less than friction levels on commercial airfields. These potentially hazardous zones can be corrected with the initiation of grooving systems. However, in 1967, the Odgen Air Material Area, which controls new tire procurement for out-of-production aircraft and the retreading of tires, determined that grooved runways were the prime cause of tire tread stripping problems [9]. Admittedly, in 20 years, improved tire design may have alleviated this type of problem. However, performance testing of military tires on grooved runways should be documented to determine if grooving is a viable option on runway touchdown zones at military installations.

Acknowledgments

This paper is a result of sponsored research conducted for the U.S. Air Force Engineering and Services Center (AFESC), Tyndall AFB, FL, and the Federal Aviation Administration Airport Technology Program. Mr. J. Murfee was the AFESC Task Officer and Mr. F. Horn and Mr. H. D'Aulerio were project managers at FAA.

Professors C. Qualls and E. Bedrick of the University of New Mexico's Department of Mathematics and Statistics are thanked for their guidance in performing the statistical analysis.

Appreciation is extended to the various base engineers and airport managers who cooperated in the test program, the various members of ASTM Committee E-17 on Traveled Surface Characteristics who have provided the authors with many suggestions and valid comments, and to the FAA Technical Center for the use of the Mu-Meter during this research effort.

References

[1] Burk, D. O., "Effectiveness of Rubber Removal Processes at Six Air Force Bases," AFCEC Memorandum 4-77, Air Force Civil Engineering Center, Tyndall Air Force Base, FL, 1977.
[2] Moore, D. F., *The Friction of Pneumatic Tyres*, Elsevier Scientific Publishing Company, New York, 1975.
[3] Moore, D. F., "Prediction of Skid-Resistance Gradient and Drainage Characteristics for Pavements," *Highway Research Record 131*, Highway Research Board, Washington, DC, 1966, pp. 181–203.
[4] Kummer, H. W., "Unified Theory of Rubber and Tire Friction," Engineering Research Bulletin B-94, Pennsylvania State University, College of Engineering, University Park, PA, 1966.
[5] Horne, W. B. and Buhlmann, F., "A Method for Rating the Skid Resistance and Micro/Macrotexture Characteristics of Wet Pavements," *Frictional Interaction of Tire and Pavement, STP 793*, W. E. Meyer and J. D. Walter, Eds., American Society for Testing and Materials, Philadelphia, 1983, pp. 191–218.
[6] Lenke, L. R., McKeen, R. G., and Graul, R. A., *Runway Rubber Removal Specification Development: Field Evaluation Procedures Development*, Interim Report DOT/FAA/PM-84/27, ESL-TR-84-40, Federal Aviation Administration, Washington, DC, July 1984.
[7] Horne, W. B., "Evaluation of High-Pressure Water Blast With Rotating Spray Bar for Removing Paint and Rubber Deposits From Airport Runways and Review of Runway Slipperiness Problems Created by Rubber," NASA TMX-72797, National Aeronautics and Space Administration, Hampton, VA, 1975.
[8] Morrow, T. H., "Performance, Reliability, and Correlation of the Mu-Meter and Saab Friction Tester," Final Report FAA-AAS-82-VI, Federal Aviation Administration, Washington, DC, Jan. 1983.
[9] Hout, R. H., "Some Experiences With Tire Wear AND Damage on Grooved Runways," in *Pavement Grooving and Traction Studies*, NASA SP-5073, National Aeronautics and Space Administration, 1968.

The Interfacial Stresses, Motions, and Wear

Seymour A. Lippmann[1]

Effects of Tire Structure and Operating Conditions on the Distribution of Stress Between the Tread and the Road

REFERENCE: Lippmann, S. A., **"Effects of Tire Structure and Operating Conditions on the Distribution of Stress Between the Tread and the Road,"** *The Tire Pavement Interface, ASTM STP 929*, M. G. Pottinger and T. J. Yager, Eds., American Society for Testing and Materials, Philadelphia, 1986, pp. 91–109.

ABSTRACT: Between the tread of the tire and the road there are distributions of interfacial pressure and horizontal stresses that affect many of the important operating properties of pneumatic tires. Among these are traction, treadwear, steering forces, noise generation, power loss, and envelopment properties. These distributions of pressure and stress are determined by the internal structure of the tire, the inflation, the load, and the operating conditions. The paper describes some of the relationships obtained from experimental studies. These same distributions also serve as clues of mechanical processes that take place within the structure of the tire. From these data we observe such matters as (1) the relationship of the lateral gradient of the interfacial pressure to the overturning moment and to the lateral walkout of the tire; (2) the mechanics of the rib to rib offset of the fore and aft shears in free rolling and steered tires; (3) the lateral stress distribution as affected by crown structure, the compressive spreading effects and the sidewall structure; (4) the dependence of the lateral pressure gradients on the characteristics of the sidewall; and (5) the effects of the above on the traction ratios (regional slip zones).

KEY WORDS: tires, roads, loads, tractive ratios, tire structures

Processes taking place in the zone of contact between the tire and the road affect many of the operating properties of the tire such as tread wear, steering characteristics, traction, noise generation, power consumption, envelopment of irregularities in the pavement, and so forth. The details of these interfacial processes are significant in that they provide clues of how the structural design of the tire relates to performance. Without this knowledge the designer

[1]Research associate, Uniroyal Tire Co., 1305 Stephenson Highway, P.O. Box 3940, Troy, MI 48007-3940.

must depend on intuition complimenting hypotheses of what is going on, ultimately solving problems by empirical correlations between alterations in structure and changes in performance, which is inefficient and tends to provide an unsubstantial basis for future work.

It is the intention of this paper to outline in general terms some of the dominant phenomena that take place in the contact patch, as observed with our interfacial stress measuring machine [1]. Included are the profiles of interfacial pressures and horizontal stresses as they are affected by the load borne by the free rolling tire and by the inflation pressure. The effects of structure of the tire are also touched on. In all instances the data will represent equilibrium conditions.

The physical measurements are acquired with a machine having a 12-m (40-ft) long road bed over which the tire travels. Nine meters (30 ft) of this bed are traversed to enable the tire to come to equilibrium. Beyond that distance there is a three-axis interfacial stress transducer in the road having a square sensing surface 5 by 5 mm (0.2 by 0.2 in.), two sides of which are parallel to the direction of travel. This transducer measures the interfacial pressure, the horizontal stress in the forward direction, and the horizontal stress in the direction at right angles to the direction of travel. In a series of successive tests the transducer can be moved to different lateral positions in the road bed and in so doing scans the distribution of stresses and pressure throughout the contact zone.

The tire rolls at 8 km/h (5 mph) along this road bed, a speed that we find to represent fairly well the phenomena that occur in most practical applications of the tire. Since data for the three channels of stress and for the position of the tire are taken every 2.54 mm (0.1 in.) of travel, the rate of data acquisition relatively rapid even at 8 km/h (5 mph), and the number of readings in a contact zone can be very large. Consequently, it has been necessary to record the readings and to analyze them with a computer. The observations described in the following sections are obtained in the manner just outlined.

The data of this report are from several investigations of P205/75 R14 tires (radial ply, belted) and are chosen to represent the phenomena discussed. Several different tires provided the measurements, and it has proven convenient to express the forces and stresses in arbitrary units. The relationships obtained are not completely general. Radial tires with different detailed profiles may exhibit somewhat different behaviors particularly with respect to lateral stress on the shoulders.

Inflation Pressure Effects

For the free rolling tire the interfacial stress distributions are largely the consequence of the inflation pressure, the bending stresses at the boundaries of the contact patch, and of the kinematics of rolling a thick toroidal shell deformed against a flat surface. The role of the inflation pressure is the most readily understood of these.

In the contact zone the load bearing membranes of the tire (the carcass and belt structures) are flattened out and by virtue of this geometric shape do not provide substantial support to the inflation pressure above the patch. This support is afforded by the reaction pressure between the tread and the road, the interfacial pressure. Because there are grooves and voids in the tread design and because the pressure under each rib or tread element must also partially support the inflation over these grooves and voids, the interfacial pressures tend to be somewhat larger than the inflation pressure. In addition there are bending stresses, and these too are supported by the interfacial pressures, particularly at the edges of the contact patch. One other effect that occurs is the reaction to bending moments acting on the tire material at the edge of contact. These moments originate in the deformed sidewall and belt structures and are reacted by gradients of pressure in the contact patch. They sometimes appear as a tendency of the central portion of the patch to lift from the road.

The general nature of the pressure distributions for a particular tire construction is displayed in Figs. 1a to c. These plots are for one of the outer ribs, one of the intermediate ribs, and the central rib of a five ribbed tire (see Fig. 2 for identification of ribs). There are four curves at different inflation pressures in each figure, together showing how the interfacial pressure at the center of the rib depends on the inflation pressure when the axle height of the tire is maintained at a fixed value. (Axle height determined at 544 kg [1200 lb] and 207 kPa [30 psi].) As expected from the above discussion, the pressure at the interface grows linearly with the inflation pressure. This is illustrated in Fig. 3 where the values of the interfacial pressures for each of the ribs at the center of the path through the contact patch as a function of the inflation pressures are plotted.

The relationships are straight lines indicating the anticipated proportionate contributions from the inflation pressures, but also features intercepts. These intercepts result from the stiffnesses of the deformed materials outside of the contact patch, which generate forces transmitted to the contact zone. From the intercepts of Fig. 3 we calculate that at the conventional inflation for this tire, 207 kPa (30 psi), about 52% of the interfacial pressure at the center of the outer rib is the pneumatic. As we will see later that is due both to the direct action of the inflation pressure over the outer rib and its adjoining grooves and also because of the pressure acting vertically on the sidewall overhanging the edge of the tread. The remaining 48% is elastic in origin caused by deforming the mechanical structures of the tire.

The central and intermediate ribs also show linear dependences on inflation pressure and bending stiffnesses, but the structural components at 207 kPa (30 psi) are quite small, only about 22%.

Thus we find that in addition to the part it plays in establishing the deflec-

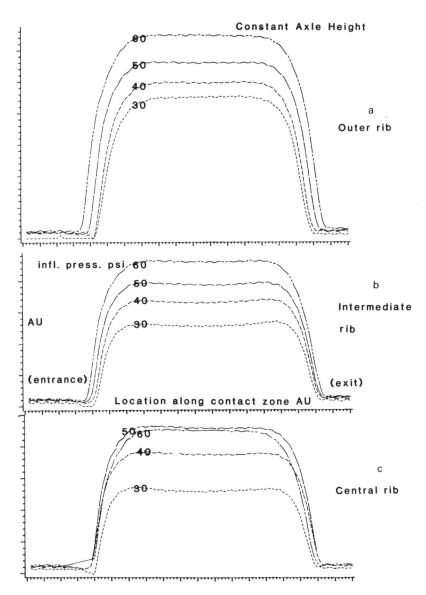

FIG. 1—*The effect of inflation pressure on the interfacial pressure distribution of a five-rib tire.*

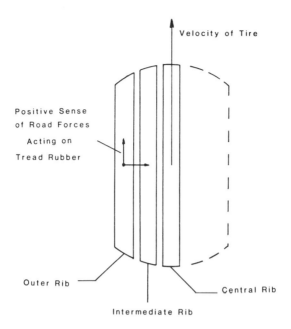

FIG. 2—*Reference diagram for (1) polarity of force traces and (2) identification of measurement locations.*

tion of the passenger tire, the main influence of the inflation pressure on the interface is that it is the dominant factor creating the interfacial pressures. However, as we shall see, the horizontal stresses are not largely developed by mechanisms that are determined by the inflation pressure.

Figures 4*a* to *b* show that the gross characteristics of the fore and aft stress remains relatively constant despite considerable changes in the inflation pressure. All curves rise similarly and fall along a similar slope, but terminate slightly differently. In the case of the outer rib in this example, the curves initially achieve different levels at the various inflation pressures though the variations from that point onward are similar. Aside from that initial difference, the mechanism that generates the fore and aft stress is apparently independent of the inflation pressure. The mechanics of these fore and aft stresses will be discussed in greater detail in the next section, but here the issue is the relative independence of the inflation.

Figures 5*a* to *c* indicate how the lateral stresses vary with changes in the inflation pressure when the deflection is held constant. The outer rib experiences large changes in lateral traction while passing through the contact patch but is only slightly affected by changes in the inflation pressure. The intermediate and inner ribs display similar variations through the patch, al-

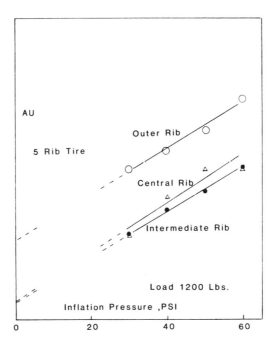

FIG. 3—*Interfacial pressures at rib centers at mid point in contact patch.*

though their initial offsets at the entrance to the contact zone are affected by the inflation. Here too it appears that the mechanism that dictates the changes in the stress distribution along the patch is insensitive to the inflation pressure. This process will also be discussed in greater detail in the following section. Again the processes behind both horizontal components of stress are largely unaffected by the inflation pressure.

Kinematics of Rolling a Deflected Tire, the Fore and Aft Stress

The fore and aft stress distribution follows from relatively simple mechanisms. As an aid in explaining these mechanisms, Fig. 6 illustrates a deflected freely rotating tire on a fixture holding the spindle stationary. Motion is induced by the translating roadbed. This particular configuration of a tire and road system enables a ready understanding of the kinematics of the rotating tire as will become evident in the following.

Briefly, in large part the fore and aft stress results from the fact that the outer diameter of the tread and the mean diameter of the belt-carcass structure under the tread are not the same. The diameters being different, then so are the outer circumference of the tread and the effective inner circumference of the belt-carcass structure. However, in each revolution of the tire, both circumferences flatten out and pass totally through the contact patch to-

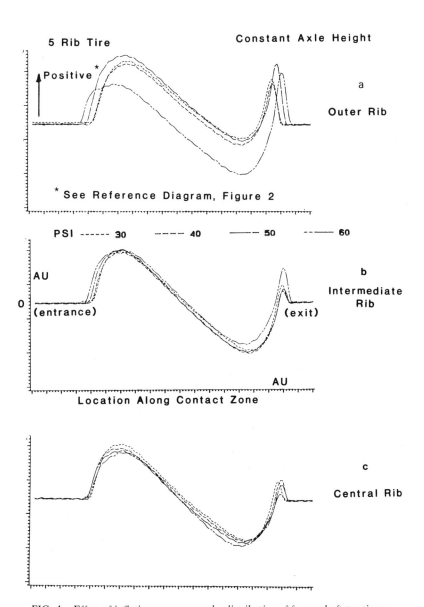

FIG. 4—*Effect of inflation pressure on the distribution of fore and aft tractions.*

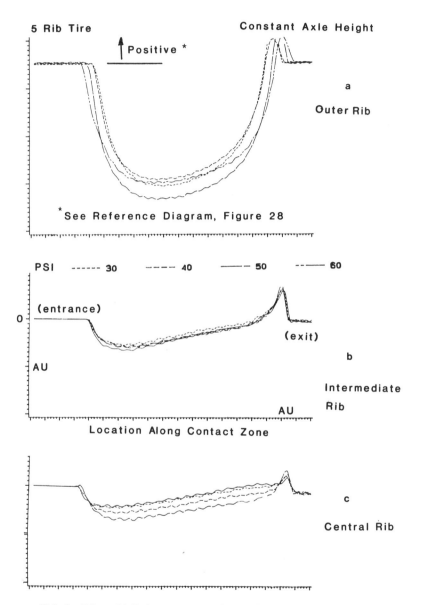

FIG. 5—*Effect of inflation pressure on the distribution of lateral tractions.*

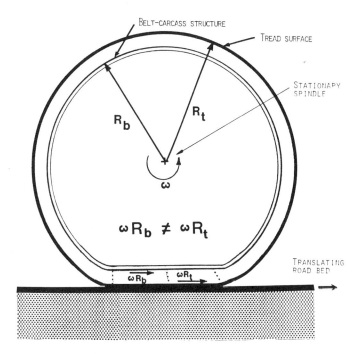

FIG. 6—*Model of formation of the fore and aft interfacial shears—based on the assumption of longitudinal incompressibility of the belt carcass structure and tread rubber—usually a satisfactory approximation.*

gether. If follows that if there is little slippage between the tire and the road, then the tread rubber between the road and the belt-carcass structure must compress longitudinally as well as shear in the fore and aft direction to allow both circumferences to pass through together. The tread surface, being adhered to the road moves through the contact patch at a constant velocity (for a constant speed of travel), and since the carcass belt structure is relatively incompressible in the fore and aft direction, it too moves through the patch at a relatively constant velocity, but not at the speed of the tire over the road surface. This difference in speeds of the two adjoining and parallel surfaces generates a linearly increasing shear of the intervening material.

There is another mechanism of interest involved in this process. If all of the ribs of a tire do not have the same effective contact length, then average shear stresses for the many ribs will not be identical. The various ribs will accumulate different amounts of fore and aft shear energy. Also because of bending at the entrance and exit of contact, the different ribs (having different structural details) enter the contact patch at a variety of energy states about which further changes occur. Because it is free rolling, the tire can adjust to this situation by rotating either forward or backward slightly to achieve a state of

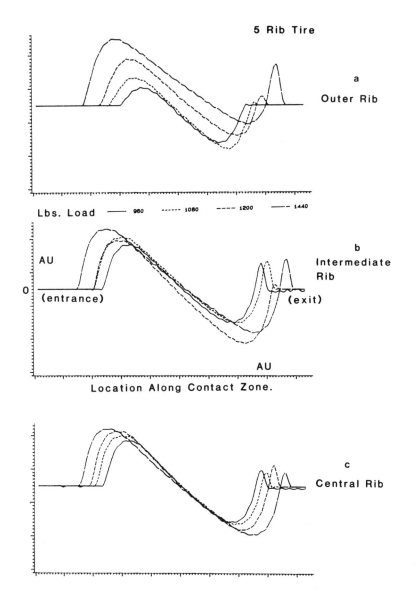

FIG. 7—*Effect of deflection load (at 207-kPa [30-psi] inflation) on the distribution of fore and aft tractions.*

minimum total strain energy. This adjusts the initial values of the fore and aft stresses of the various ribs in relation to one another. In light of the above, let us consider measurements of the fore and aft traction for a typical tire.

Figures 7*a* to *c* are curves of the fore and aft interfacial stress distributions for the same five rib free rolling tire. These data are for a 207-kPa (30-psi) inflation pressure and a number of different tire deflections (obtained by varying the loads). Except at the ends and consistent with the description noted above, in each rib there is a linear change in stress along the length of contact. For the various deflections, the span of the linear variation increases with the degree of deflection, but the slope (increase of shear with distance) remains relatively constant. The transition regions, regions in which bending stresses dominate, are in evidence at the two ends of the contact zone, and there are also the small peaks at the exits caused by slipping. As described above, the fundamental mechanics of these fore and aft stresses are neither dependent on the inflation pressure nor on the deflection of the tire. The inflation pressure, however, often affects the mechanics in a round about manner. The inflation determines the deflection of the tire, the length of contact, and how large the fore and aft force becomes. The inflation pressure also determines the interfacial pressure. Together, the fore and aft stresses, the pressures, and the lateral stresses set limits at which slipping occurs. This creates bounds to the increases in fore and aft stresses.

Sidewall Bending and the Lateral Stresses, and Interfacial Pressures in the Outer Ribs

There are several interrelated effects that occur at the lateral edges of the contact zone. Which of these effects are dominant is not immediately obvious from a cursory examination using the freebody approaches. The phenomena involved can be grouped as pneumatic in origin or caused by the elastic deformations of structures. Figure 8 illustrates the isolated pneumatic effects. The structural processes would be superimposed on the mechanisms described but are not illustrated in the figure.

The sidewalls in the vicinity of the patch are deflected to a state of high curvature in the radial direction. The curvature in the circumferential direction, on the other hand, never becomes very large. Consequently, according to the membrane equation displayed in Fig. 8 the radial upward directed tension T_x is reduced from the value it had in the undeflected state.

Also when deforming under load, the sidewall extends out laterally and also as shown in the figure. This provides a larger projected area parallel to the ground plane for the inflation pressure to act against. The downward vertical force caused by the inflation pressure bearing on the region of the sidewall that overhangs the edge of the tread is therefore larger than can be supported alone by the tension in the sidewall.

Since the system is in equilibrium, the difference in vertical forces must therefore be made up (as seen in the free body of the middle diagram) by vertical force F_v, transmitted from the interior of the contact patch. That interior force can originate in interfacial pressures at the outer rib or can be transmitted from further inward. Also as noted above, it is apparent that the sizes of those vertical components in the contact patch being pneumatic in

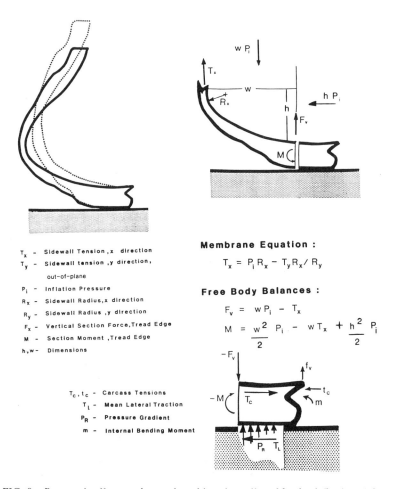

Membrane Equation :

$$T_x = P_i R_x - T_y R_x / R_y$$

Free Body Balances :

$$F_v = w P_i - T_x$$

$$M = \frac{w^2}{2} P_i - w T_x + \frac{h^2}{2} P_i$$

T_x - Sidewall Tension,x direction
T_y - Sidewall tension ,y direction,
out-of-plane
P_i - Inflation Pressure
R_x - Sidewall Radius,x direction
R_y - Sidewall Radius ,y direction
F_x - Vertical Section Force,Tread Edge
M - Section Moment ,Tread Edge
h,w- Dimensions

T_c,t_c - Carcass Tensions
T_l - Mean Lateral Traction
P_R - Pressure Gradient
m - Internal Bending Moment

FIG. 8—*Pneumatic effects at the tread road interface affected by the deflection of the tire.*

nature are therefore proportional to the inflation pressure. Furthermore, because of their relation to the curvatures of the sidewall membrane, they must increase as well with the deflection of the tire.

Figures 1*a* and 3 confirm that at the center of the outer rib, the interfacial pressure does increase linearly with the inflation pressure (when the deflection of the tire is constant) while Fig. 9*a* demonstrates that when the inflation pressure is constant and the deflection increases, again the interfacial pressure grows. Figures 9*b* and *c* inform us that the interfacial pressures under the two inner ribs are largely unaffected by changes in deflection when the inflation pressure is constant. The interfacial pressures in this central region are almost entirely a result of the support of the overlying inflation pressure as noted earlier. It follows that for the tire under consideration the vertical force

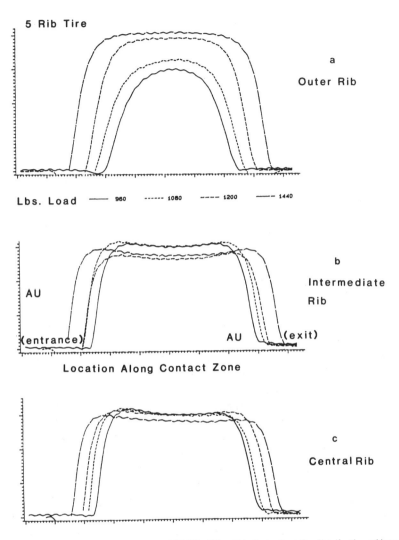

FIG. 9—*Effect of deflection load (at 207-kPa [30-psi] inflation) on the distribution of interfa-cial pressure.*

required to balance the vertical pneumatic component at the overhung side-wall is accounted for by the additional pressure under the outer rib. More-over, in general we find that the pressure under the outer rib exceeds the amount for direct support of the overhead inflation, as would be expected from this cause. Another source of excess pressure is the elastic force compo-nent described earlier resulting from bending the tire's sidewall and buttress structure.

There are bending moments at the lateral edges of the contact zone that are pneumatic in origin and that influence the interfacial stresses. We previously observed from Fig. 8 that when the tire deflects the sidewall moves out laterally while the vertical component of the inflation force increases. Both because of the repositioning of the resultant forces and because of their change in magnitude there is a deflection dependent bending moment acting on the tire at the edge of the contact zone. There is another contribution to the net bending moment resulting from the fact that the membrane tension T_x diminishes with the degree of deflection. This tension and its moment arm w form another component of the moment that is opposite in direction to that of the downwardly acting inflation pressure on the sidewall. Together these all generate the bending moment M displayed in Fig. 8. The lower diagram of the figure portrays schematically the various components available to balance this moment.

There could be a moment m bearing on the outer tread element from the inner parts of the contact zone. There could be a pressure gradient under the outer rib, a lateral stress distribution T_1 at the interface forming a couple with horizontal internal stresses $T_c - t_c$, or a couple formed form vertical stresses, F_v and f_v interacting with the resultant of the interfacial pressure distribution P_r. We can estimate which of these mechanisms are significant by observing the relationship of the interfacial stresses at the outer rib to the deflection and to the magnitude of the inflation pressure. For this purpose the outer rib is measured at five adjacent lateral locations so that pressure gradients and lateral traction gradient can be examined.

In preparation for discussing observations of the details at the outer rib, let us first consider the interactions anticipated from the adjacent ribs. We have already seen in Fig. 5 that the interfacial pressures of the inner ribs are virtually independent of the deflection of the tire while the outer rib shows considerable dependency. The same kind of relationship exists for the effect of tire deflection on the lateral tractions at the ribs. Figures 10a to c indicate that the lateral tractions at the inner ribs are much smaller than at the outer rib at the various levels of deflection, and there is much less dependency on the deflection at the inner portions than at the edge of the patch. These lateral stresses that do appear at the inner ribs usually result from assymetries in the tire caused by ply steer, offsetting of the belt, and so forth. Broadly considered the processes that develop the tractions and pressures at the outer rib are not highly coupled to the mechanics of the inner ribs, and this observation sets the stage for the discussion that follows.

In passing, it is worth noting a special event indicated in Fig. 10a, which occurred during the run at the 544-kg (1200-lb) load. At reference location 3.5 the combination of fore and aft and lateral tractions overcame the ability of the interfacial pressure to prevent slippage over the road. This occurred where the fore and aft stress attained its positive peak. The slippage resulted in a localized reduction in lateral force, and was never quite made up as that part of the tread continued through the contact patch. Such details are, of course, only observable from direct measurements at the interface.

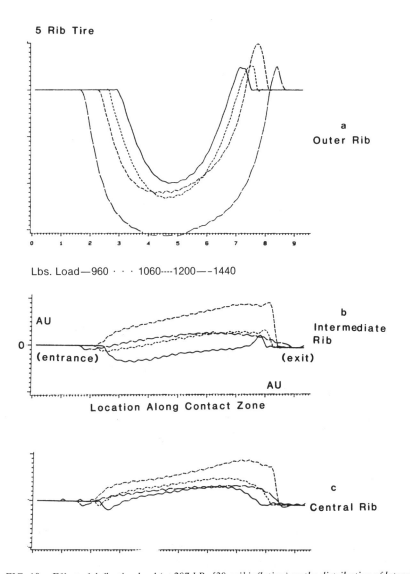

FIG. 10—*Effect of deflection load (at 207-kPa [30-psi] inflation) on the distribution of lateral traction.*

The gradient of the interfacial pressure taken in the lateral direction is one of the mechanisms for balancing the bending moment at the edge of the contact patch. That a gradient indeed exists is indicated by the slopes of the curves in Fig. 11a. These curves are for 207 kPa (30 psi) of inflation and for three different deflections (that is, loads). However, if the gradient in pressure were to counter the bending moment at the tread edge, then the pressure would be greatest at that edge and progressively smaller inward. The opposite

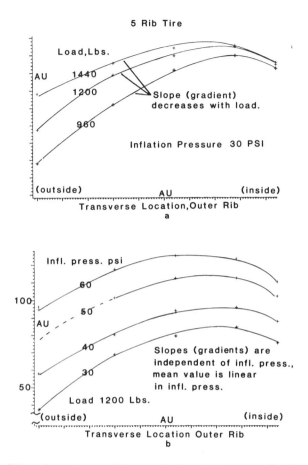

FIG. 11—*Effect of operating conditions on the interfacial pressure distribution at the mid plane in the contact zone.*

occurs with the result that the gradient augments the bending moment rather than counteracts it. This gradient appears to be a secondary effect, perhaps not at all related to pneumatic processes. For a further clue, we observe the effect of varying the inflation pressure while the deflection is held constant.

In Fig. 11*b* we see the effect of inflation pressure at four different values. The gradients of interfacial pressure do not change with the inflation pressure; the slopes remain constant. However, the average of the interfacial pressures is linear in the inflation pressure (Fig. 12). As before, the intercept denotes structural stiffness. Thus the gradient in interfacial pressure is determined by deflection while the mean pressure is partly pneumatic and partly structural. The pneumatic effect was accounted for earlier in terms of the sidewall effects and support of the inflation acting from overhead. The structural stiffness determines the gradient. The most likely process left for

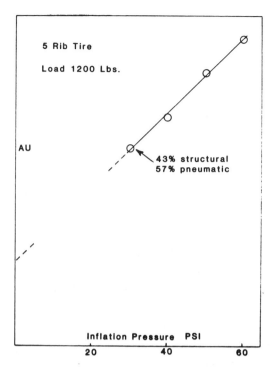

FIG. 12—*Effect of inflation pressure on the mean interfacial pressure across the outer rib.*

accomodating the bending moment then appears to be the couple from the lateral traction at the outer rib and a lateral internal tension, respectively, designated in Fig. 7 as T_1 versus $f_c - F_c$. That brings the investigation to the details of the lateral stress at the outer rib.

Figure 13a describes the distribution of lateral tractions in the outer rib and shows the effects of changes in the deflection of the tire while the inflation pressure is maintained at 207 kPa (30 psi). It is evident that a lateral gradient exists in these tractions and that the gradient (the slope) is constant across almost all of the rib. Increasing the deflection of the tire increases the average value of the lateral tractions but decreases the gradient. This dependency on the deflection at constant inflation pressure suggests but does not prove that the process by which the traction develops is elastic, not pneumatic. For further evidence, let us consider the manner in which changes in inflation pressure affect the lateral tractions at the outer rib.

In Fig. 13b we have the relation to the inflation pressure. The dependency on pressure is small, and surprisingly, it is in the reverse direction. As the pressure increases, the lateral stress dereases. There is a pneumatic effect, but it is minor and is in the opposite direction from the dominant contribution from the structural. This small pneumatic effect is in the direction that is

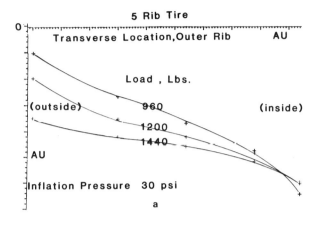

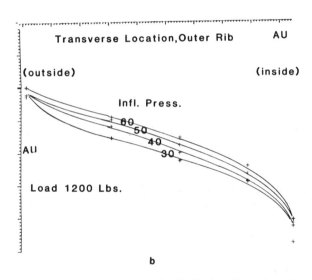

FIG. 13—*Effect of operating conditions on the distribution of lateral traction at the outer rib mid plane in the contact zone.*

expected from the schematic description of Fig. 8. The major phenomenon involves some different mechanism, and we can look to the clues already disclosed to identify it.

Superimposed on the pneumatic process described in Fig. 8 is the elastic deformation of the buttress region. The buttress bends to acquire a straighter contour than in its normal undeflected state. The neutral axis of bending in the buttress is located close to the very stiff carcass layer. Most of the internal deflection thereby occurs in the buttress rubber exterior to the carcass. This

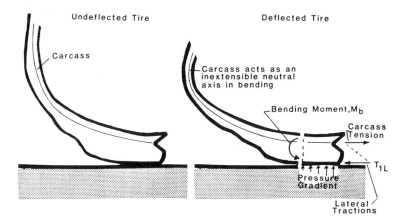

FIG. 14—*Lateral interfacial reaction at the outer rib of elastic stresses in the deflected tire.*

results in an elastic bending moment M_b as shown in Fig. 14. The surface of outer rib tends to move inward towards the center of the contact patch. The counteracting moment that develops at the rib's interface with the road consists of a lateral pressure gradient directed such that the high values tend to be at the inner edge of the rib. Also, because of frictional limitations, the lateral tractions T_{1L} (that at the surface are half of the couple that balance out the bending moment; the other half is at the carcass layer) tend to pile up at the inner edge and decrease towards the outer edge. These actions are then consistent with the behavior seen in all of the figures.

Conclusion

We have described some of the gross processes that take place in the interface of the tire and the road. There are, of course, the many minor perturbations to these effects that are related to the details of tread designs, internal structure, wear phenomena, and so forth. Beyond that, there are relationships between these interfacial events and the various performance factors of the tire, which are subjects beyond the scope of this paper.

Reference

[1] Lippmann, S. A. and Oblizajek, K. L., "The Distributions of Stress Between the Tread and the Road for Freely Rolling Tires," SAE 74102, Society for Automotive Engineers, Detroit, MI, Feb. 1974.

William E. Howell,[1] Sharon E. Perez,[1] and
William A. Vogler[2]

Aircraft Tire Footprint Forces

REFERENCES: Howell, W. E., Perez, S. E., and Vogler, W. A., **"Aircraft Tire Footprint Forces,"** *The Tire Pavement Interface, ASTM STP 929,* M. G. Pottinger and T. J. Yager, Eds., American Society for Testing and Materials, Philadelphia, 1986, pp. 110–124.

ABSTRACT: The National Tire Modeling Program is a joint National Aeronautics and Space Administration (NASA) - industry effort to improve the understanding of tire mechanics and develop accurate analytical design tools. This effort includes fundamental analytical and experimental research on the structural mechanics of tires. As an integral part of this program, local footprint forces in the normal, lateral, and longitudinal directions were measured with the use of a footprint force transducer. Measurements of forces in the footprint were obtained by positioning the transducer at specified locations within the footprint and externally loading the tire. Data obtained for various inflation pressures and external loads are presented for an aircraft tire. The tire that was tested is representative of those used on the main landing gear of B-737 and DC-9 commercial transport airplanes.

KEY WORDS: aircraft, forces, tires, footprint, structural mechanics

The U.S. tire industry and the National Aeronautics and Space Administration (NASA) are involved in a program to develop analytical tools for tire design. Langley Research Center has a major role in this National Tire Modeling Program [1]. The scope of the program consists of conducting experimental tests to determine the mechanical properties of tire materials, developing techniques to measure tire deformations and tire footprint forces, and developing analytical tools for predicting tire response. The research endeavor will build upon initial efforts to define tire deformations and structural behavior reported in Ref 2 through 5. These references are representative of the current knowledge on cord-rubber material properties and pneu-

---

[1]Aero-Space technologist, Engineering Co-op, NASA Langley Research Center, MS 497, Hampton, VA 23665.
[2]Engineering specialist, Kentron International, Inc., Kentron Technical Center, 3221 N. Armistead Ave., Hampton, VA 23666.

matic tire behavior; however information on the forces developed in a statically loaded tire footprint is extremely limited.

The purpose of this paper is to present some preliminary results of tire footprint force distributions that were obtained for a 40 by 14, Type VII, 28-ply rated aircraft tire. Data were obtained for tire inflation pressures of 0.97, 1.07, and 1.17 MPa (140, 155, and 170 psi) with external loadings ranging from 8 896 to 133 440 N (2 000 to 30 000 lb) The vertical, lateral, and drag forces that were measured in the tire footprint are presented in graphical form for the three inflation pressures at external loadings of 8 896, 71 168, and 133 440 N (2 000, 16 000, and 30 000 lb).

Footprint Force Transducer

In order to determine the forces developed in the tire-pavement interface, an instrument was designed to measure forces at ten footprint locations simultaneously. This instrument is shown in Fig. 1 with the cover plate removed to show the row of force measuring devices. These are beams that were strain-gaged to measure forces in the vertical, lateral, and drag directions with a maximum vertical load capability of 556 N (125 lb). The face of each beam is 1.27 by 1.27 cm (0.50 by 0.50 in.). There is a 0.13-cm (0.05-in.) edge

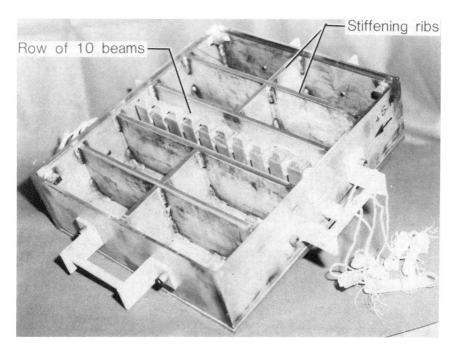

FIG. 1—*Interior view of the footprint force transducer showing the ten strain gaged beams.*

clearance between the beam face and the cover plate and each beam is mounted so that this face is flush with the cover plate. The 10 beams are positioned 3.45 cm (1.36 in.) apart, center to center. The transducer box structure is 38.1 cm (15.0 in.) wide, and the box grid structure is sufficiently stiff to keep the cover plate rigid. Both the cover plate and the face of the beams were machined to a surface finish of approximately 125.

Test Procedures

The footprint force transducer was mounted on the test fixture as shown in Fig. 2. The transducer was positioned and supported by a platen which, in turn, was supported by cables. Hydraulic cylinders were used to control the platen position and to apply the desired external load. A sheet of white paper with attached carbon paper was placed on the transducer to obtain a record of the relative position between the tire grooves and the beams. A computer was used to scan the various strain gages and to print out the force data.

The transducer was initially positioned at the center of the tire footprint, and data were recorded for external loads ranging from 8 896 to 133 168 N (2 000 to 30 000 lb) at 8 896 N (2 000 lb) intervals. The transducer was then moved 12.7 mm (1/2 in.) toward the front of the footprint and a new data set

FIG. 2—*Test arrangement of the 40 by 14 aircraft tire and the footprint force transducer.*

recorded. This procedure was continued until data for half of the footprint was obtained. The transducer was then moved to a position 12.7 mm (¹/₂ in.) behind the center of the footprint, and the procedure described for the first half of the footprint was repeated to obtain force data for the second half of the footprint. These data were then used to produce a graphical display of the footprint forces in the form of contour and three-dimensional plots.

Results and Discussion

Footprint force data obtained from the footprint force transducer are presented in Figs. 3 through 15. In Figs. 3 through 14 data are presented for the various combinations of external loads and inflation pressures. For each force and pressure combination, individual contour plots are presented for the vertical, lateral, and drag forces. Supplemental zero force values were included in each data set to clearly define the location of the tread circumferential grooves. The contour intervals for the vertical forces were set at 45 N (10 lb), and for the lateral and drag forces the contour intervals were set at 18 N (4 lb). A dashed contour line represents a negative force. The areas of dashed line contours are bounded by a solid line that is the zero force contour. Ripples in the contours are an artifact of the contour smoothing routine. The graphics

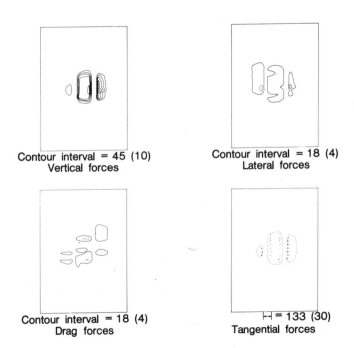

Contour interval = 45 (10)
Vertical forces

Contour interval = 18 (4)
Lateral forces

Contour interval = 18 (4)
Drag forces

⊢⊣ = 133 (30)
Tangential forces

FIG. 3—*Tire forces for an internal tire pressure of 0.97 MPa (140 psi) and external load of 8 896 N (2 000 lb).*

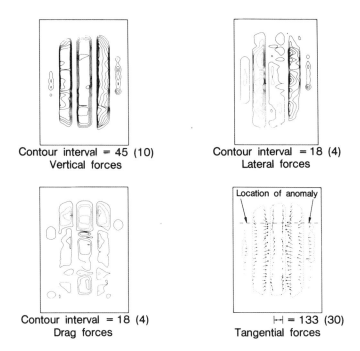

Contour interval = 45 (10)
Vertical forces

Contour interval = 18 (4)
Lateral forces

Contour interval = 18 (4)
Drag forces

⊢⊣ = 133 (30)
Tangential forces

FIG. 4—*Tire forces for an internal tire pressure of 0.97 MPa (140 psi) and external load of 71 168 N (16 000 lb).*

package, NCAR, was used to generate the contours that were smoothed through an array of 380 discrete data points.

Also included in Figs. 3 through 14 are plots of the tire footprint tangential forces obtained by combining the lateral and drag forces to show the magnitude and direction of the footprint friction forces. The length of each arrow is proportional to the magnitude of the tangential force, and the direction of the arrow denotes the direction of the friction force. The origin of each arrow indicates the location of each data point (beam location). The dashed line in each tangential force plot denotes the extent of the tire footprint.

Tire Pressure of 0.965 MPa (140 psi)

Plots of the data obtained for an external load of 8 896 N (2 000 lb) are presented in Fig. 3. Although the footprint area is small for this loading condition, substantial vertical forces were generated in the center rib. The vertical force contour plot indicates that there are steep force gradients near the groove edges. This is due to rapid transition from peak forces in the region of the rib edges to zero in the grooves. The maximum lateral and drag forces generated in the footprint are about 20 and 6% of the vertical forces, respectively.

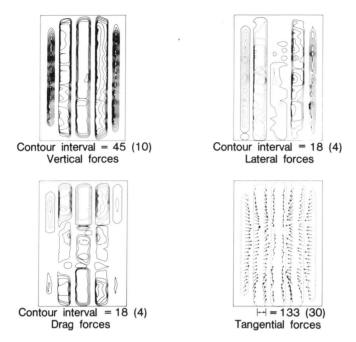

Contour interval = 45 (10)
Vertical forces

Contour interval = 18 (4)
Lateral forces

Contour interval = 18 (4)
Drag forces

⊢⊣ = 133 (30)
Tangential forces

FIG. 5—*Tire forces for an internal tire pressure of 0.97 MPa (140 psi) and external load of 133 440 N (30 000 lb).*

In Fig. 4 plots of the data for an external load of 71 168 N (16 000 lb) are presented. The increase in external loading caused an increase in the size of the footprint area. It should be noted that the vertical forces in the middle of the center rib are only slightly higher than those observed for the 8 896-N (2 000-lb) loading case shown in Fig. 3. The maximum lateral and drag forces, however, have increased and are about 30 and 20% of the vertical forces, respectively. The distribution of these frictional forces is more apparent in the plot of the tangential forces. In the center rib these frictional forces are mainly in the fore and aft directions whereas in the outer ribs the forces are directed laterally toward the center rib. Approximately one-third of the way from the top of the footprint (see arrow), there is an anomaly in the tangential forces. This anomaly is attributed to a radial mold line in the tire tread. This is the cause of the asymmetric loading.

The data presented in Fig. 5 is for an external load of 133 440 N (30 000 lb). The vertical forces in the center rib are rather uniform, and the peak values are not very much greater than those for the smaller external loads. The vertical forces in the two ribs adjacent to the center rib are also fairly uniform. The maximum lateral and drag forces generated in the footprint are about 30% of the vertical forces.

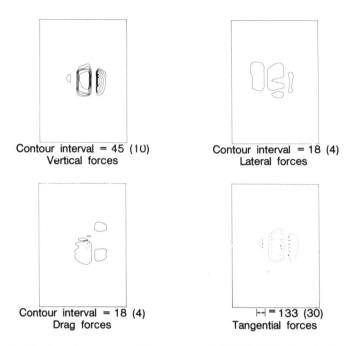

Contour interval = 45 (10)
Vertical forces

Contour interval = 18 (4)
Lateral forces

Contour interval = 18 (4)
Drag forces

⊢⊣ = 133 (30)
Tangential forces

FIG. 6—*Tire forces for an internal tire pressure of 1.07 MPa (155 psi) and external load of 8 896 N (2 000 lb).*

Tire Pressure of 1.07 MPa (155 psi)

Data obtained for an external load of 8 896 N (2 000 lb) are presented in Fig. 6. The footprint is essentially the same size as that for a tire pressure of 140 psi, and the maximum vertical force measured in the center rib is only 22 N (5 lb) greater than that shown for the similar loading condition in Figs. 3 through 5. The maximum lateral and drag forces generated in the footprint are about 10 and 15% of the vertical forces, respectively.

In Fig. 7 the maximum vertical forces in the center rib for an external load of 71 168 N (16 000 lb) are only slightly greater than those for 8 896 N (2 000 lb). The maximum lateral and drag forces, however, have increased and are about 30 and 20% of the vertical forces, respectively. The magnitude and direction of these forces are shown in the plot of the tangential forces (Fig. 7). Again, the forces in the center rib are mainly in the fore and aft directions, whereas in the outer ribs, the forces are directed laterally toward the tire center.

The data presented in Fig. 8 are for an external load of 133 440 N (30 000 lb). The vertical forces in the center rib are essentially uniform and are approximately the same as those for external loads of 8 896 and 71 168 N (2 000 and 16 000 lb). The vertical forces in the two ribs adjacent to the center rib are fairly uniform but not as uniform as those in the center rib. The lateral

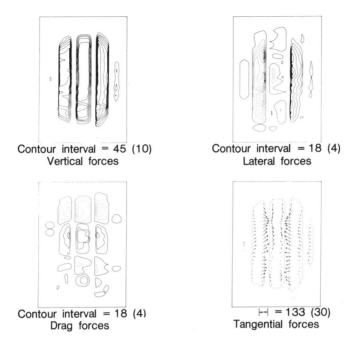

Contour interval = 45 (10)
Vertical forces

Contour interval = 18 (4)
Lateral forces

Contour interval = 18 (4)
Drag forces

⊢⊣ = 133 (30)
Tangential forces

FIG. 7—*Tire forces for an internal tire pressure of 1.07 MPa (155 psi) and external load of 71 168 N (16 000 lb).*

forces are smallest in the center rib and highest in the outer ribs. Conversely, the drag forces are relatively small in the outer ribs and are highest in the center rib. The maximum lateral and drag forces generated in the footprint are about 30% of the vertical forces. The directions of the tangential forces are similar to those in Fig. 7.

Tire Pressure of 1.17 MPa (170 psi)

In Fig. 9 the data for an external load of 8 896 N (2 000 lb) are presented. The footprint is slightly smaller than for either 1.07 or 0.97 MPa (155 or 140 psi) inflation pressures, under similar loading conditions, and vertical force in the center rib has increased by approximately 22 N (5 lb) over that for the 1.07-MPa (155-psi) case. Although the lateral and drag forces have increased, these forces are still rather small as shown by the small vectors of the tangential force plot; however, the maximum values of these forces are about 10 and 5% of the vertical forces, respectively.

The forces measured for an external load of 71 168 N (16 000 lb) are presented in Fig. 10. Although the footprint size has increased, the forces in the center rib are relatively uniform and are practically the same as those for 8 896 N (2 000 lb) of external loading. The maximum lateral and drag forces

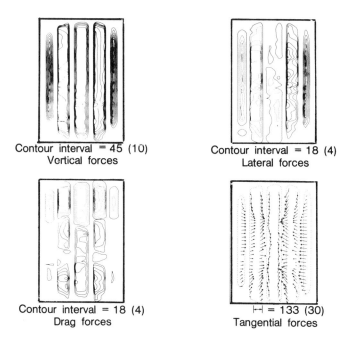

Contour interval = 45 (10)
Vertical forces

Contour interval = 18 (4)
Lateral forces

Contour interval = 18 (4)
Drag forces

⊢⊣ = 133 (30)
Tangential forces

FIG. 8—*Tire forces for an internal tire pressure of 1.07 MPa (155 psi) and external load of 133 440 N (30 000 lb).*

are about 40 and 20% of the vertical forces, respectively. In the center rib the tangential forces are basically in the fore and aft directions while those in the adjacent ribs are toward and away from the tire center. These changes in the tangential force directions indicate a significant change in the tire behavior and will require further investigation.

The data shown in Fig. 11 are for an external load of 133 440 N (30 000 lb). The footprint of the vertical forces is slightly smaller than the similar footprint for an internal pressure of 0.97 MPa (140 psi). These forces are relatively uniform and are only a few pounds greater than for an external load of 71 168 N (16 000 lb). The maximum lateral and drag forces are about 40 and 30% of the vertical forces, respectively. Note that the drag forces have increased in the outer ribs. Tangential force directions are similar to those that were first observed in Fig. 10 with the resultant loading more complex than that shown in Fig. 10. In the outer most ribs, all the force vectors are pointing toward the tire center.

Three-Dimensional Plots

In Figs. 12 through 14, the footprint force data are replotted in a three-dimensional format. For brevity, only the data for a tire pressure of 0.97 MPa (140 psi) are presented. These plots present the unsmoothed raw data and

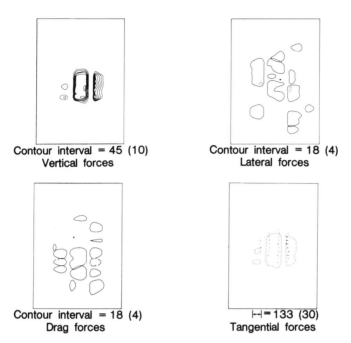

Contour interval = 45 (10)
Vertical forces

Contour interval = 18 (4)
Lateral forces

Contour interval = 18 (4)
Drag forces

⊢⊣ = 133 (30)
Tangential forces

FIG. 9— *Tire forces for an internal tire pressure of 1.17 MPa (170 psi) and external load of 8 896 N (2 000 lb).*

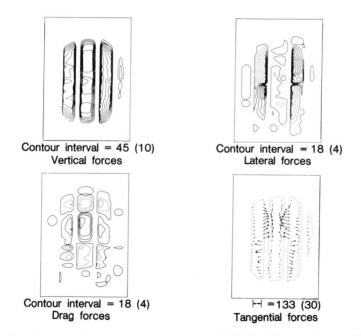

Contour interval = 45 (10)
Vertical forces

Contour interval = 18 (4)
Lateral forces

Contour interval = 18 (4)
Drag forces

⊢⊣ = 133 (30)
Tangential forces

FIG. 10— *Tire forces for an internal tire pressure of 1.17 MPa (170 psi) and external load of 71 168 N (16 000 lb).*

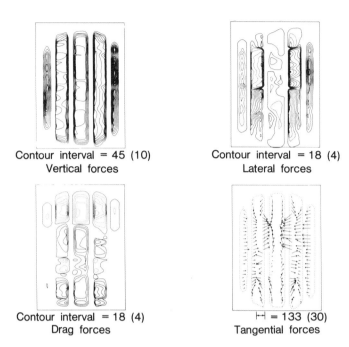

Contour interval = 45 (10)
Vertical forces

Contour interval = 18 (4)
Lateral forces

Contour interval = 18 (4)
Drag forces

⊢⊣ = 133 (30)
Tangential forces

FIG. 11—*Tire forces for an internal tire pressure of 1.17 MPa (170 psi) and external load of 133 440 N (30 000 lb).*

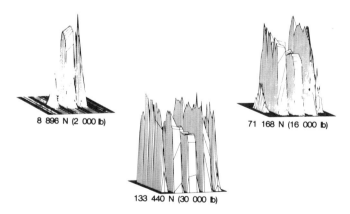

8 896 N (2 000 lb)

71 168 N (16 000 lb)

133 440 N (30 000 lb)

FIG. 12—*Three-dimensional plots of tire footprint forces for three external loads (tire pressure = 0.97 MPa [140 psi]): vertical forces.*

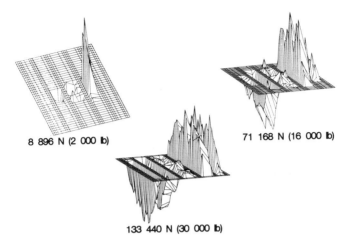

8 896 N (2 000 lb)   71 168 N (16 000 lb)

133 440 N (30 000 lb)

FIG. 13—*Three-dimensional plots of tire footprint forces for three external load (tire pressure = 0.96 MPa [140 psi]): lateral forces.*

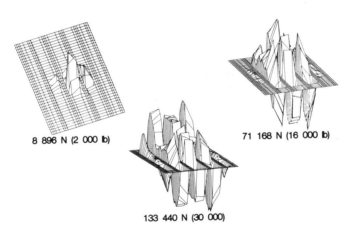

8 896 N (2 000 lb)   71 168 N (16 000 lb)

133 440 N (30 000)

FIG. 14—*Three-dimensional plots of tire footprint forces for three external loads (tire pressure = 0.96 MPa [140 psi]): drag forces.*

characteristically exhibit ragged profiles. In Fig. 12, the vertical forces are shown for a comparison at the three different external loads of 8 896, 71 168, and 133 440 N (2 000, 16 000, and 30 000 lb). The tire ribs, grooves, footprint size, and relative force values are readily apparent. Similar plots of the lateral and drag force data are presented in Figs. 13 and 14, respectively. The increased drag forces in the outer ribs are more apparent in Fig. 14 than in Fig. 11.

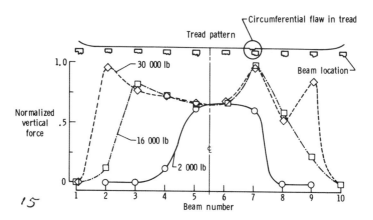

FIG. 15— *Vertical forces across the center of the footprint for a tire pressure of 1.07 MPa (155 psi).*

Vertical Forces Across Tire Center

Plots of the vertical forces across the center of the tire footprint for the three different external loads discussed in this paper are presented in Fig. 15. In this figure the vertical force is plotted as a function of the location of the ten force measuring devices. Although there should be no forces generated in the grooves, the force curves were not drawn through zero at the grooves. Instead, the curves were faired smoothly through the measured force data to show the general trends across the tire footprint. The footprint vertical forces at the 8 896-N (2 000-lb) load condition are approximately the same as the footprint forces on the tire centerline for external loads of 71 168 and 133 440 N (16 000 and 30 000 lb). Increasing the external load does not increase the vertical forces generated at the center rib, but instead increases the area of the footprint over which these forces act.

Although Beams 4 and 7 were positioned equi-distance from the tire centerline, the measured vertical forces were quite different. There is a circumferential flaw in the recapped tire tread at the location of Beam 7. About half of the face of this device was positioned on the flaw (see the beam location in the sketch in Fig. 15). Beam 7 always loaded first and, therefore, measured the largest forces. This flaw, in conjunction with the tire stiffness, appears to have relieved the load measured by Beam 8. It did not measure as much force as Beam 3, which was at a similar location on the other side of the tire centerline. An average of the measured forces at Beams 7 and 8, for external loadings of 71 168 and 133 440 N (16 000 and 30 000 lb), would give force values comparable to those measured on the opposite side of the tire. These data indicate that tire tread nonuniformities significantly influence the measured forces. With the transducer positioned symmetrically about the tire centerline, the faces of Beams 3 and 8 were only partially in contact with the tire tread. Approximately half of each of these two beams was over a groove and was not in contact with the tire, yet those two devices measured footprint forces as if their entire faces were being loaded. This surprising result strongly suggests that the tire tread is sufficiently stiff to have a significant effect on the load distribution within the footprint (also see flaw at Beam 7 in Fig. 15). This result also supports the conclusion that the local gradients are very steep along the edges of the grooves. It is apparent from these findings that the final load distribution in the tire footprint is the result of a very complicated loading mechanism and cannot be modeled accurately by treating the tire carcass as an inflated membrane alone.

Conclusions

An experimental technique has been developed to determine the forces generated in tire footprints. The data gathered by this technique and reported herein are preliminary results of measured footprint forces for a 40 by 14 transport airplane tire. The conclusions drawn from these data are as follows:

1. The center area of the tire footprint reached its maximum vertical force at a low external load and maintained that force throughout the range of loading.
2. The footprint area which exhibited this force level increased as the external load increased.
3. Tire tread nonuniformities significantly influence the measured forces.
4. The load distribution in tire footprint is the result of a very complicated loading behavior and cannot be modeled accurately by treating the tire carcass as an inflated membrane alone.

Summary

The National Tire Modeling Program is a joint NASA-industry effort to improve the understanding of tire mechanics and develop accurate analytical design tools. This effort includes fundamental analytical and experimental research on the structural mechanics of tires. As an integral part of this program, local footprint forces in the normal, lateral, and longitudinal directions were measured with the use of a footprint force transducer. Measurements of forces in the footprint were obtained by positioning the transducer at specified locations within the footprint and externally loading the tire. Data obtained for various inflation pressures and external loads are presented for an aircraft tire. The tire that was tested is representative of those used on the main landing gear of B-737 and DC-9 commercial transport airplanes.

References

[1] Noor, A. K., Andersen, C. M., and Tanner, J. A., "Mixed Models and Reduction Techniques for Large-Rotation, Nonlinear Analysis of Shells of Revolution With Application to Tires." NASA TP-2343, Oct. 1984.

[2] Clark, S. K., "Theory of Elastic Net Applied to Cord-Rubber Composites," *Rubber Chemistry and Technology*, Vol. 56, No. 2, May–June 1983.

[3] Kumar, M. and Bert, C. W., "Experimental Characterization of Mechanical Behavior of Cord-Rubber Materials," *Tire Science and Technology*, Vol. 10, Nos. 1–4, Jan./Dec. 1982.

[4] Tanner, J. A. (Compiler), "Tire Modeling," NASA CP-2264, Sept. 1982.

[5] Clark, S. K., Ed., "Mechanics of Pneumatic Tires," DOT HS 805 952, Department of Transportation, Aug. 1981.

Alan G. Veith[1]

The Most Complex Tire-Pavement Interaction: Tire Wear

REFERENCE: Veith, A. G., **"The Most Complex Tire-Pavement Interaction: Tire Wear,"** *The Tire Pavement Interface, ASTM STP 929*, M. G. Pottinger and T. J. Yager, Eds., American Society for Testing and Materials, Philadelphia, 1986, pp. 125–158.

ABSTRACT: Tire wear is the result of frictional work in the tire-pavement interface that is generated when tread surface elements go through a frictional force-slip cycle during each passage through the footprint. This review focuses on the nature of the two contacting materials in the treadwear process: the tread rubber and the pavement aggregate. To place the unique performance characteristics of rubber in their proper perspective, some text material is devoted to a brief review of the wear of materials in general and to the key role that visco-elastic behavior plays in the rubber-pavement contact.

Laboratory abrasion testers of various sorts have proven to be valuable in investigating rubber wear mechanisms, and they are reviewed, citing both the technological and the theoretical approaches. A general background on tire wear is presented by the use of a simple wear equation. Next the role of the two contacting surfaces is examined: the pavement aggregate and the tread rubber. The key pavement element of in the tread-wear process is the microtexture, that roughness of surface in the 10^{-2} mm range. Several characteristics of the tread rubber are important: the glass transition temperature, the reinforcement system (carbon black), and the general resistance of the rubber to friction induced (chemical) degradation. The influence of two of the three known external (to the tire) treadwear factors, frictional or tractive tire force intensity and "ambient-tire" temperature, are next examined. (The third external factor is the pavement microtexture.) Finally some brief information is presented on the actual loss mechanism of tread rubber principally by way of microscopic examination of worn tread surfaces and the morphology of abraded rubber particles.

KEY WORDS: wear, abrasion, friction, frictional work, mechanochemical degradation, laboratory abrasion, pavement macrotexture, microtexture

As tires perform their intended functions of providing for vehicle control by generating lateral and longitudinal forces and in cushioning the vehicle against the effects of road irregularities, the tread rubber is lost because of what has been generally called tire wear or treadwear.

[1]Research and development fellow, BFGoodrich Co., Tire Group, Research and Development Center, 9921 Brecksville Rd., Brecksville, OH 44141.

Tire wear is a complex phenomenon or set of phenomena. It is complex because it involves both physics (or mechanics) and chemistry. In a classical physics (or mechanics) problem we may deal with a material system and its associated set of stresses and strains. A description of the dynamics of such a system is frequently complex, but normally the fundamental nature and the properties of the material remain constant. When we have a complex dynamic stress-strain system that changes its properties as we observe and study it, we encounter an additional measure of complexity. That is a reasonable description of the tire wear process: a two stage complex physical-chemical process.

A very brief review of the wear of materials is presented to give some general background and to permit a full appreciation of the unique role that rubber plays in the performance of the pneumatic tire. Viscoelasticity and rubber friction are briefly reviewed to give a background for a better understanding of tire wear. Since the laboratory abrasion of rubber is a relatively simple task, with many devices built to do this testing (each constructed with the elusive goal of predicting "real-world" treadwear), a review of this work is given. A general description of tire wear centered on a simple wear equation is presented next. This helps in organizing thought on treadwear problems. The review concludes with a discussion of the two contacting counter-surfaces: the pavement and its characteristics and the role of the tread rubber. The entire review is material and material performance oriented.

Wear of Materials

Wear is one of the results that may occur from the relative motion of two contacting surfaces under conditions that produce frictional work or energy. It is defined as the loss of material from one (or both) surface during the sliding contact that generates the frictional work. Frictional work is the result of a frictional (or tangential) force acting through some finite path length. Friction and frictional work concepts will be examined in greater detail.

When a broad range of materials is considered (metals, plastics, and so forth) wear may be classified as

(1) Adhesive Wear—removal of material caused by high transient adhesion ("welding") of asperities.

(2) Abrasive Wear—caused by a cutting-rupture action of sharp angular asperities on the sliding counterface or as third bodies (particles).

(3) Erosive Wear—cutting-rupture action of particles in a liquid (fluid) stream.

(4) Corrosive Wear—from direct chemical surface attack.

(5) Fatigue Wear—caused by rapid or gradual material property changes that give rise to cracks and with their growth, a loss of material.

This list of "wear mechanisms" is usually compiled with "brittle versus ductile" materials in mind where the surface asperity deformations are mainly of a "plastic flow" character. Some elastic deformation obviously exists, but it very frequently plays a minor role in the wear mechanism for these materials.

Practical wear situations rarely involve only one of these mechanisms; a two or three way combination is frequently encountered. Complex interactions are also important. Adhesive wear may be accompanied by oxidation of the wear debris. The oxidized debris may be "soft" and act as a lubricant to reduce overall wear or it may become "hard" and cause (increased) abrasive wear.

Briscoe [1] in reviewing wear adopted the concept of "cohesive" wear, controlled by the rupture strength or energy ("toughness") of the wearing material. In this scheme a second type of wear is defined as "interfacial wear," high levels of frictional energy dissipation in very thin surface layers. High transient temperature increases are characteristic of this type of wear. Abrasive and fatigue wear (2 and 5 on the above list) are typical examples of cohesive wear; corrosive and possibly adhesive wear (4 and 1) are examples of interfacial wear.

Rubber occupies a unique role in tribology, a relatively new term that describes the sciences of rubbing surfaces with and without intervening lubricants. Rubber is used as a generic term for a broad range of polymers that possess the unique characteristic of a high level of "elastic" response to applied stress. Elastic response implies that almost all of the energy input is returned on release of the applied stress. The key words are "almost all," since no material is perfectly elastic (100% return). Part of the energy input is dissipated as hysteresis by viscous loss mechanisms, and the branch of mechanics that describes such behavior is called viscoelasticity.

Viscoelasticity

For good understanding of viscoelasticity, a brief description of rubbery or polymeric behavior is given in terms of very simple molecular structure and molecular dynamics.

A rubbery material is one that is capable of large, almost totally recoverable deformations. This unique property derives from a particular molecular structure: long, flexible, chain-like molecules that are chemically or physically attached to each other at infrequent intervals and that possess thermal energy exceeding their intermolecular attractive energy. The molecular chains form a loose, three-dimensional network in which the chains change shape and slide past each other under thermal motion, except at the points of attachment. If such attachments are formed by chemical bonding, the rubber is cross-linked or "vulcanized." Such rubbers exhibit permanent, long-lasting elasticity. In unvulcanized rubber, chain entanglements act as temporary cross-links; they eventually slip and allow the rubber to flow like a liquid on an extended time basis.

Rubber-like elasticity is developed because once strained, the molecular chains seek to return to their undeformed (more likely) or coiled conformations (from those less-probable elongated conformations) imposed on them by the deformation. Elastic restoring forces are thus entropic. Rubber molecules respond to imposed deformation by an internal flow or rearrangement of chain segments. However, molecular motions take place at a rate that depends on the thermal energy available to overcome various resistive forces that hinder relative motion of chain segments. These resistive forces are due to the internal and external barriers to changing molecular conformations. They have the effect of an internal viscosity and retard the attainment of equilibrium conformations.

When the rate of deformation requires that chains move faster than their normal mobility allows, the resistance to deformation increases and the rubber is stiffer. When the deformation rate is low relative to the rate of molecular motion, the viscous resistance to deformation is small. This rate-sensitive elasticity of rubber is termed viscoelasticity.

There are thus two distinct contributions to the elasticity of rubber: (1) equilibrium or purely elastic effects of the molecular chains comprising the network and (2) nonequilibrium, rate dependent, or viscous effects. The latter are strongly dependent upon temperature because thermal expansion greatly facilitates the motion of molecular segments. Indeed, below a characteristic temperature called the glass transition temperature, denoted T_g, thermally induced motion occurs so slowly that the material is rigid and immobile, a polymeric glass. This glass transition temperature is characteristic of the particular rubber or polymer, ranging from $-120°C$ for certain silicone rubbers up to temperatures above ambient for materials like polystyrene.

Because nearly all hydrocarbon polymers have similar intermolecular attractive forces and similar coefficients of thermal expansion, the mobility of molecular segments of all polymers increases with temperature in a similar way so that the rate ϕ_2 of thermal motion at a temperature T_2 is given by the "universal" relation of Williams, Landel, and Ferry [2]

$$\log_{10}(\phi_2/\phi_g) = \frac{17.6\,(T_2 - T_g)}{52 + (T_2 - T_g)} \tag{1}$$

where ϕ_g denotes the rate of segment motion at T_g, about 1 jump/10 s. The magnitude of the viscous contribution to stresses depends upon the rate of deformation de/dt or $\dot{e}$ (e = strain) relative to the natural mobility ϕ_2 of molecular segments at that particular temperature.

Rubber Friction

General Description

The contact area between a rubber and a rigid support substrate or counter-surface is depicted in Fig. 1. Sketch I shows the smooth surface con-

I

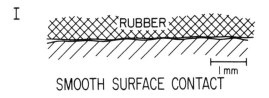

SMOOTH SURFACE CONTACT

II

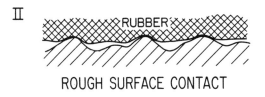

ROUGH SURFACE CONTACT

III

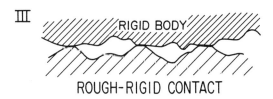

ROUGH-RIGID CONTACT

FIG. 1—*Rubber versus rigid counter surface contacts.*

tact while Sketch II shows the rough surface contact. For comparison Sketch III illustrates a dual rigid body contact. The difference between Sketch II and III is the draping action of the rubber as contrasted to the asperity versus asperity type contacts of Sketch III. Under tangential motion, the compliant rubber will undergo substantial deformation in "flowing around" and enveloping the counter-surface asperities. Note the absence of any possibility of substantial "asperity induced" deformation in the smooth surface rubber contact. Under the same circumstances the rigid-rigid body asperity contacts will exhibit a ploughing or "plastic shear" yield action.

From this visualization of rubber-countersurface contacts, three components of friction can be defined

$$F = \gamma_a F_a + \gamma_d F_d + \gamma_w F_w \qquad (2)$$

where F_a, F_d, and F_w are the frictional forces caused by adhesion, deformation, and wear or abrasion, respectively. The terms γ_a, γ_d, and γ_w are the fractional contribution of that particular friction force component, respectively.

The adhesion component is attributed to intersurface molecular or similar type bonding. This will be discussed in more detail later. The deformation component of friction is attributed to the hysteresis of the rubber. Any individual rubber surface element goes through a deformation cycle as it passes over a countersurface asperity and because of finite hysteresis or nonideal elasticity, there is net loss of energy per element per cycle.

On sharp asperity surfaces or at high-sliding velocities, a finite amount of rubber will be worn away or abraded during sliding. This will require some energy, and thus this term contributes to frictional force under certain conditions. On a macroscopic level, both adhesion and hysteresis can be attributed to the viscoelastic properties of rubber.

Theories of Rubber Friction

Under nonabrasive conditions, rubber friction is a composite of two mechanisms (adhesion and deformation) that can be separately demonstrated. The adhesion component has been attributed to a bonding of exposed surface atoms between sliding members, the breaking of which requires work. The energy lost in breaking adhesive bonds is assumed to be not fully compensated for by the energy gained upon re-making them, the difference being mainly dissipated as heat within the rubber. It is the detail of the dissipation process that presents great difficulties in all adhesion theories of rubber friction. Several reviews of these theories have appeared [3–7]. The theories can be classified as either molecular or macroscopic and one of the reviews [3] shows that they all contain a viscoelastic loss factor.

They have the common idea that bonds are formed at the sliding interface, strained, and then broken. A form of the Eyring rate theory is applied and the theories then reduce to multiplication of two principle parameters, one of which decreases with rate and the other increases. These show a maximum friction at a certain sliding speed. Schallamach's theory [8,9] provides for an increase in bond strength with speed, but the number of bonds formed decreases with speed. Bartenev [10] viewed rubber as a viscous liquid with a monotonic increase in friction with increasing sliding speed but a decrease in true contact area with speed. Both examples predict a maximum. Such theories show reasonable agreement with experimental results in sliding friction, but they predict vanishing friction at very low speeds, however rubber has a static coefficient of friction. A static coefficient indicates that adhesive bonds between rubber and track can indefinitely sustain a certain maximum tangential stress, yet on the basis of the molecular theories, bonds will break under the smallest force.

Macroscopic theories are based on different ideas. Savkoor [11] proposed that rubber adhered to the track in domains containing a number of bonds, each domain being able to sustain a small but finite force indefinitely because of an equilibrium between the breaking and making of bonds within the domain. This ensured the existence of static friction. Bulgin et al. [12] proposed a theory where rubber elements adhere to the track and are elongated until interface bonds are broken. A detached element snaps back returning part of its stored energy to the rubber sample. The energy lost is proportional to the loss tangent and inversely proportional to the hardness.

Tabor and Ludema [13] assume that interface adhesion is so strong that tearing takes place in a rubber layer about 10 nm from the interface. Using tensile strength data of rubber (as a function of temperature and rate), they deduced an effective tear strength of the interface. The variation of rubber modulus with rate of deformation was used to deduce the area of contact. The product of these gave the shear strength of the interface as a function of speed, which agreed with observation. Absolute values of theoretical friction tended to be about 10 times larger than those observed. Experimental evidence suggests no transfer of rubber onto a track at low sliding speeds, but transfer at high speeds. The former implies sliding at the interface; the latter implies that rubber itself is being sheared. This, therefore, raises the question as to whether sliding takes place at the interface or within the rubber. Finally, Kummer [14] has attempted to combine molecular and macroscopic descriptions of adhesional friction into a unified theory. Adhesion is attributed to electrostatic attraction between rubber and track.

Schallamach Waves

After 30 years, the debate continues on the mechanism of rubber friction. The theories described have ignored the nature of the counterface, the exact location of interface sliding and the possible consequences of strain crystallization of rubber molecules close to the interface, where strains are likely to be high. In practice additional factors become important, such as heat buildup and the possibility of degradation of the rubber. Schallamach described an optical study of the contact of a rubber hemisphere sliding on transparent surfaces [15]. For soft rubber sliding over a smooth, hard, clean counterface, relative motion between the two surfaces was due to "waves of detachment." The waves moved as "folds" across the rubber surface in the direction of sliding. Schallamach associated them with tangential and compressive stress gradients and the resulting elastic instability or buckling. Between these waves there was strong adhesion. The waves are called Schallamach waves.

The phenomenon is illustrated in Fig. 2, where two detached voids are shown. Since the original description, several workers have continued the line of investigation. Kendall [16] showed that for the rolling friction of smooth cylinders over smooth soft rubber the retarding force could be accounted for by considering the process as adhesive joint formation at the front of the cylinder and the propagation of a crack (rupture) at the rear, a "make-break" adhesive joint process. The energy required for the "break" operation is substantially more than the energy gained in the "make" step with a net loss of energy. The action can be described as peeling.

Roberts and Thomas [17] and Roberts and Jackson [18] have studied the surface energy and adhesion friction characteristics of rubber on smooth sub-

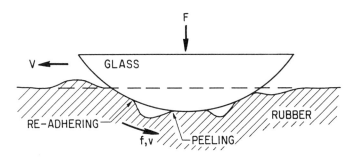

FIG. 2—*Schallamach waves, (glass) hemisphere sliding on rubber* [1].

strates and report values in agreement with this concept. From this latest work and the initial work of Schallamach, it is apparent that the sliding of rubber over smooth surfaces involves surface deformation similar in principle as in the case of rough surfaces. The mechanism is somewhat different and the buckle and peeling action is different, but surface deformation is a key element in both smooth and rough surface sliding friction.

Some of the past difficulties in the study of friction may be traced to the use of rough surfaces, which precluded optical studies of the sliding interface. It is difficult to resolve phenomena at minute asperity tips. The usefulness of smooth rubber for following interfacial events more closely is now well recognized, but in the earlier investigations smooth surfaces tended to be avoided because they appeared anomalous. They show a high friction often accompanied by gross stick-slip. The smooth rubber contacts used may be regarded as giant single asperities.

These studies provide a macroscopic theory of "sliding friction" in terms of interfacial adhesion; the interfacial adhesion itself involves both molecular forces and viscoelastic losses. As the hardness of the rubber increases the waves become finer and pass across the contact zone at higher speed. Whether this process always applies to the "sliding" of rubber over all surfaces is not known. It is possible that when the ratio of the modulus of the rubber to the surface adhesion exceeds a certain critical value true sliding occurs. On the other hand, it is possible that in this limiting case the waves are of molecular dimensions and the waves of detachment continue to operate, but on a molecular scale.

Laboratory Abrasion

General Background

Although abrasion may be viewed as a special type of wear (Wear of Materials Section), the words abrasion and wear will be used interchangeably in this part of the review. If any distinction is made between different wear mechanisms, that is, abrasive wear, it will be clear in its context and meaning.

Most of the work on laboratory rubber abrasion (wear) has been conducted on one of two types of abraders: abraders that operate at full (100%) slip, or that operate at partial slip. A circular area abrading contact, moving across a rubber surface is an example of the full (100%) slip type. A small rubber wheel rotating in contact with an abrader (grinding) wheel of equal diameter is an example of the second type. Two partial slip operational modes of the second type produce practical abrasion rates: (1) the rotational velocities of the two wheels are different (circumferential slip) or (2) the axis of the two wheels are not parallel that is, a slip angle (lateral slip) condition exists.

Examples of the full slip type are the (Williams) Du Pont or ASTM Test Method for Rubber Property—Abrasion Resistance (NBS Abrader) (D 1630), the ASTM Test Method for Rubber Property—Abrasion Resistance (Pico Abrader) (D 2228), and a German Standards Institute (DIN) rotary drum device with the rubber as the slider. Examples of the partial slip devices are the Lambourn abrader (circumferential), the Goodyear angle, and Akron abrader (slip angle). The National Bureau of Standards (NBS) device uses a hard grain abrasive paper, the Pico device uses two special blades set vertical to the rubber surface, and the Lambourn, Goodyear, and Akron devices use special Carborundum® (grinding type) wheels.

Despite nearly 50 years of effort to devise laboratory abraders that give "a good prediction" of the wear resistance of tire tread compounds in real-world situations, no abrasion device currently exists that does an acceptable job. As this review will show, this is not entirely the fault of the laboratory devices. The problem is mainly one of attempting to "hit" a moving target rather than a "stationary" one. There is no "one-point" or standardized method for measuring "real-world" tire wear because those who conduct outdoor tread-wear tests cannot control or standardize the ambient conditions of the testing environment. Variation in the environment gives variation in test results.

Although the goal of being able to predict some sort of "real-world" tire tread compound wear performance is still being pursued, one of the main benefits of laboratory wear tests has been and continues to be their diagnostic capability. Depending on the conditions of their execution (type of abrasive, speed, load, and other severity factors), they can provide insight into wear mechanisms. Some of this will be reviewed.

Unlike the situation with hard, brittle, or ductile solids, the contact mechanics and the wear of rubber is governed by the visco-elastic behavior of the rubber. Large rubber deformations arise without the extremely high contact pressures and resulting plastic flow of hard materials. The wear of rubber is primarily caused by stress concentrations produced by the countersurface texture. There are two scales of texture: (1) macrotexture, which for a pavement (as countersurface) is equivalent to the aggregate particles, that is, geometric features in the several millimetre range and (2) microtexture or surface asperities on the gross macrotexture (aggregate) particles in the 10^{-2} to 10^{-3} mm range.

The relevance of these two type of texture lies in the magnitude of the stress concentrations. If the stress concentrations are sufficiently high so that only a few asperities need pass over a given site to detach a particle, the important property is the fundamental rupture energy, most probably a tear resistance. In the opposite extreme a large number of asperity-rubber contacts must be made to produce a wear particle with some incremental "surface damage" with each contact. In this case there is a cumulative or fatigue damage aspect. Each pass over an asperity is roughly equivalent to a minute increase in the growth of a fatigue crack, and resistance to this type of damage dominates behavior. Any practical situation is some combination of these two extremes.

An important variant of the fatigue mechanism of wear is the case where chemically induced degradation of the rubber (properties) develops parallel to or before the repeated asperity stress cycles, each with its incremental increase in crack dimensions. This degradation brings about a reduction in the critical rupture energy or in the required cumulative damage to produce a wear particle.

Rubber Degradation as a Factor in Laboratory Abrasion

A fundamental problem confronts those that devise or conduct laboratory abrasion tests: What is to be done with the (rubber) abrasion debris? If no precautions are taken, this coats (smears) the countersurface or otherwise collects and interferes with the frictional contact, rubber versus abradant. Under such conditions, abrasion testing results are not valid.

The most common solution to this has been the use of a particulate material third body. This is commonly called an abrasion "dust," and its purpose is to engulf the abraded rubber and either render it innocuous in the abrasion process or to physically carry the rubber debris out of the interface. Most routinely used laboratory abrasion tests use some such dust. Magnesia (MgO), Fuller's earth, Carborundum powder, aluminum oxide, and various silicates have all been used with various abraders.

Schallamach [19] clearly showed the influence of the importance of abrasion dust in some of his pioneering work on laboratory wear and rubber degradation. Prior to his work, Brodskii et al. [20] demonstrated that certain conditions were necessary to observe degradative wear, the frictional contact must be between rubber and a smooth countersurface. Figure 3 is taken from Schallamach [19] and illustrates laboratory abrasion testing on a smooth grinding wheel device (Akron abrader).

Two natural rubber (NR) tread compounds are shown. One is without an antioxidant (AO) that protects against degradation and one is with such an antioxidant (Nonox ZA). On the left ordinant the rates of abrasion are 72 and 38, respectively, for the two compounds. These represent equilibrium values

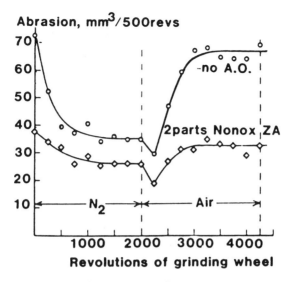

FIG. 3—*Laboratory abrasion* [19].

after a run-in period in air. The region marked "N_2" indicates what happens as abrasion tests are made in an inert N_2 atmosphere. The gradual drop in rate for both is caused by a removal of degraded layers of rubber, generated from the previous runs in air before the start of the N_2 tests. The plateau abrasion values at 2000 total revolutions are 36 and 26, respectively, for the no AO and the Nonox compounds. Thus a substantial reduction in the initial wear rates is observed; the rate of the no AO compound is reduced by a factor of one-half. The rates of both are now much closer together.

When air is admitted to the test chamber, the rates increase to nearly their original values after a period of adjustment. The dip in the rate after first admitting air is due to a reduction in wear from the smearing action of the rubber debris; this smearing being due primarily to air degraded rubber that is produced in this initial period. This lowers the rate temporarily until a new degraded layer can form and establish a new "air" rate as indicated after 3500 to 4000 total revolutions. Again the protected compound runs at about half the no AO rate.

More recently Gent et al. [21] have conducted laboratory abrasion with a blade abrader. This type of abrader was originally devised by Champ et al. [22]. Figure 4 schematically illustrates the form of the apparatus. Abrasion occurs due to the "broad front" scraping action of the blade held vertical (on a radial line) to the revolving wheel (rubber) surface. Champ et al. as well as Gent et al. have interpreted the results from such tests in terms of rubber fracture mechanics. An idealized schematic of the postulated action of the blade is shown in Fig. 5.

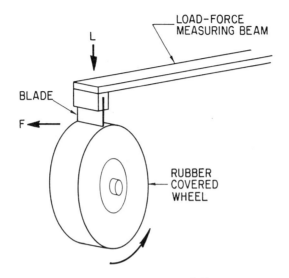

FIG. 4—*Blade abrader* [18].

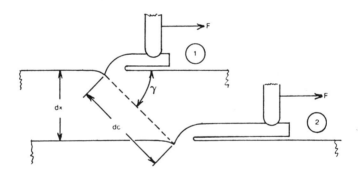

FIG. 5—*Schematic of idealized blade action; Stage 2 follows Stage 1; tongue volume increases because crack growth at base* [19].

The blade elongates (strains) a tongue of rubber in passing over the surface causing the "crack tip" at the base of the tongue to grow until it ruptures producing a wear particle. Thomas and Southern showed that the abrasion rate of gum (nonreinforced) rubbers was correlated with their fatigue crack growth rates. Rubbers that crystallize upon stretching, like NR, were exceptions, the abrasion of NR is much greater than its crack growth measurements would predict.

Blade abrasion normally produces abrasion patterns as depicted in Fig. 6. Such patterns are also observed in abrasion by grinding wheels under some conditions where the asperities on the wheels are not excessively sharp. Abrasion patterns are also observed on tires when they have been used (or tested)

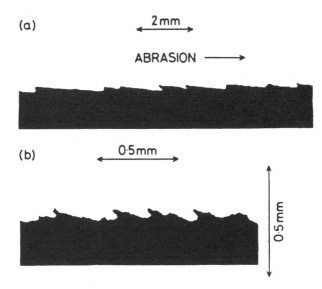

(a)

2mm

ABRASION ⟶

(b)

0·5mm

0·5mm

FIG. 6—*Abrasion pattern cross sections:* (a) *gum NR and* (b) *worn tire tread* [19].

under high severity conditions. Typically, high severity is identified with high tractive force conditions especially in the cornering mode. One requirement for the development of an abrasion pattern is a "unidirectional sliding" frictional contact. If random direction sliding conditions exist, such patterns ordinarily do not develop. The spacing between the ridges (the coarseness of the pattern) is a (direct) function of the rate of abrasion, the normal load, and the compliance or reciprocal modulus of the rubber.

Gent and Pulford [21] have summarized their work up to 1983. Rubber is abraded by two often competitive mechanisms (1) abrasion by fracture (tear, rupture) of the rubber or (2) mechano-chemical degradation of a surface layer of the rubber, with the frequent loss of surface material in the form of a sticky, oily material.

The fracture type mechanism is actually two concurrent somewhat different processes. There is a "fine scale" loss of rubber in the form of particles a few micrometres in diameter. Concurrent with this is a "larger scale" loss of large particles several hundred micrometres in diameter, where material from the upper sides of the ridge patterns is torn loose. This action is less frequent (on a time basis) than the "small-scale" highly repetitive process of small size particle removal, which takes place in the intervening areas between the ridge peaks.

The second main mechanism is the chemical breakdown of the polymer chains caused by high frictional forces on the surface layers. These intense frictional forces produce rapid chain elongation, and at isolated sites sufficient energy is stored to cause individual chain rupture. When a chain is ruptured, two free-radical ends are produced that are chemically metastable. The next step in this free-radical generation depends on the chemical nature of the rubber. For natural rubber (NR) and styrene-butadiene rubber (SBR) the next step is reaction with a free radical acceptor, oxygen being the usual such species. Such a reaction stabilizes the radical, and a fully cleaved chain is the result. The cumulative effect of chain cleavage is a reduction in molecular weight, that is, a sticky oily substance. With rubbers like cis-polybutadiene (BR), reaction of the free radical chain end with adjacent chains is the preferred action and cross-linking results. Cross-linking is the opposite of molecular weight reduction, and the product of this is a dry, powdery abraded material.

Tire Treadwear

General Background

The locus of the abrasive action at the tire-pavement interface is a layer of the rubber perhaps a fraction of a millimetre in thickness (Fig. 7). As the tire serves its vehicle functions, both this layer and the underlying rubber are subjected to compressive and (surface) shear stresses and strains. The combined action of these stresses and strains is collectively referred to as frictional work. Frictional work exists during all modes of tire operation and ordinarily produces wear of the tread rubber. The amount of wear per unit frictional work is a complex function of the intensity and the duration of the frictional work, the nature of the pavement and other environmental factors in addition to the properties of the rubber.

Simple Wear Equation

Based upon the assumption proposed by a number of investigators that wear is directly proportional to the amount of frictional work, the simplest equation that relates treadwear and frictional work is

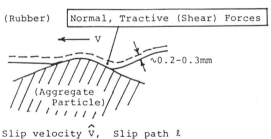

FIG. 7—*Typical "rubber-pavement aggregate particle" contact.*

$$R_W = AE_F \qquad (3)$$

R_W = rate of wear, amount of rubber lost from a unit surface per tire revolution,

A = abradability = the amount of rubber lost per unit area per unit frictional work under specified interface conditions, and

E_F = the frictional work per unit area, per revolution, for a typical tread element.

One may object to Eq 3 as being too simple and maintain that a more complex relationship must surely apply. The true relationship eventually may prove to be more complex although in the development given below, much of the complexity is carried by the term A. If in fact a more complex relationship is found to exist, the adoption of this simple relationship and the treatment given below is not invalidated; the analysis will only need to be appropriately expanded building on this treatment as a foundation. One important point, the abradability A is not a material constant (for any particular tread material). The value of A is a function of the rubber, the pavement, the temperature (at the interface), and interfacial contaminants.

The lack of a specific constant value for A would seem to limit the value of Eq 3 as an aid in solving treadwear problems. This is both true and false. It is true that Eq 3 cannot be used in the sense that each material has a relatively constant A value. However the most important use of Eq 3 is its role in organizing thinking in the analysis of tread-wear problems.

This is illustrated in Fig. 8. Factors that contribute to abradability A are shown on the left. Factors that contribute to frictional work E_F, are indicated on the right. Without a clear differentiation between abradability factors and frictional work factors, discussion of treadwear tends to be confused.

All abradability factors are independent of frictional work factors, except tire interface temperature. All frictional work factors influence the tire interface temperature since tire wear is in general not an isothermal process and any change in a right-hand E_F factor increases the expended interface energy thereby raising the transient sliding temperature. The dashed line indicates this interaction. It is implicitly understood therefore that an increase in frictional work increases interface temperature in addition to other direct consequences of increased frictional work.

The use of the diagram of Fig. 8 aids in the organization of experiments to study tire wear; it also aids interpreting the results of the experiments and tread-wear phenomena in general.

In current work in our laboratories on treadwear, tests are conducted by way of three separate, but interrelated and complimentary approaches:

(1) regular vehicle convoy or fleet tests,
(2) tests with an instrumented cornering wear trailer, and
(3) laboratory tests, with an abrasion tester.

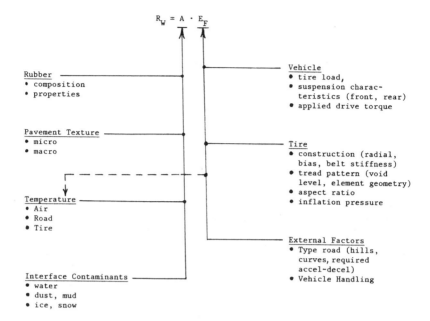

FIG. 8—*Analysis of treadwear problems—simple wear equations.*

Convoy tests with regular highway vehicles are indispensable because they are "essentially identical" to ordinary vehicle operation for a substantial portion of the vehicle use population. They represent a random input of tire forces, and they can be conducted at various times of the year to study some "seasonal-environmental" factors as well as other treadwear parameters.

Tests with a cornering trailer instrumented to control and measure cornering forces via slip angle variation are also of great importance. Such tests produce greatly accelerated wear at slip angles of 1 to 2°. With a basic understanding of tire force generation mechanics, important tire wear characteristics can be determined, that are difficult or impossible with ordinary convoy testing. An example is the measurement of tire wear temperature coefficients.

Finally, for a fundamental understanding of the "rubber-abrasive" interface, the control of certain aspects of the frictional contact between rubber and the abrasive is necessary. This is best accomplished with laboratory abrasion testers. Such operational factors are slip velocities, normal loads, ambient temperature, extent of interface sliding, and the presence or absence of "third bodies," for example, dust, abrasive detritus, and water. This part of the overall approach to tread wear is still in the preliminary development stages. No results will be reported on this particular type of abrasion.

Pavement Characterization

General Background

The principle method of characterizing pavements is by means of road surface texture. As previously stated, two scales of texture are recognized: macrotexture and microtexture. Macrotexture is defined by the size, distribution, and geometrical configuration of the individual aggregate particles and the voids surrounding such particles. A high-macrotexture pavement has large, often angular aggregate particles that stand proud from the underlying base of asphalt or concrete and thus generate a large void volume between the particles.

The microtexture of a pavement is characterized by the degree of surface roughness or rugosity of the individual aggregate particles. The scale of roughness or harshness is thus 10^{-1} to 10^{-2} mm or less, usually beyond observation by the unaided eye.

The petrographic or chemical nature of aggregate materials is also important in regard to their microtexture and their resistance to polishing action by continued contact with tires. Limestone of various graded varieties is noted for its tendency to polish. Granites and quartzite containing aggregates are generally hard and hold their microtexture, sharp edges, and angularity much better than limestones.

Pavements gradually change over a period of months or years depending on traffic density, to a pseudo-equilibrium state of macro- and microtexture. The macrotexture gradually increases because of the wearing away of the asphaltic binder material thus providing a greater void between aggregate particles. The microtexture decreases, mainly because of a surface polishing of the aggregate particles. The prefix "pseudo" is used because it has been conclusively shown that seasonal variations in such measurable pavement properties as skid, friction or traction resistance do exist. Williams et al. [23] and Bond et al. [24] in the United Kingdom have pioneered in the study of pavement texture.

As shown in Fig. 9, the seasonal change in wet skidding resistance correlates with the seasonal change in the microtexture. During the summer months, the microtexture decreases because of intense traffic polishing, and during the winter it increases as a result of water, frost, and other forms of weathering action. The photomicrographs in Fig. 9 illustrate changes in microtexture of the order of 0.005 to 0.02 mm that occur as a result of the natural weathering action and the polishing action of traffic, which is dominant during the summer. Under extremes of traffic density (areas of heavy braking or cornering) the polishing effect (high relative slip between the tire and pavement) will mask the effect of natural weathering processes.

Figure 10 taken from a publication by Sabey [25] also indicates the influence of "seasonal-weathering" variations in the percentage of wet road acci-

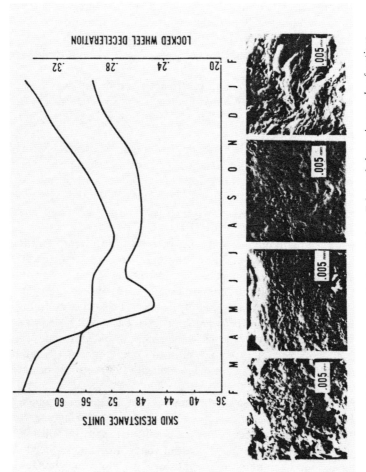

FIG. 9—*Skid resistance versus month of year (Feb. to Feb.) and photomicrographs of sections taken from sections monitored for skid resistance* [24].

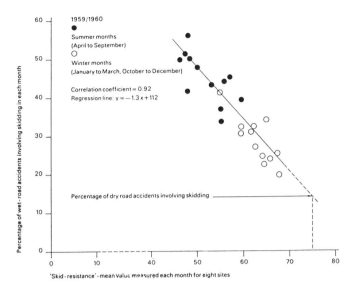

FIG. 10—*Percentage wet road accidents with skidding versus skid resistance (monthly basis) for conditions in the United Kingdom* [25].

dents involving skidding. The percentage decreases as the skid resistance increases. All the "summer month" plotted points occur at the low skid resistance end of the regression curve; all the "winter" points occur at the high-end. The changes in microtexture are responsible for the change in skid resistance summer versus winter.

In the United States the same conclusions have been reached on the weathering effect of pavements. Kummer [26] attributed the increase in microtexture of pavements (in periods of increased rainfall) to a chemi-mechanical roughening. This effect is pronounced for limestone aggregates. He attributes increased microtexture development in low-temperature wet conditions as a result of an acidic attack from increased concentration of atmospheric carbon dioxide (CO_2) dissolved in the water. The mechanical roughening component is due to a coarser particle size for the detritus or debris particles worn off the aggregate at low temperature (winter months). The tire acts as a lapping tool in this mechanical roughening.

Figure 11, Kummer et al. [27], shows a manifestation of the transient nature of the microtexture increase because of rainfall. The low equilibrium level of skid resistance (about 12 SN) is substantially increased in the terminal stages of the three-day rainfall period caused by a microtexture increase. Several days are required to reestablish an equilibrium microtexture.

Quite recently, Whitehurst and Neuhardt[2] have documented the changes in

[2]Whitehurst, E. A. and Neuhardt, J. B., in this publication, pp. 61–71.

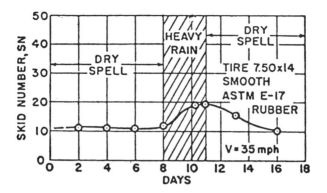

FIG. 11—*Transient nature of pavement skid resistance with rainfall* [27].

skid resistance of the reference skid test surfaces developed by the Federal Highway Administration for skid trailer calibration. Figure 12, taken from their publication, shows the month-to-month variation of skid resistance for the years 1975 to 1983 on Primary Reference Surface 1 (PRS-1) located in Ohio. This is a surface with finely graded silica sand (No. 10-16 gradation) and an epoxy binder. Again in agreement with the work done in the United Kingdom, high skid resistance is found during the winter months and low skid resistance during the summer months. Note the relatively constant seasonal variation for all the years tested. All skid resistance results are for wet slide traction by way of the ASTM Test Method for Skid Resistance of Paved Surfaces Using a Full-Scale Tire (E 274) procedure.

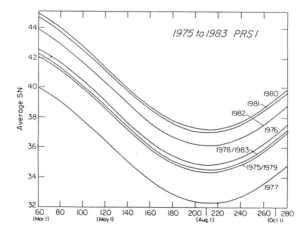

FIG. 12—*Seasonal variation in skid resistance of reference skid surface (PRS-1) (in Ohio) for years 1975 to 1983 (see Footnote 2).*

These results show that surfaces that are not subject to constant daily traffic also go through a cyclic seasonal microtexture change. These test surfaces were of course subjected to the "traffic" of testing, with the high tire-pavement tractive forces characteristic of such testing. Whether this is equivalent to the less intense frictional work characteristic of low torque or free rolling tires that constitute normal traffic conditions remains to be seen.

Tire Wear Versus Pavement Texture

Other than occasional references in the trade literature to the fact that newly prepared pavements are abrasive and give high rates of treadwear, the scientific literature on treadwear versus pavement texture is sparse. The main contribution is a paper by Lowne [30] in 1971. The treadwear of passenger tires was measured on a series of test pavements at the Transportation and Road Research Laboratory (and Proving Ground) in the United Kingdom. Two types of tests were conducted: (1) very accelerated wear on a special test vehicle at 20° slip angle and (2) tests on ordinary vehicles that were driven in a "figure 8" handling pattern with high cornering input.

Both sets of tests were in agreement, and they showed that the microtexture was the dominant factor in determining treadwear. Macrotexture played a minor role, with increased macrotexture giving increased wear. Lowne showed that treadwear W was given by a multiple regression equation of the form

$$W = -9.2 + 90 \, (S_{50}) + 18T \qquad (4)$$

where S_{50} is the wet cornering traction coefficient at 50 km/h for a smooth no tread pattern tire and T is the macrotexture depth, normalized to a reference surface as 1.

Parameter S_{50} is a measure of microtexture. The statistical importance of S_{50} and T is given by the confidence level values 0.95 and 0.75, indicating that S_{50} is substantially more important. Wet traction testing has shown that S_{50} is quite responsive to the microtexture of pavements. Thus we may conclude that the microtexture of a pavement, which must of necessity include the angularity (sharp edge) factor, is the controlling pavement characteristic in determining the influence of pavement texture on treadwear.

The Role of the Tread Rubber

Characterizing Tread Rubbers

There are a wide range of physical and chemical measurements that can be made to characterize both the base or gum rubbers and the fully formulated tread compounds. However, all tread rubbers and their tread compounds respond to an imposed strain in a visco-elastic manner. One of the key parameters in the visco-elastic response of polymers (rubbers) is the glass transition temperature, denoted by T_g.

The main function of tread rubbers is to provide a high level of grip with the pavement. High friction or grip has been shown to be a function of visco-elastic response; thus the T_g of a rubber should play a role in good frictional contact. Frictional work is the causative factor for treadwear; thus a connection between wear and T_g is logical.

It must be emphasized that T_g is one of several factors that determine the absolute wear rate of a tread compound. Two other factors play an important role: the reinforcement system (carbon black and processing oil) and the cure system (organic chemicals, sulfur zinc oxide, and fatty acid) that are needed to cure or cross-link the rubber to increase its elastic response characteristics and reduce its viscous response behavior. Thus

$$\text{rate of wear} = f(T_g)(R)(C) \tag{5}$$

where

T_g = glass transition temperature,
R = reinforcement system (carbon black, process oil), and
C = cure system (accelerator, sulfur, zinc oxide (ZnO), fatty acid, and other materials).

Figure 13 illustrates the influence of T_g on treadwear in Southwest Texas tests at the San Angelo uniform tire quality grading (UTQG) Test Course in three seasons of the year: winter, spring, and summer. There are two "rubber blend" systems used, SBR/BR and NR/BR. (SBR = styrene-butadiene rubber, BR = cis-polybutadiene rubber, and NR = (natural) polyisoprene rubber.) The open points represent these blends, the lower the T_g the greater the BR content of any blend. The solid points are for 100% SBR and 100% NR.

The concept of treadwear index will be used to discuss relative treadwear or tread-wear resistance. The treadwear index (often abbreviated TWI) is the ratio of tread life of two compounds multiplied by 100. The reference or control compound tread life is placed in the denominator, thus an index greater than 100 indicates superior tread-life performance for the experimental or candidate compound.

The tread rubber T_g has a substantial influence on treadwear rate. At low tread-wear ambient (air) test temperatures (5°C), rate of wear is directly related to T_g for both SBR/BR and NR/BR blends. At high treadwear test temperatures (29°C), the strong (5°C) wear dependence on T_g gives way to a mild (direct) dependence for SBR/BR and to a negative or inverse relationship for NR/BR blends. The opposite behavior of the NR/BR blends is due in part to the discovery that low T_g rubbers have a high "rate of wear" temperature coefficient, that is, they are more temperature sensitive. As test temperature

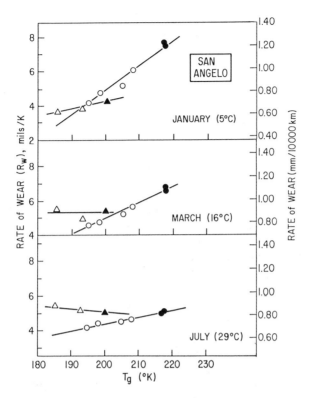

FIG. 13—*Rate wear versus* Tg *for San Angelo during Jan., March, July,* Δ = NR/BR *with* ▲ = *100% BR, and* ○ = *SBR/BR, and* ● = *100% SBR* [31].

is lowered the treadwear index of low T_g rubbers increases compared to all SBR (=100) control compound. Thus, winter tests favor a superior tread-wear performance for BR rubber or BR rich blends. The other contributing factor that produces a differing behavior SBR/BR system versus NR/BR is the lower carbon black content for the NR/BR blends compared to the SBR/BR, 45 versus 76 phr (phr = parts per hundred of rubber). Thus the relative influence of T_g is highly dependent upon the season, mainly the ambient temperature of tire use. It is also dependent upon the degree of reinforcement (carbon black level and type) in the compound.

The Rubber Reinforcement System

Rubber reinforcement is defined as an enhancement of a particular performance property. Stiffness (modulus), rupture strength (tear, tensile), and abrasion resistance are the three most important properties considered. Carbon black when suitably mixed into the rubber "reinforces" in all three of these categories.

Studebaker [*32*], Dannenberg et al. [*33*], Biard and Svetlik [*34*], and others have reported on the variation in wear index (relative wear resistance) of tread compounds with different carbon blacks as test severity is varied. It is generally recognized that higher structure and smaller particle size blacks confer enhanced wear resistance under high test severity conditions.

Veith [*28*] has reported on special wear tests conducted to assess the effect of the colloidal or morphological properties of carbon blacks. Veith and Chirico [*31*] investigated the influence of the carbon black reinforcement system and studied the four components of this system: (1) the morphology or structure of the carbon black, measured by a special laboratory test and referred to as DBP absorption, (2) the specific surface area of the carbon black, evaluated by electron microscope (EMA), (3) the concentration of carbon black in the compound, and (4) the concentration of process oil. The process oil, which is an adjunct to the carbon black is required for proper mixing and processing during tire manufacturing. It is considered as part of the reinforcement system. Another important carbon black variable, the surface activity, was held constant for the work described. A comprehensive study of the influence of these four factors on the rate of treadwear over a very wide range of tire use or severity conditions was conducted.

The influence of each factor or component of the reinforcement system increases as test severity is increased. Carbon blacks with high structure and surface area are substantially superior to blacks with normal structure and surface area at the higher test severities. At the higher severities, increased oil produces higher wear rates. The rate of wear passes through a minimum as compounds with increased carbon black are tested at any severity level. The carbon black content at this minimum wear rate shifts to higher values as the test severity is raised.

Accelerated trailer tests conducted at a series of specific cornering force levels (0.10 to 0.30 g range) give strong evidence that the treadwear index of typical tread compounds demonstrates crossovers or inversion of index values. If the linear extrapolation is accepted, compounds that show superior wear resistance compared to a reference compound at high severities, show smaller magnitude inferior wear resistance at low severities. Figures 14 and 15 illustrate wear index versus cornering force for the trailer tests.

Both figures show the marked differences in relative wear resistance as reinforcement system variables are varied. In general, high black levels, low oil, high EMA, and DBP promote superior high severity wear resistance. Compounds with EMA and DBP values that show superior wear resistance at high severities, show a small degree of inferior wear resistance at low severity in the region of 0.05 g. Compare compounds 1 and 4 in Fig. 14 and compounds 7 and 11 in Fig. 15. Additional work, subsequent to that described here and scheduled for future publication, again confirms such crossovers. Other investigators [*5,35–37*] have also reported on such phenomena. The reports of these investigators dealt mainly with the wear resistance inversion influence of

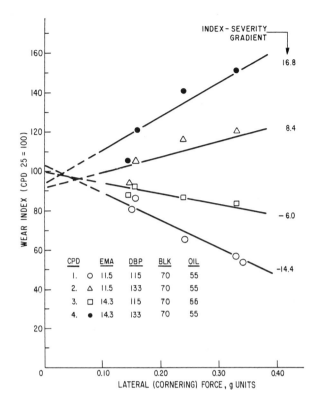

FIG. 14—*Wear index versus lateral force* g *in cornering trailer tests (Compounds 1 to 4)* [31].

different tread rubbers. In this work the tread rubber (blend) was maintained constant, and the effect is directly attributable to the interaction of the carbon black reinforcement system and the testing severity level. Thus, the crossover or wear index inversion phenomena is a general one and is of paramount importance in the understanding of treadwear.

(Tread Compound) Chemical Degradation Versus Treadwear

The influence of an antioxidant on the treadwear of NR compounds is illustrated in Table 1. The wear index of antioxidant containing compounds increases relative to the control as the level of antioxidant is increased. An improvement of some 25 to 30 index points is found at the 1 to 2 phr level. There is a good correlation between accelerated cornering trailer tests [28] and test car data.

Additional accelerated treadwear data have been obtained in cornering trailer experiments [28] on two pavements. The first is referred to as a "blunt" pavement, and the second is termed a "harsh" pavement. The blunt

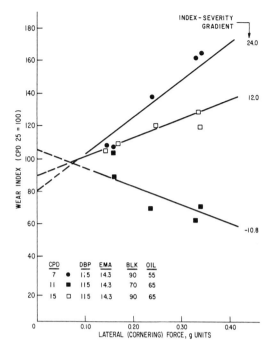

FIG. 15—*Wear index versus lateral force g in cornering trailer tests (Compounds 7, 11, and 15)* [31].

TABLE 1—*"Blunt" pavement tire wear effect of antioxidant in NR.*[a]

| | Wear Rating or Index | |
Antioxidant Content, phr	Test Trailer at 1° Slip	Test Car
0	100	100
0.4	106	111
0.8	. . .	124
1.6	129	120

[a]Antioxidant is N-phenyl N-cycle hexyl *p*-phenylene diamine. NR with 50 phr HAF, 5-phr oil, CBS cured.

surface is a concrete road polished and worn by traffic for several years, the "harsh" surface is a newly laid concrete highway. The terms "blunt" and "harsh" describe microtexture level.

Table 2 shows that the wear index of tread compound B versus A is a function of the texture of the pavement. On the blunt pavement, B is superior to A while on the harsh pavement A is superior to B. The difference between the

TABLE 2—*Effect of pavement type on wear rating of two tread compounds.*

Date	Tread Compound[a]	Texture of Pavement	Wear Rating or Index	Absolute Wear Rate Control, mil/k
		ACCELERATED TESTING		
9-10	A	blunt	100	35
	B		126	
10-3	A	harsh	100	250
	B		73	
10-6	A	harsh	100	60
	B		78	
10-8	A	blunt	100	55
	B		114	
10-13	A	blunt	100	190
	B		130	
		TEXAS FLEET TESTING		
	A	Texas roads	100	20
	B	harsh	68	

[a]Tread A = SBR/BR 65/35 blend tread compound similar to the ASTM Test Method for Skid Resistance of Paved Surfaces Using a Full-Scale Tire (E 274). Tread B = chlorobutyl/SBR 60/40 blend with lower carbon black level than A.

two is some 40 to 45 index points. The data for the individual runs shown in chronological order by date are presented to demonstrate that the phenomenon was repeatable.

Tread A is similar to the standard ASTM skid tire tread compound while B is a chlorobutyl/SBR blend with lower carbon black content. Compound B would have a margin of superiority in wet traction capability. Tests conducted on the harsh pavement correlate fairly well with Texas fleet tests. The Texas roads probably did not exactly duplicate the harsh road of the accelerated testing, and this is no doubt is partly responsible for the small difference.

This reversal of rating is explained on the basis of a change in the predominant mechanism of wear on the two pavements. Kragelskii [37] has reported on the tensile-tear versus fatigue wear mechanism. Laboratory abrasion on very harsh surfaces (silicon carbide paper) is almost entirely tensile-tear failure wear, and such laboratory wear tests invariably fail to predict tire wear. Wear on blunt surfaces in air is due to a degradation of physical properties from the shear-temperature conditions of frictional contact. Particles are removed when oxidative degradation in the surface layer proceeds to a certain critical point. Data obtained by Brodski [20] on wear tests conducted both in air and nitrogen on Monocorundum® paper and a blunt knurled metal surface show that in air the wear index of butyl versus OE-SBR (as 100) was 58 on the abrasive paper and 83 on the knurled or blunt surface. This is an increase of 25 index points and qualitatively agrees with the tire tests described above when considering the differences in rubber composition and other test details. He also showed that the wear rate of butyl is the same in air and nitrogen, illustrating that it is not sensitive to the air degradation effects suffered by SBR and other unsaturated rubbers.

The above example showing a change in the *A* versus *B* wear rating with road surface microtexture change illustrates the interaction of the material factors that affect tire wear. Tread materials interact with roadway materials; neither can be ignored when considering treadwear.

Treadwear Versus Temperature, Rainfall

Tire temperature is important both for its effect on absolute wear rate and on relative rating of different tread compounds. The surface temperature of a tire is the important temperature parameter. This is governed by (1) the transient surface temperature pulse induced by frictional work in passage through contact, (2) the ambient air and road temperature, and (3) temperature caused by hysteretic heat generated within the tire.

Schallamach [38] has shown that the "static" tire surface temperature measured within 1 to 2 min after a vehicle is stopped (after previous running) is proportional to the transient temperature in the contact area. For tires tested under constant load, angle and speed conditions, the "static" surface temperatures measured in this way follow ambient pavement-air temperatures. Temperature coefficients for tire wear rate obtained in this way are positive. Table 3 shows data obtained by two investigators. The agreement is quite good considering that there were differences in time, tread composition, road surface, and measuring technique.

These data show that wear rate increases as temperature increases. It is important to note that the (1973) coefficients were calculated from wear rate data obtained over a short time span, one to two weeks, on pavements in a state of equilibrium polish or microtexture level. Both sets of data were obtained by the use of instrumented cornering trailers under accelerated wear conditions.

Schallamach's data are illustrated in Fig. 16. Although there is considerable scatter, there is an unmistaken positive trend of wear rate versus tire surface temperature. Some of the scatter seen in this plot may be explicable

TABLE 3—*Temperature coefficient of wear* α.

Source	NR	SBR
Schallamach and Grosch [28]	0.04	0.02
Veith [29]	0.04	0.02

NOTE: $W = W_{50} [1 + \alpha (T - T_0)]$; $\alpha \times 100 = \%/°C$.
W_{50} = wear rate at $T_0 = 50°C$.

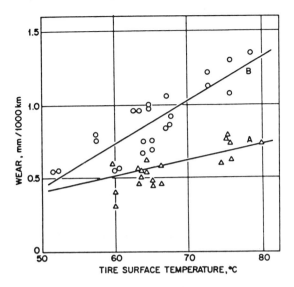

FIG. 16—*Wear of NR (○) and SBR (Δ) at 1° slip angle versus tire ambient temperature* [29].

by changes in roadway abrasiveness as outlined in the next paragraph. In Fig. 17, the wear is expressed in mil/K, and in Fig. 18 it is expressed as g/K (K = 1000 miles) Equivalent results are obtained by the two methods. Good linearity is obtained in both plots with the exception of the points labeled R and HR. These are discussed below.

The points represented by R and HR illustrate the influence of changes in pavement microtexture and how this will influence tire wear rate. The points marked R denote wear rate measured one day after moderate rainfall, ap-

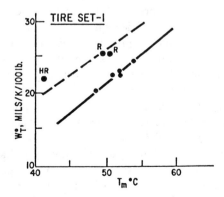

FIG. 17—*Normalized wear rate (mils/K/100 bf cornering force) versus tire surface temperature* [28].

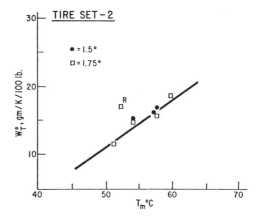

FIG. 18—*Normalized wear rate, g/K/100 lbf of cornering force for SBR compound versus tire surface temperature at two slip angels* [28].

proximately 0.5 cm (0.2 in.) during the previous 24-h period. These are wear rates on dry pavement, after the rain. The pavement is a blunt concrete highway with a surface polished by several years of use. The point denoted by HR (heavy rain) was after a three-day period where a total of 2.54 cm (1.0 in.) of rain fell. These R and HR points show the increased treadwear compared to the curve, at the particular temperatures in question. The 2.54-cm (1-in.) total rainfall over three days increased the dry wear rate by 47%.

Such effects are due to pavement surface etching. The rain combined with dissolved atmospheric agents (SO_2, NO_2, and CO_2) that chemically react with the surface to increase its microtexture. This increases pavement abrasiveness as discussed in the previous section.

These data serve to illustrate the extreme danger in using fleet wear rates, winter versus summer, to assess tire wear temperature coefficients. This has been done by some investigators [39,40], and negative temperature coefficients and zero temperature coefficients have been reported. Unless independent measurements are made to guarantee equivalent pavement microtexture, such seasonal wear rate changes cannot be used for this purpose. Temperature coefficients of tire wear must be assessed when all other factors that effect wear rate are held constant.

An example of the reduction in wear rate caused by an actual water film on the road is given in Table 4. The reduction in wear rate on a harsh pavement, a new concrete highway, is 30%. Note how the "static" tire temperature is lowered 15°C by the water. Schallamach has suggested that this is the major effect of a water film or wet road, that is, to lower tire surface temperature. Using a temperature coefficient $\alpha = 0.02$, the wear rate for dry pavement that would give a 34°C tire temperature has been estimated in the table. The estimated value is in good agreement with the wet data. The difference (76 versus 71) may be due to direct lubrication effects.

TABLE 4—*Effect of wet pavement on wear rate.*[a]

Pavement Condition	f[b]	Tire Static Temperature, °C	Pavement Temperature, °C	Relative Wear
Dry	228	49	20	1.00
Wet	216	34	18	0.71
Estimate dry	...	(34)	...	0.76

[a]On (harsh) high/microtexture pavement, for SBR compound.
[b]f = cornering stiffness, lbf/degree slip angle.

Rubber Loss Mechanism and Microscopic Examination of Tire Tread Surfaces

The words "loss mechanism" refer to the way in which rubber is bodily removed from the surface of a tire tread. The exact loss mechanism has until recently been a matter of speculation. There are two schools of thought. The first is the complete rubber degradation mechanism. In this the surface of the rubber is completely degraded into small molecular fragments that are eliminated in gaseous or volatile form. The second maintains that rubber is removed from the tread surface in particulate form, with a probably broad size range depending upon the severity of the tire use.

The most recent and extensive work on the mechanism of the loss of rubber from the tire tread is the work of Dannis [41]. He found no evidence for the loss of rubber by a volatile or gaseous mechanism, instead the loss was attributed to a physical or particulate erosion process. Small particles of rubber are removed from the tread surface because of tangential forces by a peeling process as previously discussed.

Samples of abraded rubber were collected from tires mounted on a vehicle that was driven on public roads. A special vacuum system was employed at the rear of the tire. The size distribution was found to be log-normal, that is, the log of the (equivalent) particle size had a normal distribution. The mean size depended somewhat on vehicle speed and on the road surface characteristics. The particle (equivalent) diameters ranged from 3 to 100 μm with a mean of the order of 12 μm. The collected wear debris had a high nonrubber content, mainly silica or mineral particles that result from the fragmentation of the road aggregate.

Of equal importance, Dannis found that the rubber particles are readily bio-degraded by common soil bacteria. Thus, the rubber wear debris particles are airborne for a period of time, settle out of the air on soil (beside the roadways), and with the help of rain the debris is washed into the soil and biodegraded.

There is ample evidence that the mechano-chemical degradation mechanisms cited in the Laboratory Abrasion Section are also operative in tire use and testing. Boonstra et al. [42] and Martin and Biddison [43] both reported that on SBR and SBR/BR blends a sticky film was present on the surface of the tire treads after road testing. This adhered tenaciously even after (surface) washing with soap and water. Boonstra et al. also observed that the tire surfaces contained substantial amounts of the elements silicon, aluminum, and potassium.

Smith and Veith [44] also studied tire tread surfaces after wear testing and also the wear particles that are abraded from tires under high cornering conditions. These were collected by a technique similar to Dannis [41]. They examined the particles and the tread surfaces with a scanning electron microscope, energy dispersive X-ray analysis, and transmission electron microscopy of ultrathin sections.

On the worn tread surface of an SBR compound containing 75 phr N285 carbon black and 45 phr oil, a liquid-like layer composed of an intimate mixture of degraded rubber and road silt was observed on the worn tread surfaces. The thickness of this layer is variable but generally in the micron and submicron region, except where rubber was about to be thrown off as a debris particle. Several collections of rubber debris particles were also examined and found to have the same composition of degraded rubber and road silt that was observed on the tread surface.

These observations are in agreement with the results of Boonstra et al. with respect to the analysis of road silt materials on tread surfaces. Since the silt is within the thin layer of degraded rubber, it cannot be washed off the tread surface with soap and water.

These results emphasize the importance of considering the abrasion of tire treads as a three-bodied system: the tread compound, the road surface, and the road silt or detritus. Previous references to the presence of road silt particles on worn tread surfaces implied their incidental nature. This study shows that road silt penetrates into and becomes a part of the substructure of worn tread surfaces. Furthermore, the internal morphology of this substructure is identical to the morphology of the tread debris thrown off from the tread surface.

Conclusions

Treadwear is the result of frictional work in the tire-pavement interface. The nature of the two surfaces, the rubber and the pavement, and the conditions of interfacial contact; these jointly determine the magnitude of treadwear. The important features of the rubber are the glass transition temperature T_g, the degree of reinforcement by carbon black or other material, and the propensity to degradation of the cross-linked rubber compound.

The main characteristic of the pavement that determines the rate of wear is the fine scale or microtexture; the 10^{-2}, 10^{-3} mm scale. The main external world condition, in addition to the pavement microtexture, is the ambient pavement air temperature under which frictional work is generated. Another important external world factor is the force spectrum under which tires operate. This in essence influences the actual interface temperature, which is paramount in the understanding treadwear.

This review attempts to place these key factors into an appropriate perspective, against a background of abrasion of typical nonrubbery materials.

References

[1] Briscoe, B., *Tribology International*, Vol. 14, 1981, p. 231.
[2] Ferry, J. D., *Viscoelastic Properties of Polymers*, 2nd ed., Wiley, New York, 1970.
[3] Moore, D. F., *Friction and Lubrication of Elastomers*, Pergammon Press, New York, 1972.
[4] Moore, D. F. and Geyer, W., *Wear*, Vol. 22, 1972, p. 113.
[5] Schallamach, A., *Rubber Chemistry and Technology*, Vol. 41, 1968, p. 209.
[6] Tabor, D., *Advances Polymer Friction and Wear*, Plenum Press, New York, 1974.
[7] *Tribology in the 80's*, Vol. I, Sessions 1-4, NASA Conference Publication 2300, *Proceedings of International Conference*, Cleveland, OH, 18-21 April 1983.
[8] Schallamach, A., *Proceedings of the Physics Society*, Vol. B66, 1953, p. 87.
[9] Schallamach, A., *Wear*, Vol. 6, 1963, p. 375.
[10] Bartenev, G. M., *Kokl. Acad. Nauk.*, Vol. 96, 1954, p. 1161.
[11] Savkoov, A. R., *Wear*, Vol. 8, 1967, p. 222.
[12] Bulgin, D., Hubbard, G., and Walters, M., *Proceedings of the 4th Rubber Technical Conference IRI*, London, 1962, p. 188.
[13] Tabor, D. and Ludema, K., *Wear*, Vol. 9, 1966, p. 329.
[14] Kummer, H. W., *Engineering Research Bulletin B94*, Penn State University, University Park, PA, 1966.
[15] Schallamach, A., *Wear*, Vol. 17, 1971, p. 301.
[16] Kendall, A., *Wear*, Vol. 33, 1975, p. 351.
[17] Roberts, A. D. and Thomas, A. G., *Wear*, Vol. 33, 1975, p. 45.
[18] Roberts, A. D. and Jackson, S. A., *Nature*, Vol. 257, 11 Sept. 1975, p. 257.
[19] Schallamach, A., *Journal of Applied Polymer Science*, Vol. 12, 1968, p. 281.
[20] Brodski, G. I., Sakhuovski, N., Rezinikovski, M., and Evstratov, V., *Soviet Rubber Technology*, Vol. 19, No. 8, 1960, p. 22.
[21] Gent, A. N. and Pulford, C. T. R., *Journal of Applied Polymer Science*, Vol. 28, 1983, p. 943.
[22] Champ, D. H., Southern, E., and Thomas, A. G., *American Chemical Society (Coatings Division Paper)*, Vol. 34, No. 1, 1974, p. 237.
[23] Williams, A. R., Holmes, T., and Lees, G., *Society of Automotive Engineering*, Paper 720162, Detroit, MI, 1972.
[24] Bond, R., Lees, G., and Williams, A. R., *The Physics of Tire Traction*, Plenum Press, Elmsford, NY, 1974, p. 339.
[25] Sabey, B. E., *Journal of British Granite and Whinstone Federation*, Vol. 5, No. 2, 1965.
[26] Kummer, H. W., *Rubber Chemistry and Technology*, Vol. 41, 1968, p. 895.
[27] Kummer, H. W. and Meyer, W. E., "Tentative Skid Resistance Request for Main Rural Highways," NCHRP Report 37, National Cooperative Highway Research Project, 1967.
[28] Schallamach, A. and Grosch, K., *Wear*, Vol. 4, 1961, p. 356.
[29] Veith, A. G., *Rubber Chemistry and Technology*, Vol. 46, 1973, pp. 801 and 821.
[30] Lowne, R. W., *Rubber Chemistry and Technology*, Vol. 44, 1971, p. 1159.
[31] Veith, A. G. and Chirico, V. E., Rubber Chemistry and Technology, Vol. 52, 1979, p. 148.
[32] Studebaker, M. L., Rubber Chemistry and Technology, Vol. 41, 1968, p. 373.
[33] Dannenberg, E. M. et al., *Rubber World*, Vol. 131, 1955, p. 131; *Rubber Age*, New York, Vol. 85, 1959, p. 431.
[34] Biard, J. and Svetlik, F., *Rubber Chemistry and Technology*, Vol. 26, 1953, p. 731.
[35] Geesink, H. and Prat, I., *Rubber Chemistry and Technology*, Vol. 31, 1958, p. 166.
[36] Miller, R. F., Marlowe, R., and Ginn, J. L., *Rubber and Plastics Age*, Vol. 42, 1961, p. 968.
[37] Kraghelski, I. and Nepomnysschi, E., *Wear*, Vol. 8, 1965, p. 303.
[38] Schallamach, A., *Journal of IRI*, Vol. 1, 1967, p. 40.

[*39*] Kienle, R. N., et al., *Rubber Chemistry and Technology*, Vol. 44, 1971, p. 996.
[*40*] Snyder, R. H., *Tire Science and Technology*, Vol. 1, 1973, p. 202.
[*41*] Dannis, M. L., *Rubber Chemistry and Technology*, Vol. 47, 1974, p. 1011.
[*42*] Boonstra, B., Heckman, F., and Kabaya, A., *Rubber Age*, Vol. 104, No. 4, 1972, p. 33.
[*43*] Martin, F. and Biddison, P., *Rubber Chemistry and Technology*, Vol. 46, 1973, p. 586.
[*44*] Smith, R. W. and Veith, A. G., *Rubber Chemistry and Technology*, Vol. 55, 1982, p. 469.

Wade K. Shepherd[1]

Diagonal Wear Predicted By a Simple Wear Model

REFERENCE: Shepherd, W. K., **"Diagonal Wear Predicted By a Simple Wear Model,"** *The Tire Pavement Interface, ASTM STP 929*, M. G. Pottinger and T. J. Yager, Eds., American Society for Testing and Materials, Philadelphia, 1986, pp. 159-179.

ABSTRACT: Diagonal wear on tires is a significant problem that can cause noise and vibration, and reduce the useful life of the tire. A wear model is used to show how diagonal wear can develop across the tread under certain conditions of toe and camber on a non-drive axle.

In a simple wear model, tread wear is taken to be proportional to abrasion and sliding length. Triaxial stress measurements made in the laboratory on the tread blocks of rolling tires provide data for the wear prediction model. Under nonzero toe and camber the magnitude of the predicted wear is increased and its pattern becomes diagonal; a higher wear rate is predicted near the leading edge of contact on one side of the tire and near the trailing edge on the opposite side. This prediction agrees with the diagonal wear pattern seen on tires run on the road at similar toe and camber settings.

KEY WORDS: tires, wear, tire contact, tire stress, tread wear, tire testing methodology

Tread wear has long been a concern of the transportation industry [*1–3*]. As radial tires have become dominant in the passenger tire market, irregular types of wear have become more common because of the longer tread life. Also, the increasing popularity of front wheel drive (FWD) cars has caused tire wear problems peculiar to this type of vehicle to become more prevalent [*4–6*]. One problem, seen mainly on the rear axle of FWD cars, is "diagonal wear." It is characterized by a series of flat spots on the tread, running diago-nally from one shoulder to the other (Fig. 1). Diagonal wear is often found on both sides of the affected car with the diagonal pattern running in opposite directions on the left and right sides of the car (Fig. 2).

Data from the field indicate that the alignment of the rear suspension is a major factor in the generation of diagonal wear. Toe and camber settings on

[1]Senior scientist, Michelin Americas Research and Development, P.O. Box 1987, Greenville, SC 29602.

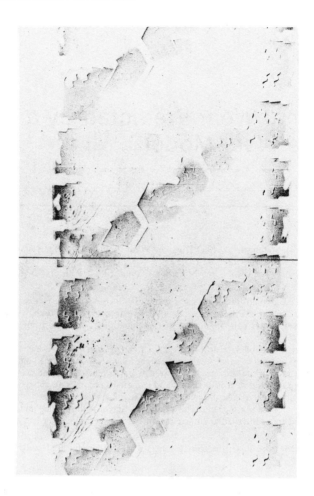

FIG. 1—*Tire track showing diagonal wear.*

vehicles with diagonal wear are often found to be excessive. The orientation of the diagonals also changes depending upon whether the suspension is set to toe-in or toe-out. In addition, there appears to be a correlation between diagonal wear and driving habits. Freeway driving at constant speed tends to worsen the problem.

Changes in the toe and camber settings on a rolling tire change the stress distribution in the contact patch with a corresponding change in the wear pattern [7,8]. The present work was done to characterize the stress distribution under conditions known to induce diagonal wear and to utilize a simple model to predict the resulting changes in the wear pattern.

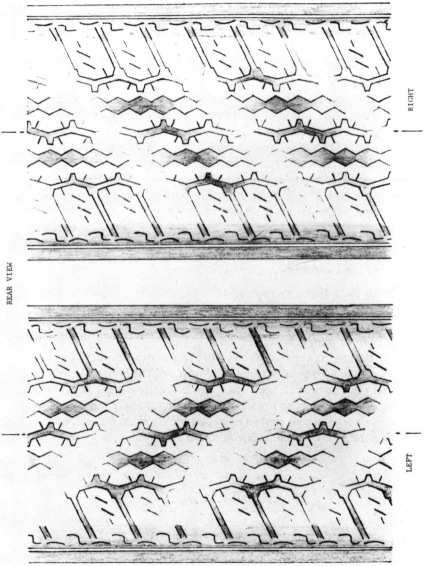

FIG. 2—*Tire diagonal wear.*

Test Program

A test program was instituted to measure the XYZ stress development curves on tire tread blocks under closely controlled conditions. Measurements were made using a flat bed test machine where the tire parameters (slip angle, camber, and load) could be set accurately and the tire position closely controlled. Tire test parameters are listed in Table 1.

Test Coordinate System

The data below are presented using a right-handed rectilinear system with the Y and Z axes reversed in direction from the Society of Automotive Engineers (SAE) convention (Fig. 3). Slip and camber angles of the test coordinate system are related to the toe and camber on a car as shown in Table 2.

The slip angles reported are referenced to the steer angle required to produce zero lateral force on a rolling tire at 0° camber. This reference angle is generally between 0.1° and 0.2° from the geometric zero. Stresses are reported as those exerted upon the tire by the ground.

Tire Stress Measurements

One tread block is chosen from each rib, and the X, Y, and Z stresses are measured as it traverses the contact patch (Fig. 4). A computer controlled measurement system is used that isolates rectangular sections on the tread typically 20 to 40 mm on a side (Fig. 5).

Typical XYZ stress curves are shown in Fig. 6 for the shoulder blocks of a radial tire rolling with zero slip angle and camber. The horizontal axis is the distance traveled by the tire; the vertical axis is the stress seen. The curves are like those usually seen when the stresses on rolling tires are measured [9,10]. The X stress is driving near contact entry and braking near the exit, and the Y stress is normally of opposite sign on the two shoulders.

TABLE 1—*Tire test parameters.*

Dimension	P195/75R14
Pressure	240 kPa
Z-load	500 kg
Cambers	−2,0,+2°
Slip angles	−0.5,0,+0.5°
Rim	5.5JJ14
Rolling speed	0.5 km/h

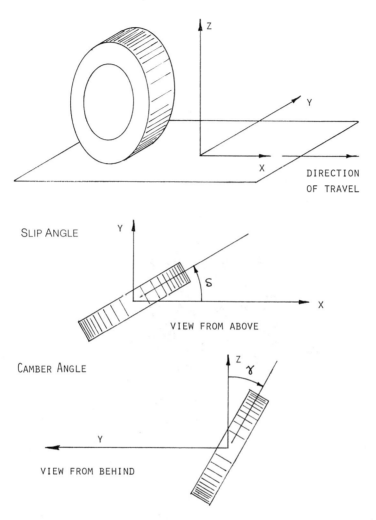

FIG. 3—*Test coordinate system.*

TABLE 2—*Test machine versus car coordinates.*

Test Coordinates	Car Coordinates	
	Left Side	Right Side
Camber +1°	camber+1°	−1°
Slip angle+1°	Toe 1° out	1° in

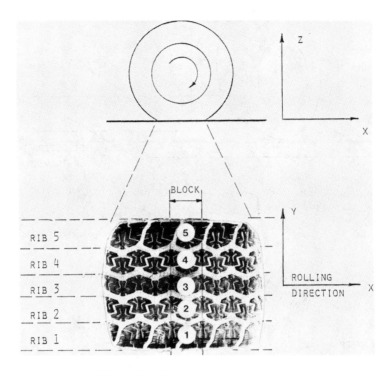

FIG. 4—*Partitioning the tire for measurement.*

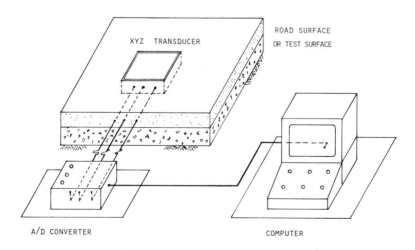

FIG. 5—*XYZ stress measurement.*

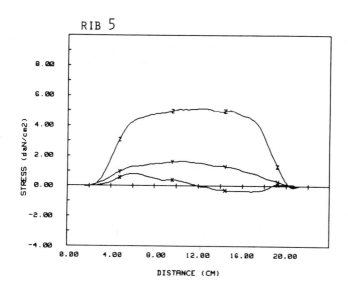

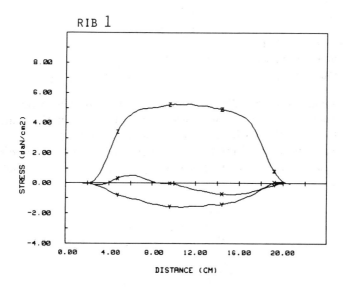

FIG. 6—*Typical* XYZ *stresses.*

Wear Model

Model

Numerous models have been proposed to relate contact stresses to various types of rubber wear [11-15]. In this paper a simple model is used to predict the wear produced by the tire contact stresses. Wear is taken to be proportional to the product of an abrasion term and the length a tread-block slides during contact

$$W = AL \tag{1}$$

where

A = abrasion term and
L = sliding length.

The abrasion term A includes a constant B (which depends on the road surface, tread compound, temperature, and other factors [16-20]) and the normal stress σ_z raised to a power n greater than 1 [21]

$$A = B\,\sigma_z^n \tag{2}$$

where

B = abrasion coefficient,
σ_z = normal stress, and
n = exponent (1 to 2.2).

The sliding length is obtained by assuming that the tread-block is Hookean in shear and slides when the tangential stress is larger than a threshold stress σ_o where $\sigma_o = \mu_o \sigma_z$, with μ_o being a constant coefficient of friction. The sliding produces wear and reduces the tangential stress leading to a relieved stress term $\sigma_r = \sigma_t - \sigma_o$, which is calculated in conjunction with the wear calculation

$$L = \frac{C}{K}(\sigma_t - \sigma_o),\ \sigma_t > \sigma_o$$

$$L = 0,\ \sigma_t \le \sigma_o \tag{3}$$

σ_t = tangential stress (resultant of σ_x, σ_y),
σ_o = sliding threshold stress,
C = contact area of block, and
K = shear stiffness of block.

From Eqs 2 and 3 one obtains

$$W = \frac{BC}{K} (\sigma_t - \sigma_o) \sigma_z^n, \ \sigma_t > \sigma_o$$

$$W = 0, \ \sigma_t \leq \sigma_o$$

(4)

Wear Calculation

The data used in the wear calculation consist of N digitized measurements of σ_x, σ_y, and σ_z, which are made as the tread block passes through contact. Vectors are used in calculating the wear increments because the various shear stresses are not necessarily colinear. The wear is calculated from the measured data as follows.

For $i = 1$ to N, calculate the tangential and threshold stresses ($\sigma_{r1} = 0$)

$$\vec{\sigma}_{ti} = \vec{\sigma}_{xi} + \vec{\sigma}_{yi} - \vec{\sigma}_{ri}$$

$$\vec{\sigma}_{oi} = \mu_o \sigma_{zi} (\vec{\sigma}_{ti}/\sigma_{ti})$$

and calculate the wear increment and relieved stress

$$W_i = (BC/K) (\sigma_{ti} - \sigma_{oi}) \sigma_{zi}^n, \ \sigma_{ti} > \sigma_{oi}$$

$$W_i = 0, \ \sigma_{ti} \leq \sigma_{oi}$$

(5)

$$\vec{\sigma}_{r(i+1)} = \vec{\sigma}_{ri} + \vec{\sigma}_{ti} - \vec{\sigma}_{oi}, \ \sigma_{ti} > \sigma_{oi}$$

$$\vec{\sigma}_{r(i+1)} = \vec{\sigma}_{ri}, \ \vec{\sigma}_{ti} \leq \vec{\sigma}_{oi}$$

The total predicted wear is the sum of the wear increments

$$W = \Sigma \ W_i, \ i = 1, N$$

(6)

Figure 7 shows the predicted wear (shaded area) for a typical shoulder tread block. A profile of the predicted wear across the tire is produced by applying the same treatment to a block from each rib.

Effects of Slip Angle and Camber

Under the conditions of zero camber angle and zero lateral force used to approximate straight ahead rolling, the contact stresses are well-balanced and the footprint is relatively symmetric. If the alignment is changed, the stresses become unbalanced and the footprint is distorted. In the footprints

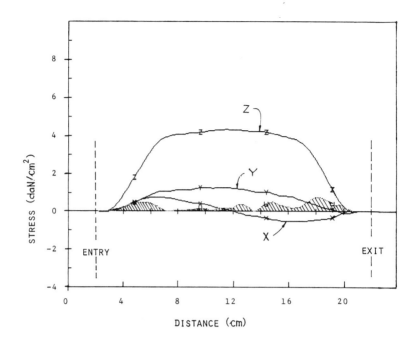

TOTAL WEAR   W = 4.6 (ARBITRARY UNITS)

FIG. 7—*Predicted wear on a rib.*

and stress examples below, large slip angle and camber are chosen to simulate vehicle alignments that have produced diagonal wear.

Rolling Footprints

Rolling footprints are shown for a P195/75R14 tire loaded to 500 kg at 240 kPa for several slip and camber angles (Figs. 8 and 9). The footprint distortions resulting from either camber or slip angle will reinforce or cancel when combined depending on the signs of the angles.

At −0.5° slip angle and 2.0° camber the footprint attains a symmetry similar to that of zero slip and camber. As will be seen below however, slip angle and camber distort the footprint by different mechanisms so the stresses generated by one are not canceled by adjusting the other.

Slip Angle Contribution

Figure 10 shows the contribution to the normal and tangential stresses on the shoulders of a tire from a slip angle of 0.5°. The "contribution" curves are

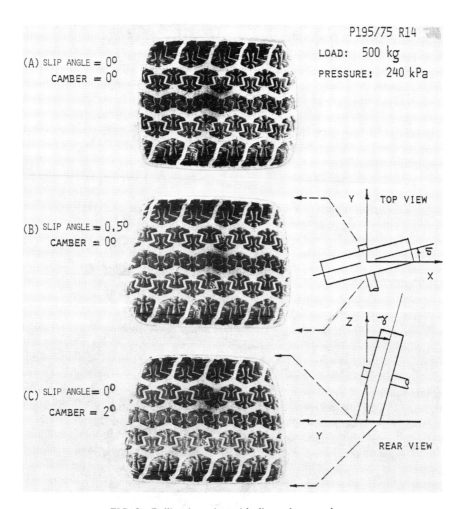

FIG. 8—*Rolling footprints with slip angle or camber.*

derived by subtracting the 0.0° curves from the 0.5° curves. The peaks at the beginning and end of the stress contribution curves are seen when the contact lengths are different for the compared conditions.

In general, the slip angle contribution to XYZ stress level increases linearly from entry to exit of the contact patch as can be seen from the slope of the contribution curves. The changes in the stress patterns on the two ribs are sizeable and all tend to have an unbalancing effect. Some of the changes act to increase the wear rate while others would reduce it, so a tool like the wear model is needed to find which effects dominate.

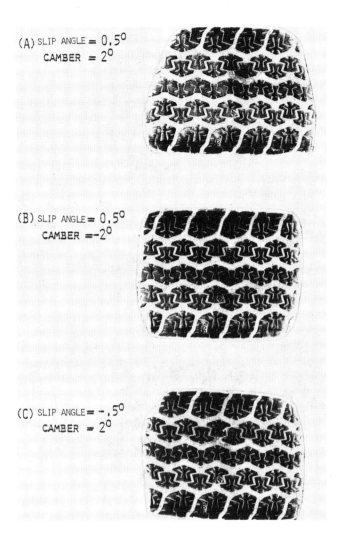

(A) SLIP ANGLE = 0.5°
     CAMBER = 2°

(B) SLIP ANGLE = 0.5°
     CAMBER = -2°

(C) SLIP ANGLE = -.5°
     CAMBER = 2°

FIG. 9—*Rolling footprints with slip angle and camber.*

Camber Contribution

Camber imposed on a rolling tire changes the contact stresses in a different manner from slip angle. The contribution of camber to the contact stress is relatively static as seen from the nearly zero slope of the contribution curves (Fig. 11). The various stress contributions all tend to increase the wear rate on Rib 1 while decreasing it on Rib 5.

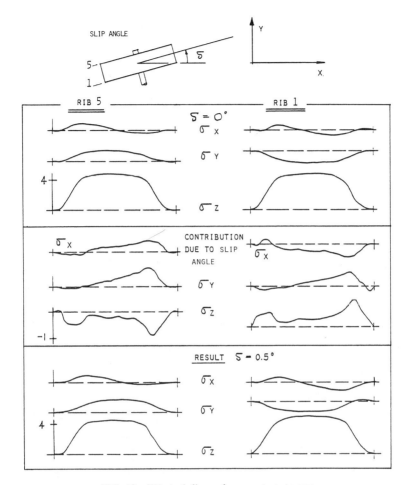

FIG. 10—*Effect of slip angle on contact stresses.*

Predicted Wear

Table 3 illustrates the changes predicted in the wear rate from the contributions to the XYZ stresses of the 0.5° slip angle or 2° camber. The change in slip angle increases the predicted wear on both shoulders while the camber change causes an increase on one shoulder and a decrease on the other.

Besides predicting the total wear rate on the ribs of a tire, the model used here also indicates where in the contact patch the wear is likely to occur. The changes in the stress patterns caused by slip angle and camber causes the wear regions to shift. The wear centroid (the point with half the wear before and after) is marked on the shoulder ribs and connected in Fig. 12 to show the shift. Also, high wear areas are emphasized to illustrate the wear trends.

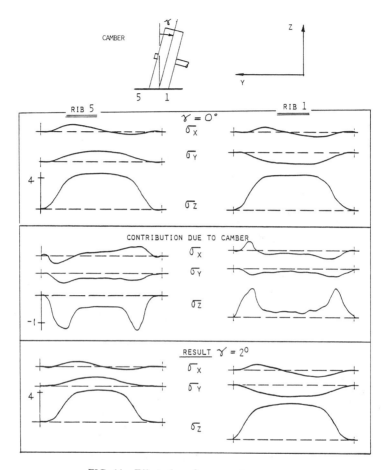

FIG. 11—*Effect of camber on contact stresses.*

TABLE 3—*Effect of alignment change on wear rate for*
XYZ stress components.

Stress Component	Slip Angle = 0.5°		Camber Angle = 2°	
	Rib 1	Rib 5	Rib 1	Rib 5
X	+	−	+	−
Y	−	+	+	−
Z	+	−	+	−
Total	+	+	+	−

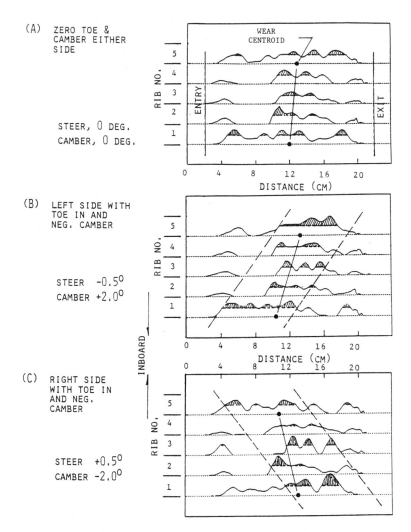

FIG. 12—*Effect of toe and camber on predicted wear.*

Figure 12*a* shows a relatively symmetric wear pattern for a tire run at zero slip angle and camber. Figures 12*b* and 12*c* show the shift in the wear pattern for a tire run under conditions equivalent to toe-in and negative camber on a car. In Fig. 12*b* (left side of car) the high levels of predicted wear are shifted toward the rear of the contact patch on Rib 1 and toward entry on Rib 5. In Fig. 12*c* (right side of car) the shift is in the opposite direction. This means that wear tends to occur nearer the entry into contact on the inside ribs and nearer the exit from contact on the outside ribs.

The track made by the tire on the ground would then be an arrow pointing forward in the direction of travel (Fig. 13), and the pattern on the tires as seen from the rear of the car would be an arrow pointing downward (Fig. 13).

This pattern corresponds to the diagonal wear pattern seen on tires with toe-in and negative camber. However, the predicted wear curves from the contact stresses do not lead directly to the diagonal wear. They predict a tendency for the diagonal wear pattern to develop but do not indicate the places on the tire where the diagonals will form. There are clearly other factors in the initiation and development of diagonal wear.

Nibble Vibration

On a rolling tire the diagonal wear pattern creates a variation in the X and Y forces in the contact patch that tends to induce torsional vibrations about the Z axis (nibble). Tests were undertaken to characterize these vibrations on

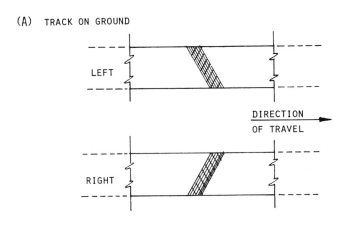

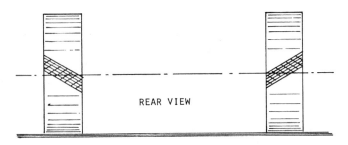

FIG. 13—*Predicted wear pattern: toe in and negative camber.*

cars with new tires and tires with diagonal wear patterns. The tests measured the frequency content of the nibble on the road under highway driving conditions.

Test Apparatus

A matched pair of accelerometers was mounted on a horizontal bar attached to the right rear hub. The output from the accelerometers was fed through a differential amplifier (to isolate the nibble vibration) to a spectrum analyzer to generate nibble spectrum (Fig. 14).

Nibble Results

The results of the nibble tests indicate that resonances in the tire and suspension system can have a significant effect on diagonal wear formation. The amplitude of the nibble spectrum increases with increasing speed for new tires but the frequency content is virtually independent of rolling speed (Figs. 15 and 16). There is a wide resonance band between 300 and 400 Hz.

The same resonance band exists for worn tires but with a higher amplitude. A comparison of the worn tire spectra at 64, 80, and 96 km/h (40, 50, and 60 mph) shows that the amplitude is higher at 64 and 96 km/h than at 80 km/h (Fig. 17). This indicates that the vibration of the worn tire is tuned to certain speeds.

Wear Test

To further test the effect of toe settings on the generation of diagonal wear, two cars were chosen that were as nearly identical as possible except for differ-

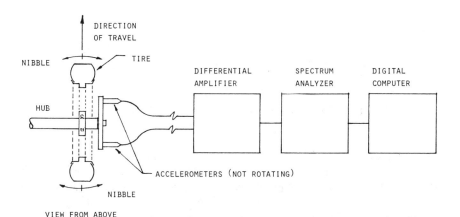

FIG. 14—*Nibble measurement system.*

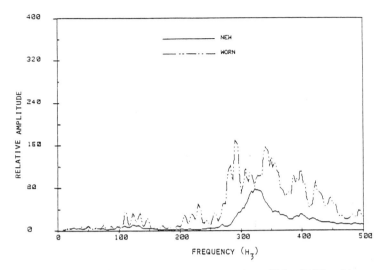

FIG. 15—*Nibble spectrum: new versus worn tire at 80 km/h (50 mph).*

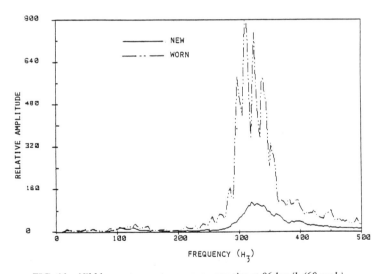

FIG. 16—*Nibble spectrum: new versus worn tire at 96 km/h (60 mph).*

ences in the rear toe settings. New tires were mounted on these cars, and they were run over a suburban and rural course for 35 800 km (22 400 miles) with the wear being monitored regularly. Vehicle test conditions are listed in Table 4.

The rear tires from Vehicle 2, which had the higher toe settings (13.2 versus 5.5 mm), developed diagonal wear patterns and experienced an average 65%

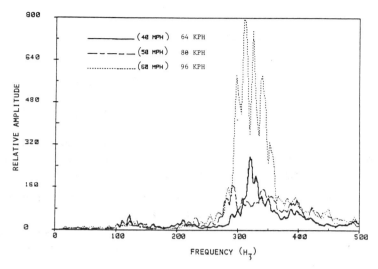

FIG. 17—*Nibble frequency: worn tire at different speeds.*

TABLE 4—*Wear test vehicle parameters and results.*

Parameter	Vehicle 1		Vehicle 2	
Front alignment	Left	Right	Left	Right
caster	1°50′	0°50′	1°10′	1°00′
camber	1°59′	1°59′	2°10′	1°20′
toe	−5.1 mm	−5.1 mm	−5.5 mm	−5.5 mm
Rear alignment				
camber	−0°43′	−0°59′	−0°29′	−0°46′
toe	+5.5 mm	+5.5 mm	+13.2 mm	+13.2 mm
Test results	normal		diagonal	
type wear	145 600 km		52 800 km	
prdicted life	(91 000 miles)		(33 000 miles)	
Loads/wheel	Tires		Inflation Pressure	
rear: 250 kg	Michelin P175/80R13		200 kPa	
front: 400 kg	4.5JJ13 rims			

reduction in estimated life compared to those on Vehicle 1 based on tread weight loss and tread depth at the most worn groove. The higher toe setting is thus seen not only to increase the wear rate but to change the pattern of wear and generate the irregular diagonal wear. A single test, such as this, is not conclusive, but it illustrates dramatically the effect of the suspension settings upon tire wear.

Conclusion

Wheel alignment is seen to be the primary cause of diagonal wear. It develops according to the following scenario:

1. It is necessary to have a strong Y force or an unbalanced X force or both on the tire. Since the diagonals are found to run in opposite directions on the left and right sides of the car, the forces must also have opposite orientations on the two tires.

2. Once diagonal wear is initiated, the pattern produced depends upon car speed and the resonances in the tire/suspension system. Driving at a given speed would thus tend to tune the tire to a particular pattern.

A simple wear model using data from laboratory tire stress measurements has been used to predict the occurrence of diagonal wear under excess toe and camber. This shows once again the value of combining physical measurements and mathematical analysis in helping to increase our understanding of tire performance.

Acknowledgments

The author wishes to express his gratitude to his colleagues at Michelin Americas Research and Development Corporation and at Manufacture Francaise de Pneumatique Michelin, who provided invaluable assistance and advice during the tests and analysis for this paper.

References

[1] Ambelang, J. C., *Tire Science and Technology*, Vol. 1, No. 1, Feb. 1973, pp. 39–46.
[2] Gusakov, I., Bogdan, L., and Schuring, D. J., "A Laboratory Technique for Evaluating Tire Tread Wear," SAE Paper 770872, Society of Automotive Engineers, Detroit, MI, Sept. 1977.
[3] Dudley, E. A., Bauer, R. F., and Reilly, P. M., *Tire Science and Technology*, Vol. 7, Nos. 3-4, July-Dec. 1979, pp. 43–57.
[4] Carrier, H., *Tire Review*, Vol. 79, No. 8, 1979 Monograph, pp. 26–30.
[5] Wikinson, T., *Modern Tire Dealer*, Vol. 63, No. 6, May 1983, pp. 14–17.
[6] Mavrigian, M., *Modern Tire Dealer*, Vol. 64, No. 10, Oct. 1984, p. 36.
[7] Moore, D. F., *Wear*, Vol. 61, 1980, pp. 273–282.
[8] Schallanmach, A. and Grosch, K., in *Mechanics of Pneumatic Tires*, S. K. Clark, Ed., U.S. Department of Transportation-National Highway Traffic Safety Administration (US-DOT-NHTSA), Washington, DC, 1982, Chapter 6, pp. 365–474.
[9] Lippman, S. A. and Oblizajek, K. L., "The Distributions of Stress Between the Tread and the Road for Freely Rolling Tires," SAE Paper 74072, Society of Automotive Engineers, Detroit, MI, Feb. 1974.
[10] Browne, A., Ludema, K., and Clark, S. K., in *Mechanics of Penumatics Tires*, S. K. Clark, Ed., U.S. Department of Transportation-National Highway Traffic Safety Administration (USDOT-NHTSA), Washington, DC, 1982, Chapter 6, pp. 271–303.
[11] Schalamach, A., *Rubber Chemistry and Technology*, Vol. 41, No. 1, 1968 Monograph, pp. 209–244.
[12] Oblizajek, K. L. and Lippmann, S. A., "Predicting the Tread Wear of Non-Driven Front Axle Tires from Laboratory Measurements," SAE Paper 740073, Society of Automotive Engineers, Detroit, MI, Feb. 1974.

[13] Novopol'skii, V. I. and Tarnovskii, V. N., *International Polymer Science and Technology*, Vol. 7, No. 4, 1980, pp. T66–T69.

[14] Gan'kin, Y. A. and Ermilov, V. N., *Vestnik Mashinostroeniya*, Vol. 62, No. 3, 1982, pp. 45–46.

[15] Jain, V. K. and Bahadur, S., *Wear*, Vol. 79, 1982, pp. 241–253.

[16] Satake, K., Sone, T., Hamada, M., and Hayakawa, K., *Rubber Chemistry and Technology*, Vol. 44, No. 5, 1971 Monograph, pp. 1173–1185.

[17] Kienle, R. N., Grosch, K. A., and Scott, C. E., "Material Properties Affecting Traction and Wear of Passenger Tires," SAE Paper 720161, Society of Automotive Engineers, Detroit, MI, Jan. 1972.

[18] Bergman, W. and Crum, W. B., "New Concepts of Tire Wear Measurement and Analysis," SAE Paper 730615, Society of Automotive Engineers, Detroit, MI, May 1973.

[19] Cotten, G. R. and Dannenberg, E. M., *Tire Science and Technology*, Vol. 2, No. 3, Aug. 1974, pp. 211–228.

[20] Rougier, P., Barquins, M., and Courtel, R., *Wear*, Vol. 43, 1977, pp. 141–150.

[21] Schallamach, A. and Grosch, K., in *Mechanics of Pneumatic Tires*, S. K. Clark, Ed., U.S. Department of Transportation–National Highway Traffic Administration (USDOT–NHTSA), Washington, DC, 1982, Chapter 6, pp. 406–407.

Tire Pavement Interaction Generated Vibration and Noise

Marion G. Pottinger, [1] *Kenneth D. Marshall,* [1]
James M. Lawther, [2] *and Donald B. Thrasher* [1]

A Review of Tire/Pavement Interaction Induced Noise and Vibration

REFERENCE: Pottinger, M. G., Marshall, K. D., Lawther, J. M., and Thrasher, D. B., **"A Review of Tire/Pavement Interaction Induced Noise and Vibration,"** *The Tire Pavement Interface, ASTP STP 929*, M. G. Pottinger and T. J. Yager, Eds., American Society for Testing and Materials, Philadelphia, 1986, pp. 183-287.

ABSTRACT: The tire/pavement interface zone is the origin of a major portion of the ride vibration, ride noise, and environmental noise disturbances associated with road vehicles. It is appropriate to view these separate problems as one comprehensive systems problem involving the road, the tire, the vehicle, and human response to noise and vibration stimuli. A flow chart is used to discuss the general systems problem. Main branches of the flow chart are examined based on a thorough review of the pertinent literature. Relevant and previously unpublished information is included in the paper.

KEY WORDS: noise, vibration, tires, pavements, human vibration sensitivity, road roughness, tire roughness, shake, spring rate, wheel hop, vibration modes, tire vibration modes, tire enveloping, noise mechanisms, tire uniformity, automobile suspension responses, chassis beaming, panel modes, vehicle cavity modes, vehicle transmission loss, boom, conicity, harshness, nibbling, plysteer, road roar, thump, waddle, wiggle, human acoustic sensitivity, human acoustic and vibration sensitivity

The tire/pavement interaction is the source of a nearly bewildering array of noises and vibrations. These noises and vibrations can not only disturb the passengers in a vehicle but also those who live and work near heavily traveled highways.

This paper is an overview of tire/pavement interaction generated noises and vibrations that directly produce human annoyance. This paper is intended to serve as a study guide to the literature for those who may be new to

[1]Associate research and development fellow, manager of tire performance, and senior research and development associate, respectively, BFGoodrich Tire Group, 9921 Brecksville Rd., Breckville, OH 44141.

[2]Associate professor (retired), Pennsylvania State University, University Park, PA 16801.

the field, and also for the practicioner who wishes to delve more deeply into an unfamiliar part of the subject.

Tire/pavement interaction generated noise and vibration problems are complex systems problems as portrayed in Fig. 1. There is an intimate involvement of the tire, the pavement, the vehicle, the environment, and subjective human response.

In Fig. 1, the forces generated at the tire/pavement interface are considered to be the source of various problems. These forces arise when tire or pavement irregularities or both perturb the steady state tire deformations causing some of the tire/vehicle kinetic energy to be transduced into vibrational or acoustic energy. These complex forcing functions excite the tire-vehicle system, the pavement, and the atmosphere.

In this paper, we are concerned with those system paths leading directly to the vehicle passengers or through atmospheric noise transmission to individuals in the vicinity of the highway (Paths A and B in Fig. 1). Paths leading to vehicle structural fatigue, highway structural fatigue, and cargo damage are

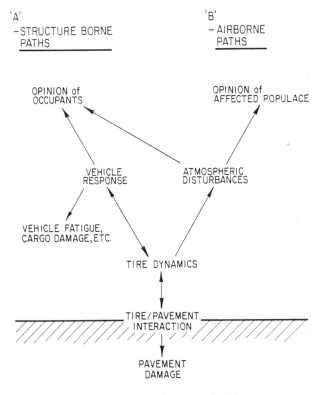

FIG. 1—*The tire/pavement interaction generated noise and vibration flow diagram.*

also shown in Fig. 1, but these are not discussed in this paper. This paper also does not discuss moving load excitation of highway structures or highway deterioration because of vibration, a long-term source of increasing noise and vibration levels.

Figure 2 presents an overview of the portion of the frequency spectrum of concern for in-vehicle problems. In the tire/vehicle industry, descriptive terms are commonly applied to the various portions of the spectrum for road induced behavior, tire induced behavior, tire responses, and vehicle responses. The terms are defined in Appendix A. Also shown are two curves that typify, but do not fully describe, human responses to vibration and noise. A consideration of Figs. 1 and 2 points out the formidable complexity of the problems originating from tire/pavement generated noise and vibration.

In this paper, we first discuss certain aspects of the individual pavement, tire, vehicle, environmental, and human characteristics listed in Table 1. Various combinations of these characteristics will then be tied together to take a brief look at five problems: shake, roughness, harshness, in-car noise, and environmental noise. The author responsible for each section is listed in Appendix B.

Since many of the illustrations used were drawn from older references and are in English units, Table 2 is included for the convenience of those who may be confused by traditional units.

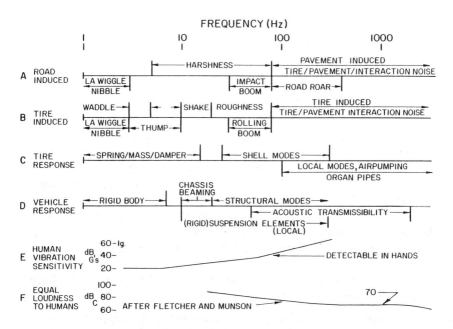

FIG. 2—*The noise/vibration problem.*

TABLE 1—*Systems characteristics for discussion.*

Road roughness
Tire spring rate
Tire modal characteristics
Tire enveloping behavior
Tire uniformity
Automobile suspension responses
Chassis beaming
Higher chassis modes
Vehicle panel and cavity modes
Vehicle transmission loss
Human vibration response
Human acoustic response
Combined human acoustic and vibration response

TABLE 2—*English to metric unit of measurement conversions.*
English unit × multiplier = equivalent SI unit.

English Unit	Conversion	SI Unit
Inch	2.540×10^{-2}	metre
Foot	3.048×10^{-1}	metre
Mile	1.609×10^{0}	kilometre
Feet/second	3.048×10^{-1}	metre/second
Miles/hour	1.609×10^{0}	kilometre/hour
Inches/second^2	2.540×10^{-2}	metre/second^2
Feet/second^2	3.048×10^{-1}	metre/second^2
Pounds force	4.448×10^{0}	newton
Pounds mass	4.536×10^{-1}	kilogram
Pounds/inch^2	6.895×10^{3}	Pascal

Pavement Surface Undulations

In this section, we treat the quantitative characterization of highway pavement surfaces. Surface characterization is of interest to vehicle and tire designers since the pavement surface is the driving function in many ride quality analyses and the generator of mechanisms for traction, rolling resistance, wear, and exterior as well as interior noise. Surface characterization is also of interest to the highway engineer for he must assure that minimum levels of performance are available from the pavement surface with regard to each of the above functions, assuming typical vehicle and tire mixes. We try to bring out the two distinct points of view, beginning with that of the highway engineer.

Highway pavement surface undulations are classified according to wavelength regimes as

(1) topographical undulations—wavelengths > about 50 m,
(2) road roughness—wavelengths between about 10 cm and 100 m,

(3) road macrotexture—wavelengths between about $1/2$ mm and 10 cm, and

(4) road microtexture—wavelengths < about $1/2$ mm.

The above wavelength regimes apply for measurements along a longitudinal profile of the highway lane. Others will define the end points of the wavelength regimes somewhat differently as, clearly, there are no sharp demarcations between regimes.

The temporal frequency of vibrations experienced by a tire traversing a pavement is related to the wavelength by the relationship

$$\text{temporal frequency} = \text{axle speed} \div \text{wavelength} \tag{1}$$

Thus, a tire moving at an axle speed of 100 km/h (27.8 m/s), traversing a sinusoidal undulation with a wavelength of 27.8 m, would experience vertical displacement excitations at a frequency of 1 Hz. Since human body sensitivity to vibrations extends to frequencies at least as low as $1/2$ Hz and since the ear's sensitivity to noise extends upwards beyond 10 kHz, the undulations in Regimes 2 and 3 are the ones significantly affecting these aspects of ride quality. The microtexture regime is important for skid resistance and may be important in adhesion processes governing tangential tread vibration excitation at tread release.

Roadway Roughness Measurement and Characterization—
Viewpoint of Highway Engineers

The difference in design perspective between the highway engineers and the vehicle system engineers has resulted in the use of different parameters for assessing both the roadway roughness and the macrotexture. This section pertains to the highway engineer's viewpoint. He must, for example, be able to tell a paving contractor what kind of surface specifications he has to meet, and after the road is built, must be able to determine if the contractor is in compliance. Later, he must be able to survey the pavement on a regular basis to determine any need for resurfacing.

The paving contractor, the pavement construction foreman, and the designers of pavement surfacing machinery must be able to relate to highway engineering specifications, and the highway engineer must know the limitations of the men and equipment laying down the highway surfaces. For the most part, today's construction contracts include only fairly rudimentary roughness parameter requirements. Federal standard specifications for portland cement concrete (PCC) roadway construction, for example, indicate roughness in terms of maximum deviation of the longitudinal profile from a reference line defined by a 10-ft (3-m) rolling straight edge [1]. The standard requirement for PCC is that no more than 8% of a 2500 yd (2286-m) lot of jointed pavement will indicate deviations in excess of $1/8$ in. (3.2 mm). Plant mix bituminous pavement is required to be tested with a 10-ft (3-m) straight edge both at right angles to and parallel to the roadway centerline. Testing in this instance is done at selected sampling locations, and the maximum allowable deviations anywhere between any two adjacent points of contact of the straight edge and the pavement are $1/4$ in. (6.35 mm). Roadway design grades are constant between adjacent stations (100-ft [30.5-m] spacings) and are faired to maintain continuity at grade changes. (Of course, individual contracts may be specified more completely.)

Straight edge acceptance requirements are coupled with requirements on the type and quality of the paving machines, and with the general qualitative requirement that pavement lines, grades, and cross sections conform "reasonably" with those specified on the plans. Taken all together, and considering the ride softening features of today's automobiles, pavements as newly constructed, offer good ride quality in terms of today's subjective and objective standards. (Admittedly, passenger judgement of what is "good" is conditioned by the range of pavements to which he has been exposed).

After a pavement is ready for vehicles to move on it, more sophisticated testing can be done, and a more detailed surface characterization is possible. (Earlier analysis of the design profile might be helpful, but the paving contractor is given flexibility, and the as-built profile may deviate from the design profile substantially in adhering to line, grade, and section.)

At least a dozen instruments and instrument modifications have been developed to follow a longitudinal profile and to deduce one or more measures of that profile. Traditionally, these instruments have been categorized in two classes: "response type" measuring systems and "absolute" measuring systems (profilometers). The "response type" systems are distinguished by their use of the frame of a vehicle or vehicle trailer as a sprung mass for referencing roadway elevation variations. The profilometer or "absolute" systems incorporate a so-called inertial reference against which the undulations of a road profile may be compared during movement along the profile. The class of "response type" roughness instruments includes, among others, the Bureau of Public Roads (BPR) roughometer [2], the Portland Cement Association (PCA) meter [3], and the Mays-meter [4]. Various versions of these instruments have been developed, both by the individual states and by others in this country and abroad. A review of these instruments, and of profilometers as well, has been made by Wambold et al. [5].

Examples of "absolute type" road roughness measuring instruments are the Carey, Huckins, Leathers, and others (CHLOE) system [6, 7] and various versions of the General Motors Research (GMR) Laboratory profilometer [8, 9]. An appendix to Gillespie's 1980 report on calibration of response type systems also discusses profilometer units [10]. Primary U.S. patent classes/subclasses for the roughness and texture measuring art are 73/105 and 73/146.

Although accelerometers and pendulae are often distinguished as "absolute" instruments, they also invariably measure the motion of a "sprung" mass, just as do "response type" instruments. Spatial and frequency filtering is thus inherent in the so-called "absolute" systems, too. The differences in the two categories are really differences in the natural responses of the two types of systems. The "absolute" systems have flat, or controlled, responses over a temporal frequency range corresponding to or exceeding the range of frequencies produced by traversing the undulation wavelengths relevant to road roughness at measurement speeds. The "response type" instruments have responses with resonance peaks inside the desired range. As is well known, the response behavior of a mechanical system is most sensitive to minor perturbations in its element properties in the vicinity of its resonances. For these and other reasons, there have been difficulties in maintaining calibration of the "response type" instruments [10]. Moreover, the reduced sensitivity of "response type" systems to undulations at wavelengths corresponding to off-resonant frequencies makes accurate reconstruction of the true road profile by inverse filtering difficult (the necessary inverse filters magnify measurement errors in this wavelength regime).

Since one of the uses of measurements made by the "absolute" systems is to predict the output of a typical "response type" system, the response of a typical response type system (a selected 1/4-car suspension response) is now being simulated using a standard software accessory built into advanced profilometer processors [11].

What had earlier been the major advantage of response type systems, the fact that they could be run at freeway speeds, is now being overcome in the newer profilometers. Contact-wheel engagement with the pavement is being replaced with noncontact engagement using white light [5], coherent (laser) light [12], infrared [13], or acoustics [14,15]. The displacement pickup subsystems in all these noncontact systems sense displacements relative to the vehicle frame, then subtract out absolute vehicle frame motion at frequencies within the band of interest. The latter is sensed by a frame-mounted accelerometer whose output is then double integrated to obtain the "absolute" displacement reference. The accelerometer signal is initially conditioned by filters to remove displacement components at topography wavelengths and also to eliminate spurious high-frequency noise.

Swift [16] proposed mounting an accelerometer directly on the contact roller, thus producing "absolute" contact point accelerations, or (with integrations, "absolute" contact velocity or displacement). At first glance, such a system is simpler to implement than the relative displacement systems with inertial references. There is, however, one problem that makes implementation difficult. Very short wavelength impacts at the contact point introduce high-acceleration levels at the accelerometer output, even though the associated displacements are very small. The accelerometer itself must be fairly sensitive in order to bring the long wavelength (low-frequency) content of the undulation signal to levels above instrument noise. The impact-produced acceleration levels at the output of the contact point accelerometer can easily exceed the overload levels at low noise accelerometer preamplifier inputs. Perhaps because of such implementation difficulties, the GMR type profilometer has been given more attention than the Swift concept.

Roadway Roughness Parameters for Pavement Servicability Ratings

A principal measurement parameter of the response type roughness meters is the accumulated magnitude of displacement above a preset "zero elevation" reference (or, in other cases, the accumulated magnitudes of both positive and negative displacement about the preset zero). This measure is usually referred to a fixed length of roadway and is given in inches per mile. Figure 3 shows a graphical representation of an undulating function, together with derived functions that may be called the positive variation function, the negative variation function, and the total variation function [17]. All are functions of the horizontal position along the roadway.

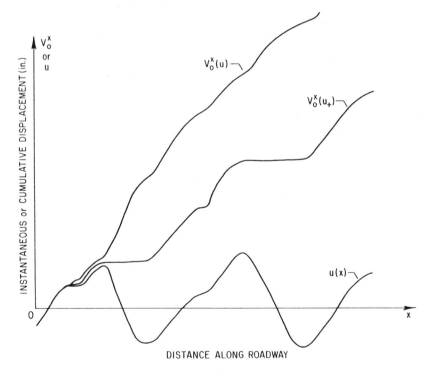

FIG. 3—*Profile relative displacement function* u(x), *its positive variation function* $V_0^x(u_+)$, *and its total variation function* $V_0^x(u)$.

Although not usually discussed in such terms, a ratchet motor, such as that in the BPR roughometer, generates a scroll advance of an amount that at any time is essentially proportional to the value of the positive variation function $V_o^x(u_+)$ of the undulating relative displacement u. (We denote the positive variation function illustrated in Fig. 3 as $V_o^x(u_+)$, signifying the accumulated positive-going profile excursions u_+, over the distance $[o,x]$. Similar notation applies to the negative variation function and the total variation function.) A Mays meter accumulates displacement increment magnitudes and produces a paper advance proportional to the value of the total variation function $V_o^x(u)$. At the end of a run of r miles, the value $(1/r)\, V_o^r(u)$ in inches per mile is noted and reported as the roughness attribute of the test roadway. Gillespie et al. have indicated [10] that for random stationary Gaussian undulations, the inches-per-mile statistic equals their "average rectified velocity (ARV)" in inches per second, divided by vehicle speed in miles per second, therefore

$$\text{ARV} = V_o^r(u) \div T_r$$

where T_r is the time to travel r miles.

The values of $V_o^r(u)$ and ARV give no indication of the distribution of road roughness according to wavelength. This was recognized early on with the BPR unit, and attempts were made to estimate the wavelength distributions by tuning the roughometer suspension system to different frequencies [18].

The PCA roadmeter measures a somewhat different statistic, namely, the number of times per mile of roadway that the relative undulation magnitude crosses or reaches each of a set of equally spaced threshold levels. This yields a distribution of threshold "window" crossing frequencies. In practice, a single parameter, the PCA meter measure, is formed by taking a weighted sum of crossing counts per mile, each term in the sum being weighted by the square of the index of the threshold window (that is, the zero window has zero weighting, the smallest nonzero threshold magnitude has a weighting of one, the next smallest a weighting of four, and so on.) Figure 4 shows an undulating relative displacement function with windows and indices as indicated.

Usually, the PCA measure includes as an overall multiplying factor the square of the incremental displacement magnitude between threshold levels, so that the statistic is given in square inches per mile. When this factor is left out, the measure is in weighted counts per mile. When, in addition, the weighting factors in the summation are all replaced by unity, the system simply counts steps in the undulation magnitude. In this case, the sum of all counts, multiplied by the size of the step, gives the variation function once again. This is borne out by the analysis of Gillespie et al. [10].

Early profilometers, like CHLOE, were essentially traveling straight edges, with deviations in the profile slope relative to the edge or profile displacement from the edge as the basic measure. CHLOE slope outputs were processed to yield a number proportional to profile slope variance over a measured dis-

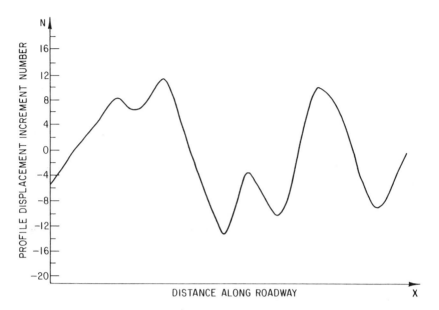

FIG. 4—*Typical section of pavement profile relative displacement function superimposed on displacement increment number scale as in PCA meter windowing.*

tance. This measure is the one that correlated best with subjective ride comfort judgements in the American Association of State Highway Officials (AASHO) tests (now AASHTO, the "T" standing for Transportation) of the early 1960s. The platform lengths of traveling straight edges implemented mechanically have been much shorter than the longest wavelengths of interest in roughness determination. The spatial filter action introduced by the finite length produced undesired peaks and nulls in this wavelength regime. A longer baseline length, using a tracked laser beam, has been developed for airport runway assessment [12]. The system has not yet been given much attention by highway departments at this time.

Some of the earliest roughness profiles were taken by rod and transit techniques [19,20]. The processing of the resulting sampled profile by power spectrum analysis was an early example of sampled data processing via the Digital Fourier Transform. (Modern laser-aided survey techniques should be very useful for defining calibration strips for testing higher speed profilometers.)

The inertial reference profilometers, of which the original GMR unit [9] and its digitally processed follow-on version [11] are well known examples, have a baseline length limited only by the length of run that can be made in a time equal to the time constants of the integrators that convert the accelerometer outputs to displacements. This length is much longer than the longest wavelengths of interest in the roughness measurement. High-pass filtering is actually introduced (in the temporal frequency domain) to prevent topography undulations from overloading the instrument. Because the filtering is done in the temporal frequency domain and not the spatial frequency domain, the filter must be adjusted for each new profile scanning speed. The latest instruments simply require a speed input selection. The filtering is automatically switched in, accordingly.

With the availability of rapid scan profilometry, enhanced by noncontact relative displacement sensors, there is now no reason why any measure of the roadway profile cannot be implemented either in real time (for instruments including on-board digital computation capabilities) or off-line, on the recorded profile data. Such recordings are typically made for both wheel tracks simultaneously, and synchronism of the data taking for the two tracks is state of the art. The road servicability indices are readily generated by (1) processing the profile data with, say, the response of a quarter car or half car model and (2) supplying the model output as input to the computation of the requisite index algorithm. This much is already being done. From the highway engineering point of view, the remaining work is in improving the noncontact sensors and in developing profile processing algorithms that will offer control of the resurfacing processes. Algorithms are already in existence for estimating the material needs in bringing a rough profile into compliance with preset smoothness requirements [11].

Roadway Roughness Measurement and Characterization: Viewpoint of Vehicle Suspension Designers

From the viewpoint of the vehicle suspension system designer and others involved with assuring ride comfort and low-acceleration transport of material, something more is needed in roadway roughness characterization. For an earlier review of road roughness, see Quinn [21]. Finite-element analysis techniques for automobile frame and passenger compartment vibration, and for low-frequency panel vibrational excitation of compartment noise, are now being used in the industry [22]. Roadway roughness must be characterized so that the correct forcing functions may be applied to the vibration models. Early characterization, based on the power spectrum analyses of many roughness profiles, was done in terms of a power law approximation to the vertical displacement function. Dodds and Robson [23] suggested an equation for the displacement power spectral density (dimension: square feet per cycle/foot) as

$$\phi(\eta) = \begin{bmatrix} \phi(\eta_o) \left(\dfrac{\eta}{\eta_o}\right)^{-W_1} & \eta \leq \eta_o \\ \dfrac{}{} \\ \phi(\eta_o) \left(\dfrac{\eta}{\eta_o}\right)^{-W_2} & \eta \geq \eta_o \end{bmatrix} \qquad \eta = \text{spatial frequency} \qquad (3)$$

where $\phi(\eta_o)$ is a constant dependent on the roadway, to be determined from a profile spectral density plot, η_o is the spatial frequency at which the typical break in the slope of the density function occurs, and W_1 and W_2 are the typically nonnegative slope-determining exponents of the spectrum in the two defined ranges. Dodds and Robson estimated the spatial break frequency to be around 1/20 cycle/ft (0.15 cycles/m) for the roadways they examined, with $\phi(\eta_o)$, W_1 and W_2 dependent on the quality of the road. These authors give a table with ranges of the three parameters for different qualities of road.

A difficulty with the straight power-law characterization of the roughness spectrum is that for typical values of W_1, the integral of the power spectral density (that is, the mean square displacement), increases without bound as the lower integration limit approaches zero. This is a problem with roughness analyses involving computation of the total rms displacement. Gillespie has suggested an alternative representation of the power spectral density, which yields a total rms measure less sensitive to the lower spatial frequency cutoff. His suggestion is

$$\phi(\eta) = \frac{G}{4\pi^2\eta^2}[1 + \eta_o^2/\eta^2], \text{ ft}^2/\text{cycle/ft} \qquad (4)$$

for the elevation spectral density, or

$$\phi_{z1}(\eta) = G\left[1 + \frac{(\eta_o)^2}{\eta}\right], \left(\frac{\text{ft}^2}{\text{ft}}\right) \text{cycles/ft} \qquad (5)$$

for the slope spectral density, where G is a road constant.

The Gillespie representations do not agree with the Dodds and Robson representation at very high or very low spatial frequencies, though in the operating range and with values of the parameters properly chosen, agreement can be satisfactory. This is to be expected since both developments derive from roughness data in the report of LaBarre et al. [24].

Twin profilometers, recording profiles in both left and right tire tracks, have been the practice in recent years, and new noncontact techniques are in final development stages to obtain in a synchronous manner, a set of longitudinal profiles spaced across the vehicle width [5]. Dodds and Robson have suggested [23] that for some pavements, the synchronously recorded profiles may not be necessary, since an assumption of isotropy may be used. In this case, data from a single profile permit computation of the roll, pitch, and elevation spectral densities of any reference vector in the frame of the vehicle. When isotropy cannot be assumed, synchronized measurements of both wheel paths must be made. More generally, the roadway may be regarded as an undulating elevation function in two dimensions. The statistics of such fields have been treated by Longuet-Higgins in the 1950s [25] following on Rice's analysis of one-dimensional waveforms [26]. Concepts, such as waveform straight-crestedness, and the two-dimensional wave vector of a surface are discussed in this treatment, as are spatial correlations and spatial frequency cross spectra. Use of cross spectra among tire contact points is discussed by Robson [27] and, earlier, in the extensive study of off-road dynamics by VanDeusen [28]. Helms has noted that the near symmetry of the passenger car about a central roll axis leads to useful transformations of the left and right roughness profile functions into orthogonal (roll and elevation) coordinates. Symmetry then permits the roll and elevation axis responses to be studied separately [29].

Macrotexture Measurement and Characterization

Measurement of pavement macrotexture and macrotexture characterization arose initially out of skid resistance considerations, and were concerned with accessing the paths for water to "squeegee" out from under the tire tread rubber during engagement with wet roads. Most closely related to this effect was a measurement called the outflow meter measurement [30], with its characterizing parameter, an hydraulic coefficient indicative of the time required for a given volume of water under a given initial head to escape beneath an annular surface seal of given diameter and annulus proportion. The coarser the macrotexture, the quicker the water escaped.

A similar measure, called the Sand Patch test, was a determination of the mean depth of pavement texture that could be filled to pavement "surface" level with a given volume of sand (ASTM Test Method for Measuring Surface Macrotexture Depth Using a Sand Volumetric Technique [E 965] [31]). The greater the depth, the coarser the texture. A comparable test is done with putty. A more detailed appraisal of the macrotexture of the pavement surface is obtained through stereo-optics. Schonfeld has developed a quasi-subjective four-parameter scheme for rating macrotextures from stereo photograms [32]. (His observables include stone height, width, angularity, and surface density. He also measures two microtexture parameters, and he rates the wet skid resistance of pavement in terms of all six.) More generally, high resolution photogrammetry is a technique for recording the two-dimensional surface, then obtaining whatever subsequent texture measures one requires.

As is the case with road roughness, the focus of macrotexture measures has shifted to the profile, and to those parameters characterizing the pavement that are derivable from the profile. Again, early emphasis has been on wet skid resistance, and attempts have been made to relate such macrotexture profile parameters as rms height, mean slope magnitude, and meander length per foot of scan to the skid resistance of the pavement (or the percent rate of change of skid resistance with test speed.) Profile spectral analysis has, more recently, become a common basis for characterization. Typical macrotexture spectra for different pavement types are shown in Fig. 5 [33]. The sharp drop off in spectral density with wave number, already perceived with pavement roughness spectra, is seen to characterize the high end of the ma-

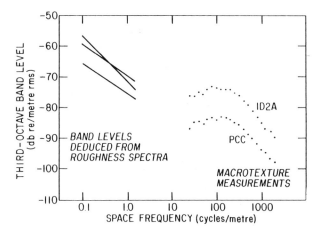

FIG. 5— *¹/₃-octave spectra of pavement profiles in the roughness and macrotexture regimes.*

crotexture regime as well. The juncture of the roughness spectrum with the low wave number region of the macrotexture region is not well characterized. Macrotexture profilometers in general have too short a baseline for measuring spectra at wavelengths of the order of 1 ft (30 mm) while the roughness profilometer analyses tend to disregard wavelengths as short as this. The envelopment filtering of some roughness profilometers precludes making measurements at such short wavelengths, while the sampling intervals of those computing from profile samples are too long (typically 6 in. [15 mm] or so). Generally, in fact, this wavelength limitation is deliberately imposed for roughness determinations. Unfortunately, the borderline between roughness and macrotexture wavelengths is where some of the dominant tire/pavement noise excitation sources are found.

Tire Effects

The tire is a major component in the system vibration and noise problem for highway vehicles. It serves as an isolator and an excitation source all at the same time. We have chosen to examine tire isolation properties in terms of spring rates, modal properties, and enveloping. The examination of tire excitation properties is in terms of uniformity effects. Tread pattern excitation effects are not discussed.

Tire Spring Rate Behavior

Tire spring rates are an important determinant of ride comfort and vehicle dynamic behavior at low frequencies. Vertical (or radial) spring rate is the most important and most studied of the tire spring rate characteristics. Because of limitations in space, we will confine our discussion to only vertical spring rate and keep the discussion of measurement methods short. For an extended discussion of measurement methods and data on vertical, lateral, and circumferential spring rates, see Pottinger et al. [34].

Vertical spring rates may be measured either statically or oscillating [34–36]. Static measurements [34] typically are derived from an analysis of load/ deflection data taken in a manner analogous to a simple stiffness test for a mechanical spring. Oscillating data [34–36] are obtained by exciting a simple vibrating system at low frequency and calculating the effective spring rate on the basis of the frequency for the first natural resonance. The equivalent viscous damping of the tire can be obtained from the frequencies of the half power points and the natural frequency of the system [35], from the system amplitude magnification, or from the free decay log decrement [37].

All that has been said to this point is exactly analogous to standard mechanical measurements made for any spring or damping element or both. The important difference between tires and other mechanical spring elements is that tires roll. The consequence of this is that tire spring rate and damping depends strongly on the change from the nonrolling to the rolling state. Figure 6, drawn from Rasmussen and Cortese [35], is an excellent illustration of this fact. The effective tire spring rate is sharply different for rolling and nonrolling tires. Vertical spring rate at low frequencies is not, however, very frequency dependent. Thus, the use of a constant is a reasonable first approximation. Phillips showed this through mobility measurements [38] of which Fig. 7 is an example. The damping characteristics of tires are also greatly altered by rolling (Fig. 8). Chiesa and Tangorra have noted this effect [36].

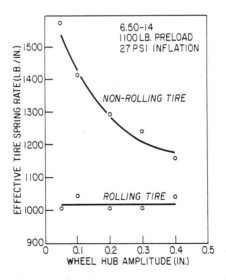

FIG. 6—*Spring rate for an oscillating tire* [35].

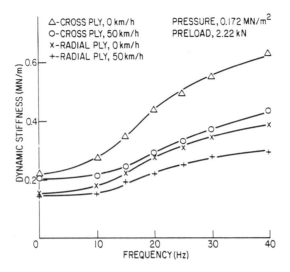

FIG. 7—*Tire dynamic stiffness* [38].

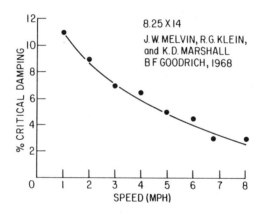

FIG. 8—*Tire damping.*

The effect develops fully as the tire speed increases from 0 to 16 km/h with most of the effect occurring in the first 8 km/h.

Pottinger et al. [34] have demonstrated support for the hypothesis that part of the change from nonrolling to rolling may be due to increased freedom in the footprint boundary condition for a rolling tire. This is equivalent to a reduction in the coefficient of friction in the footprint of the nonrolling tire.

Chiesa and Tangorra [36] also observed that a load/deflection curve for a rolling tire leads to "substantially coinciding results" for spring rate with those obtained from a rolling bouncing tire, "except at very slow speeds." This approximate equivalence offers a simplification in the testing necessary to obtain data indicative of tire behavior at normal road operating speeds. These data will be called the "tire rolling spring rate" and are used in the rest of this section.

Keeping the information just discussed in mind, we will briefly discuss the effects of load, speed, inflation pressure, aspect ratio, rim width, and belt material on radial tire rolling spring rates. See Figs. 9 through 14, which are from Pottinger [39].

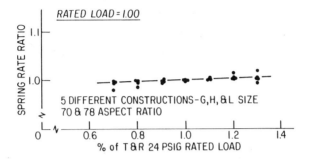

FIG. 9—*Effect of load on 50-mph (80-km/h) vertical rolling spring rate for steel-belted radials* [39].

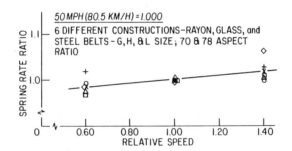

FIG. 10—*Effect of speed on vertical rolling spring rate of radial tires* [39].

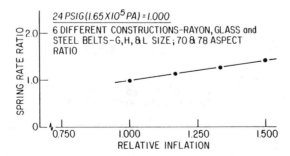

FIG. 11—*Effect of inflation pressure on radial tire vertical rolling spring rate at 50 mph (80-km/h)* [39].

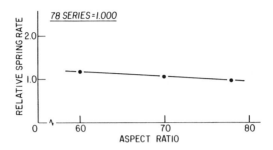

FIG. 12—*Effect of aspect ratio on radial tire spring rate for tires on design rim at 24 psig (166 kPa)* [39].

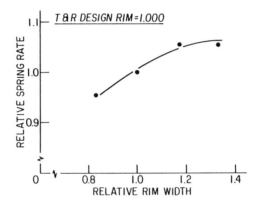

FIG. 13—*Effect of rim width on the vertical rolling spring rate of GR70-15 radial tires* [39].

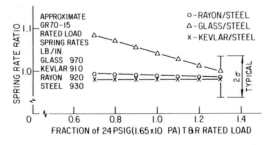

FIG. 14—*Effect of belt material on radial tire vertical rolling spring rate at 50 mph (80 km/h)* [39].

Figure 9 shows that radial tire rolling spring rate is almost constant over a broad range of loads. This is true regardless of tire size and aspect ratio.

In the normal operating speed range, rolling spring rate shows a slight linear increase with speed (Fig. 10). However, remember that the vertical spring rate decreases abruptly as you pass from the nonrolling through the low-speed rolling state, speeds less than 16 km/h [36].

Rolling spring rate increases linearly with inflation pressure (Fig. 11). This has been well known for many years [35,36]. Rolling spring rate exhibits a slight linear increase as aspect ratio decreases (Fig. 12). Because of changes in the shell shape of the tire, spring rate increases nonlinearly with increases in rim width (Fig. 13). Belt materials have little influence on radial tire spring rate for conventional (nonracing) tires (Fig. 14). Tire vertical damping is small except at a very low speed (Fig. 8). This was also found by Pottinger et al. [34] and Chiesa and Tangorra [36].

Modal Behavior

As the excitation frequency increases, the tire is no longer adequately represented as a collection of springs and dashpots. Its dynamic response approaches that of a composite toroidal shell structure. The shell modes, particularly those related to vertical and longitudinal oscillations of the wheel hub, become dominant factors in vibration performance. The shell modes related to vertical and longitudinal wheel hub oscillations are the radial and torsional modes. The radial and torsional modes can be studied for understanding purposes based on simplified ring or thin shell on an elastic foundation models similar to those proposed by Tielking [40], Bohm [41], and Fiala and Willumeit [42]. In these references the radial modes are emphasized.

For a radial tire with a fixed hub, but a free periphery, the radial modes are characteristically like those shown by Bohm [41] (Fig. 15). The frequencies

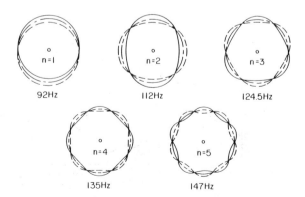

FIG. 15—*Radial natural frequencies and mode shapes for a 155R15 at 147-kPa inflation pressure* [41].

vary with tire size, construction, and inflation pressure, but the mode shapes are constant.

The addition of the tire footprint constraint or boundary condition alters the mode shapes as illustrated in Chiesa et al. [43]. Potts et al. [44] show mode shapes for both the free tread band and footprint contact cases for the same tire. However, it is important not to be confused by the language in Potts et al. [44]. The standing tire resonances are referred to as the anti-resonance condition of the free tread band tire. And, as might be expected, the maximum transmissibility of the tire occurs at the standing resonance conditions. This is nicely illustrated in Fig. 16, which comes from Potts and Csora [45]. The high stiffnesses in Fig. 16 are indicative of small amplitude excitation of a standing tire (Fig. 6). Soedel and Prasad [46] have obtained a theoretical relationship that allows the engineer to predict the standing tire modes from the free periphery modes.

Phillips [38] states that the first radial natural frequency for the standing tire is dominant in noise transmission from the road. Chiesa et al. [43] also show that this is true (Fig. 17).

Torsional resonances are important to vibration transmissibility according to Barson and Dodd [47] and to noise transmissibility below 60 Hz [38]. However, little appears in the literature on the torsional modes except for footprint to wheel hub transmissibility data by Barson et al. [48]. Figure 18 is an example of longitudinal transmissibility [48]. Tielking's model [40] illustrates the fact that the radial and torsional vibrations are coupled. Basically, if you have one, you have both.

Mobility measurements by Mills and Dunn [49] (Fig. 19) show clearly that the static tire is stiffer than the rolling tire, as discussed in the section on tire spring rate. The first vertical resonant frequency drops as the tire's rotational speed increases but only by a modest amount, as also noted by Barson and Dodd [47]. This softening was predicted by Tielking [40].

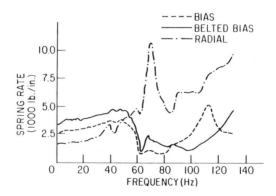

FIG. 16—*Transmissibility (spring rate) variations over frequency of input for bias, belted bias, and radial tires, all in H78-15 size* [45].

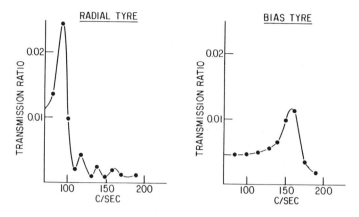

FIG. 17—*High-frequency portions of the transmission curves, after being cleared of the lower frequency components arising from the tire's vibration as a rigid body and spring system* [43].

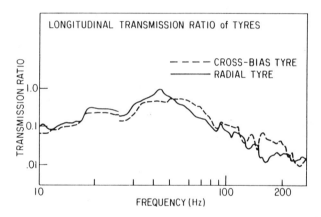

FIG. 18—*Comparison of longitudinal transmission ratios of cross-bias and radial-type tires* [48].

Damping also drops as the tire rotational speed increases. This supports the data in Fig. 8. In Fig. 19, the decrease in damping shows up as an increase in the amplitude of the 13- to 15-Hz vibration of the measuring head (mounted on the tire spring). Although the damping is small for the rotating tire, it is very important because it is all the damping present in the suspension system beyond 30 Hz (Fig. 20) [48]. This damping is strongly influenced by generic tire type and, thus, sidewall characteristics [43,48].

Before leaving the work of Mills and Dunn, it is worth noting the predominance of the first vertical mode in Fig. 19.

Mills and Dunn [49] presented data (Fig. 21) that clearly show that tire design within a generic tire type can influence tire vibration response. The

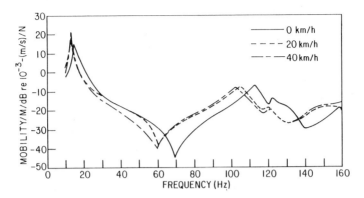

FIG. 19—*The frequency variation of driving point mobility with rolling speed for a 165R13 at 2240-N load and 172 kPa* [49].

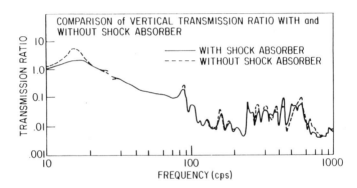

FIG. 20—*Effect of shock absorber on vertical tire transmission ratio* [48].

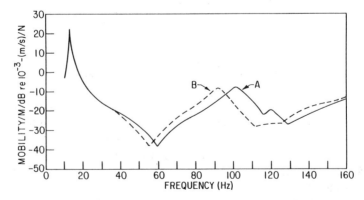

FIG. 21—*The frequency variation of driving point mobility at 50 km/h for two 165R13 radials at 2240-N load and 172 kPa* [49].

literature provides some information as to tire construction variables that are important to changing radial tire properties. Reduction of carcass angle below 90° has a strong effect on resonant frequencies (Fig. 22). Potts and Csora [45] found the same type of effects in their transmissibility data. In the late 1960s, the Metzler Tire Co. tried to popularize a high carcass angle (near to pure radial) tire to take advantage of the strong influence of carcass angle.

Belts do not strongly influence radial tire modal natural frequencies. This can be seen by examining the data in Pottinger [39] or the transmissibility data of Potts and Csora [45] (Fig. 23), which involves an eightfold change in belt bending stiffness and a significant change in crown mass. There is a slight change in transmissibility amplitude.

Enveloping

"The most obvious task of the tire is to damp and reduce the effects of road irregularities on the vehicle and on the passengers, giving a comfortable ride, which, on a normal road, the suspension alone is unable to guarantee" [50].

Enveloping deals specifically with the tire's ability to damp and reduce the effects of road irregularities. We will discuss these in terms of the forces at a fixed spindle, first qualitatively and then quantitatively, neglecting tire resonance effects. After this discussion, the effects of tire resonances will be added to give a more or less complete picture of the character of spindle forces caused by the tire passing over a road surface irregularity.

At long road undulation wavelengths, 1 m or more, the tire can be treated as a vertical spring and dashpot excited by a point follower. In this case, the fundamental absorber characteristics of the tire come into play.

As road undulation wavelengths are reduced so as to approach, and finally become less than the length of the tire contact patch, local tire shell stiffnesses and deformations become fundamental to the forces generated by the tire.

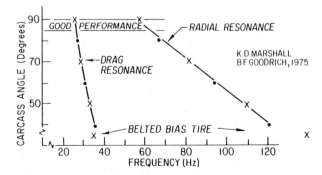

FIG. 22—*First mode natural frequencies as a function of carcass angle for rolling GR78-15 tires. Drag is fore-aft. Radial is vertical.*

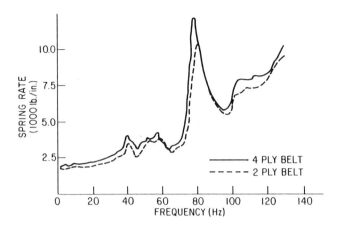

FIG. 23— *Transmissibility (spring rate) variation over frequency of input for 4-ply and 2-ply fabric-belted radials* [45].

The tire partially engulfs short wavelength road surface irregularities in a process called enveloping. The spindle force history is no longer simply related to the profile of road irregularities.

This section concentrates on the enveloping forces that are the forces arising from road seams, tar strips, stepoffs between pavement slabs, and so forth.

As Julien and Paulsen [51] showed in 1952, a slowly rolling tire encountering a short bump, or cleat, wider than its tread produces spindle forces with the character shown in Fig. 24. The precise form of the curve obtained is dependent on the size and shape of the bump, the tire size, the tire deflection, the tire structure, and the tire inflation pressure. Julien and Paulsen observed the following:

1. If all other variables are fixed, the magnitude of the vertical force is linearly dependent on inflation pressure.

2. High tire deflections produce lower vertical forces and slightly higher longitudinal forces.

3. The tire's response to an upward road elevation change is not exactly the same as its response to a downward change.

4. Tire response amplitude is not linearly dependent on obstacle size (the envelopment process is not linear).

In spite of its importance, the subject then rested at this state of knowledge until the mid 1960s. At that point in time, Lippmann and Nanny [52] published a mechanistic look at the process, and presented some interesting ideas:

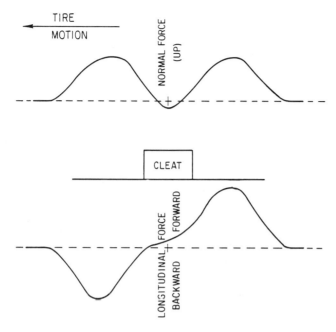

FIG. 24—*Typical character of forces from enveloping a small cleat at low speed* [51].

1. A valid way to look at enveloping forces is as response spectra (Fig. 25 [52]), which always contains two maxima for each force direction.

2. All types of tires probably have qualitatively similar enveloping characteristics. This is based on the data in both this paper and an earlier paper by Lippmann et al. [53].

3. A linearized first approximation to the process using tire characterizing functions can give the ability to approximately compute spindle forces for any road surface irregularity.

Barone [54] investigated dynamic enveloping, the enveloping process at road speeds. His work (Fig. 26) indicates that Lippmann and Nanny's third contention is not valid for obstacles with a length equal to or shorter than that of the tire footprint. Barone's normalized *PD* curves come from data like that in Fig. 27 [39]. Very important is the fact that in all cases, the principal vibrational frequency observed was independent of the particular size or form of the object enveloped. The tire behaves as a linear constant parameter system in having a constant ring down frequency independent of excitation amplitude. Furthermore, almost all the response is first mode response for the particular sense of vibration occurring, normal or longitudinal.

Building on the observations in the literature, Bandel and Monguzzi [50] proposed a tire envelopment model for generating an effective black-box

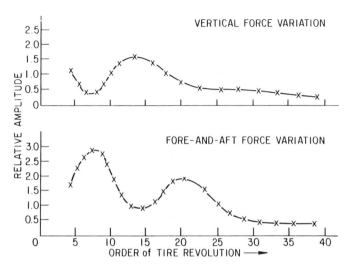

FIG. 25—*Harmonic analysis of force responses to cleat (tire = 8.15-15/2; cleat = 0.50 in. (1.27 cm) wide, 0.25 in. (0.64 cm) high; inflation = 30 psi (207 kPa); deflection = 1.00 in. (2.54 cm); speed = 2.5 mph (4 km/h))* [52].

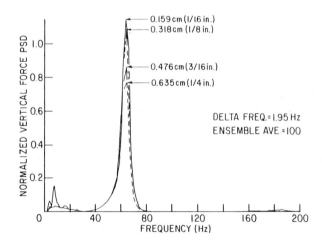

FIG. 26—*Vertical spindle force response (cleat width 5.08 cm = 2.0 in)* [54].

model of fixed axle spindle forces. Their model treats the tire as an equivalent second order system in both the vertical and longitudinal directions, the system being excited by the basic low-speed (nonresonant) force input. The resultant spindle forces agree well with experimental values (Figs. 28 and 29). It is still necessary, however, to obtain the basic form of the low-speed enveloping force function and the tire modal resonant frequencies experimentally.

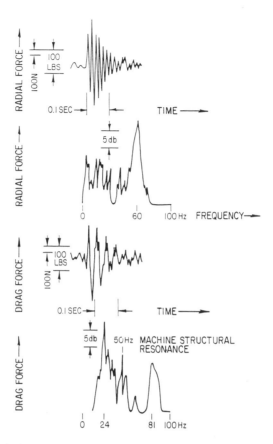

FIG. 27—*Typical maximum axle force responses for tire on high stiffness test system over a ¹/₈-in. (0.32 cm) high × 1 in. (2.54 cm) long full width cleat* [39].

However, the model does give an accurate representation and is simple enough to use as part of a general vehicle model. As finite-element modeling develops, it should be possible to compute the input data required to develop the parameters in the Bandel and Monguzzi model. This would be done by using finite-element analysis. The analysis would be used to compute the natural frequencies and stiffnesses required by adaptive footprint models [55–57]. The adaptive footprint models would yield the approximate low-speed spindle forces.

Designing the tire to reduce the basic enveloping forces can only be partially effective since about 75% of the effect is pneumatic [51,52]. The only helpful design measure substantiated in the literature, outside of using a high aspect ratio [51], is to keep the tread band out-of-plane bending stiffness as low as possible [39,58].

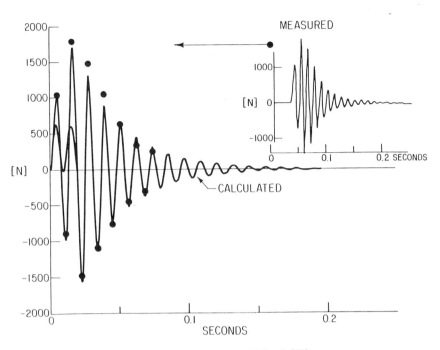

FIG. 28—*Vertical force at 52 km/h* [50].

Uniformity

Operating tires are self-excited as well as being excited by road irregularities. Tire self-excitation arises from nonuniformities in the tire shell. These nonuniformities in the tire shell may come from either manufacturing imprecision or from tire tread variations arising in the design of the tread pattern. This discussion will deal with general uniformity characteristics and some of the particular manufacturing imprecisions responsible for nonuniformity excitation. This discussion does not specifically deal with tire tread pattern design effects.

Because of the deformation characteristics of the tire shell and the kinematics of rolling, a free rolling tire can exert three cyclically varying forces and two cyclically varying moments on the vehicle spindle (Fig. 30). Any of these cyclically varying forces and moments can potentially become an important source of ride disturbance to passengers in a vehicle if the vehicle has the appropriate sensitivity characteristics. This will be illustrated later in the paper. However, the majority of uniformity difficulties have arisen because of variations in radial (normal) force or in drag (tractive or longitudinal) force. We will emphasize these forces in this discussion.

As the tire revolves, each of the forces and moments exerted on the spindle by the tire changes through one complete cycle in each tire revolution (the

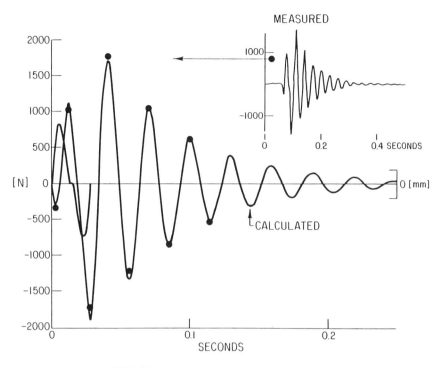

FIG. 29—*Longitudinal force at 35 km/h* [50].

data are periodic). To study these changes, it is necessary to measure quantities that accurately represent the character of the excitations applied to the vehicle spindle. Historically, three effective approaches have been used: measurement of loaded tire runout or its derivatives [59-61], measurement of the forces and moments exerted on a simulated roadway (drum, road-wheel, or dynamometer wheel) [62-65], and measurement of the forces and moments applied to the wheel spindle of a tire running on a simulated roadway [66-70].

The measurement of free radial runout is another method that has been tried, but it is a significantly less effective approach as it ignores everything about the tire except dimensional irregularities [61,64].

Before discussing the merits of the three useful methods for measuring tire uniformity, it is necessary to look briefly at how any of these signals is typically analyzed. Since any uniformity variation is completely periodic, it may be conveniently represented in terms of Fourier series harmonic coefficients [71]. Figure 31 is a representative example of a single uniformity signal and its harmonics, as drawn from Daberkoe [72]. Evidence in the literature suggests that the first ten harmonics of uniformity variation can contribute to passenger discomfort. Figure 2 presents a spectrum of the potential problems, many of which will be discussed later in this paper. With this back-

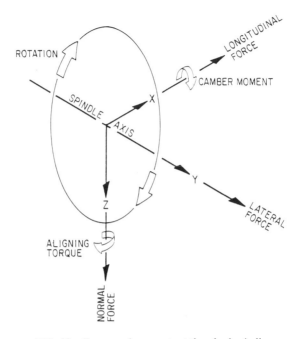

FIG. 30—*Forces and moments at the wheel spindle.*

ground in place, we may now resume our discussion of uniformity measurement methods.

Loaded Radial Runout Devices

Loaded radial runout is simple to measure. A tire loaded by a compliant mechanism is rotated against a drum. The change in axle height gives an effective measure of the tire induced force variations in the radial (or normal) direction. Measurements of the other excitations are not available. Loaded radial runout measurements at high speeds are complex because machine resonance occurs at low frequencies for a loaded radial runout machine [60,61]. This is due to the necessity of making the spindle support quite compliant.

Force Variations at the Roadway (Factory Type Uniformity Machines)

Tire forces and moments exerted on the drum of a uniformity machine by a tire running at a fixed axle deflection are measures of the contact patch forces and moments that excite the tire. These forces and moments are valid indicators of the excitations present at the wheel spindle at low frequencies where the tire vibration modes are not excited. The contact force and moment resultants are sensed by load cells applied to the axle of the small, light alloy drum

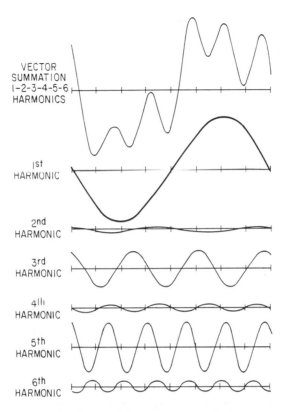

FIG. 31—*Force variation, one tire revolution* [72].

against which the tire rotates (usually at a rate of 1 rps). Measurements taken on this type of machine are generally effective for vehicle problems that occur below 15 Hz, the type of problem that is usually caused by first harmonic variations or residual steady state lateral forces and aligning torques. The uniformity machines presently used in tire manufacturing plants follow this design because of its relative simplicity and ruggedness, and because tire mounting and dismounting can be automated. Most existing machines of this type measure only normal and lateral forces. At one time, the machines in use at Dunlop [63] also measured aligning torque.

Force Variations at the Tire Axle (Research or High-Speed Uniformity Machines, HISUM)

The tire forces and moments exerted at the spindle on which the tire rotates are measures of the forces and moments that excite the vehicle. The spindle forces are sensed by load cells applied to the tire rotation spindle. These are valid indicators of the excitations applied to the vehicle spindle for any frequency where uncompensated machine resonances do not distort the results. Through careful design, machine resonances can usually be pushed to high enough frequencies to allow a valid determination of the approximate force and moment variations over the entire range of vehicle problem frequencies [66,68-70]. Uniformity machines of this type are not used in manufacturing plants because they are complex and expensive, and because tire mounting is not easily automated. Machines of this type are laboratory devices specifically aimed at understanding tire uniformity behavior involving higher harmonics, and the interactions between tire and vehicle resonances. They are the only machines capable of dealing with these systems problems [66]. These machines usually measure all the spindle forces and moments at various speeds from typically 8 to 120 km/h.

Uniformity Characteristics

The characteristics of tire uniformity will now be discussed based on measurements from force measuring uniformity machines (types listed above). As previously mentioned, normal and longitudinal force variation will be emphasized because of their importance.

The signal shown schematically in Fig. 31 would be typical of the character of a radial force variation curve obtained at low speed, 1 rps (the first harmonic frequency is 1 Hz). In this signal, the first harmonic dominates. As tire speed increases, the frequency associated with each harmonic is given by Eq 6

harmonic frequency (Hz) = harmonic number $\times$ tire rotation rate (rps) (6)

When the frequency of a radial harmonic becomes an appreciable fraction of the first natural frequency of the tire, significant force amplification occurs at the spindle. Figure 32 is an example of this process for a radial fifth harmonic. Acceleration data for the front spindle of a car, force data from a tire spindle measuring machine (HISUM), and a drum measuring machine are compared. As mentioned earlier, the drum measuring machine (factory type machine) is not effective for analyzing this type of problem. It really does not show the response amplification as the fifth harmonic passes through tire resonance. The HISUM shows the correct behavior. It is worth noting two other things: the tire natural frequency depends on the diameter of the test surface, and the vehicle vibration response is clearly a systems problem. The peak in the car response at 17 to 18 mph (27 to 28 km/h) is the first vertical resonance of the suspension system (wheel hop).

The successive excitation of tire natural modes by lower and lower harmonics as the speed rises is occurring for all the tire modes, not just radial direction modes. This gives rise to strong excitations of particular modes in narrow frequency bands. Marshall et al. [69] and Marshall and St. John [68] give a clear discussion of the process and consequences.

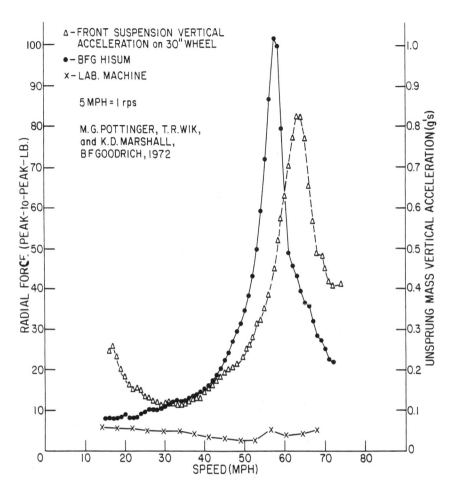

FIG. 32—*5th harmonic uniformity generated normal forces and suspension vertical accelerations.*

Besides the process of resonant interactions, tire uniformity force levels may change because the effects of some manufacturing irregularities are themselves speed sensitive. That is, the excitation itself, for some mechanisms, grows as speed rises. This was first noted by Lippmann [67], who probably constructed the first effective high-speed uniformity machine. Figure 33 is a specific example drawn from Lippmann's paper. Walker and Reeves [70] published results for many radial tires showing clearly that uniformity generated forces at the tire spindle depend on the square of speed in all cases for longitudinal force. In many, but not all, cases, normal force is also influenced by speed. Indeed longitudinal force variation is so speed sensitive that low-speed measurements are useless [70]. One might think of predicting the effec-

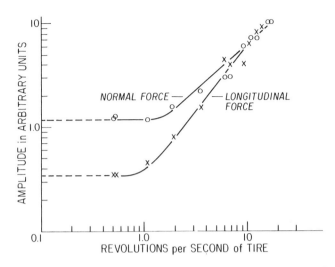

FIG. 33—*Change in uniformity forces for a tire with a heavy tread splice* [67].

tive longitudinal force at speed from radial force measurements, but it is important to note that radial and longitudinal force are poorly correlated [70], so such predictions will not be accurate.

Many of the manufacturing irregularities that produce tire uniformity force variations have been documented. A list of items from the literature applicable to causing normal force variation in both radial and bias tires would include: heavy tread splices [67], lightness at the tread splice, and tread thickness variation in general [73], nonsymmetry in setting the tire beads so that bead-to-bead cord length varies around the tire [73], tire building drum and mold irregularities [73], carcass stiffness variation [63], and runout [63]. For bias tires, other specific sources are cited. Walker and Reeves [70] proved theoretically that any source of rolling radius fluctuations will excite longitudinal force variations.

It is worth noting that the overall mass variation in the tire/wheel/brake/hub assembly gives rise to unbalance forces, like those in an unbalanced motor rotor. These are the forces corrected by balancing the tire/wheel assembly assuming a balanced brake/hub assembly [63,70]. These are not the uniformity forces we have been discussing. The uniformity variation generated forces always exist even in the case of perfectly mass-balanced assemblies.

Some have proposed adding a deliberate imbalance to cancel first harmonic normal force variation. This is not practical [70]. It works only over a narrow speed range, and you can not simultaneously cancel the first harmonic of both normal and longitudinal force variation.

Since the first harmonic of normal force variation is particularly important, a great deal of work has been done in an attempt to reduce rotating assembly levels to a low value. For the tire itself, this has taken the form of controllably grinding a small amount of rubber from the tire shoulders to change the footprint pressure distribution and thus reduce the first harmonic of normal force variation (Fig. 34) [74]. This process was pioneered by Hofelt [75]. Grinding is not an effective way to reduce higher harmonic forces at road speeds. Hamburg and Horsch [64] demonstrated this with road test results for tires ground to almost zero normal force variation (Fig. 35). Tire roughness is caused by higher harmonics of force variation.

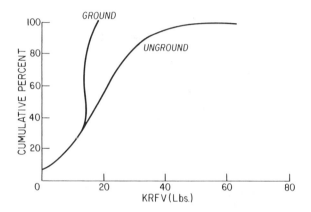

FIG. 34—*First harmonic effects of grinding upon quality of tires. Population statistics expressed as cumulative percent* [74].

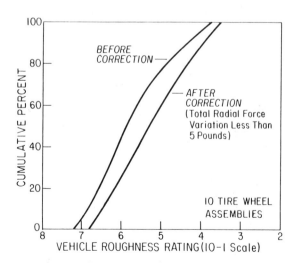

FIG. 35—*Change of vehicle roughness rating because of radial force variation correction, single front tire run on a chassis roll* [64].

The out of roundness of nontire components rotating on the car spindle contributes to nonuniform forces at the spindle [61, 74]. By alternately compressing and extending the tire spring, eccentric rotation components can generate forces equal to or larger than those generated by the tire itself. Thus, it is necessary that the hub be round, that the wheel pilot be snug and on center, and the bead seats on the wheel be concentric with the pilot hole in the wheel. Wheels have been steadily improved, a major improvement occurring about 1970 (Fig. 36) [74]. Match mounting is also often used to produce the lowest obtainable level of assembly first harmonic forces (Fig. 37) [75]. In this

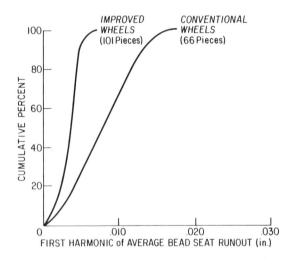

FIG. 36—*Cumulative distribution for improved and conventional wheels* [74].

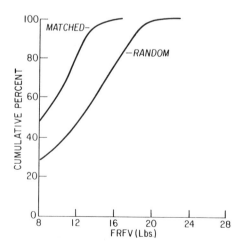

FIG. 37—*Comparison of random and matched tire/wheel assemblies* [75].

process, the low point of wheel first-harmonic bead-seat-runout variation is matched to the high point of the first harmonic of the normal force variation for the tire.

In addition to the force variations we have been discussing, there are three steady state effects, important to vehicle on-center handling that are also classified as uniformity effects. These effects cause the vehicle to deviate from a straight path. The steady state effects are called conicity, ply steer, and tire induced torque steer. Conicity and ply steer (their source and their effects) can be understood on the basis of three papers [63, 76, 77] given some knowledge of vehicle dynamics.

Tire conicity and ply steer are effects caused by residual steady state lateral force and aligning torque. Tire induced torque steer is not discussed within the literature. Since none of these problems is a source of vibration, we will not discuss them further.

Vehicle Vibrational Response

In this section of the paper, we will consider the vibrational behavior of the vehicle. The manner in which the vehicle interacts with the vibrational behavior of the tires, along with specific ride problems, will be discussed later in this paper. In order to facilitate this discussion, it will be convenient to visualize the vehicle as being made up of a number of different components, and to examine the vibrational behavior of each component as though it were isolated from its neighbors: rigid body, suspension, chassis, body panels, engine, and so forth. This component approach is quite common, but the reader should keep in mind that this methodology implicity assumes that the whole question of component interaction will be handled at some later stage of the analysis. This method is useful because the overall systems problem is broken down into a number of simpler and more manageable sub-problems, each of which demonstrates certain important characteristics of the vehicle. It is these characteristics that we wish to emphasize, since in a survey paper we can only scratch the surface of a topic as complex as vehicle vibrations. The included references, and the additional literature referenced therein, can serve as a guide to the reader seeking more detailed information. The majority of the findings from this discussion are also tabulated in Fig. 2.

Rigid Body Vibrations (Low Frequency, 0.5 to 5 Hz)

In this frequency range, the predominant modes of vibration are related to the rigid body motions of the vehicle body. "Rigid body" refers to the fact the chassis/body of the vehicle moves as a lumped mass on the springs or the tires or both [78–81]. In the vertical direction, the vehicle body will bounce, pitch, and roll on the springs of the suspension system (in the Society of Automotive Engineers [SAE] notation this corresponds to a vertical translation in the

z direction, and rotation about the y and x axes, respectively). The vibrational frequency of these modes is usually in the range of 1 to 3 Hz, and the shock absorber damps out the motion after a few cycles of oscillation (assuming the source of the excitation has been removed). The contribution of the tires to these motions is quite minimal since the spring rate of the tires is three to five times greater than that of the suspension springs. The deflection of the suspension springs absorbs the vast majority of the energy present in these modes. A variety of investigators have included this type of vibrational behavior in vehicle ride models [38, 78, 80, 83, 84].

The vehicle has three other rigid body modes: longitudinal and lateral deflection and yaw motion (x and y translation and rotation about the z axis, respectively). The frequencies of these vibrational modes generally occur between 3 and 5 Hz and may be coupled to other suspension or chassis modes or both [79, 81, 82]. In this instance, the direction of motion is such that the suspension is considerably less compliant (that is, the suspension is much stiffer in the x and y directions than the z direction). For these motions, the tires and the suspension bushings play a dominant part in determining the frequency of vibration. The relative responsiveness of these modes is also usually much less than those occurring in the vertical direction [81], and, hence, they are often ignored in vehicle models.

Suspension Vibrations (5 Hz and Above)

The vibrational behavior of the vehicle suspension is extremely important since the suspension provides the direct link between the tire and the remainder of the vehicle. The vibrations delivered by the tire to the vehicle at their point of connection may be amplified or attenuated depending on the dynamic response of the suspension components. The resulting vibrations appear at the connection points between the suspension and the chassis, and eventually disturb the passengers. For this reason, vehicle suspensions have been the subject of extensive experimental and analytical investigations for many years. The comments that follow are based on information found in Refs *38*, and *78* through *92*.

Suspension systems may be divided into two generic classifications: those where the wheels on the left and right side of the vehicle are truly independent and those where there is some type of more or less rigid connection between the wheels (a drive axle that connects a gear case to the wheels through universal joint would not be considered a rigid link).

1. *Independent.* Virtually all front suspensions, A-frame or strut, and independent rear suspensions, strut and trailing arm or its brethren.

2. *Linked.* The majority of suspensions found on the rear of a vehicle. The old leaf spring Hotchkiss and the newer torque arm suspensions used with rear wheel drive vehicles, and the newer open-channel axles used with front wheel drive vehicles.

From a suspension designers point of view, these two classifications of suspension types present unique challenges, but from a dynamics point of view as it relates to vehicle vibration and noise problems, there are many similarities. The principal difference is that while independently sprung wheels will interact primarily through the steering mechanism to cause problems, such as tramp, shimmy, flutter, and wheelfight, the linked suspension necessitates that the two wheels undergo truly coupled motion such as axle fore-aft, side and yaw shake, and axle windup (definitions from Ref 93). The equations of motion can be quite complicated, but such complexities need not concern us here. There is sufficient similarity between the various types of suspensions that we may address the problem in total and handle the exceptions as needed.

We begin by considering the vibrational behavior of the suspension in the vertical direction. The most common model for a vibrating suspension is the classical second order spring-mass-damper system, where both the tire and the suspension spring contribute to the overall spring rate of the model (Fig. 38) [38,78,80,82–89]. The resonant frequency occurs between 10 and 20 Hz and is generally referred to as wheel hop (this is discussed in more detail later in the paper), and the shock absorber provides essentially all the damping available to the system. At frequencies above about 30 Hz, the shock absorber is valved so that its damping diminishes rapidly and the small amount of damping present in the tire becomes very important in limiting the motion of the system. Indeed, unless the shock absorber is properly valved, it can actually appear as a dead-short between the spindle and the chassis. In addition, at certain frequencies, various components of the suspension may them-

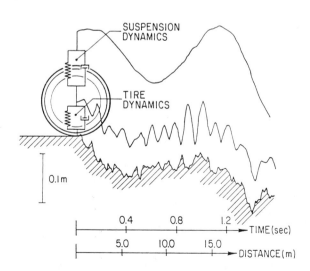

FIG. 38—*Road profile, motion of front tire and suspension/body contact point* [84].

selves exhibit resonant modes of vibration. Bending and twisting of A-arms and struts, and surging resonances of springs are a few of the more common problems [89–91]. When these situations occur, generally in the frequency range of 50 to 300 Hz, the vibrations that are transmitted across the suspension are greatly increased over what would otherwise be present [79,82,89]. This situation is illustrated in Fig. 20, where the effect of the shock absorber and the presence of various suspension resonances can be easily seen. The peak in the curve at approximately 85 Hz is the vertical resonance of the tire itself. The primary difference between independent and linked suspensions is that while the independent suspension can be expected to have a single wheel-hop resonance in the 10 to 20-Hz frequency range, the linked suspension will exhibit a pair of resonances, one where the wheels move in phase, and a second resonance at a slightly higher frequency where the wheels move out of phase [79].

With respect to the actual vibrational level transmitted across the suspension and entering the vehicle chassis, both the suspension spring and the rubber suspension bushings play an important part in this story (Fig. 39) [82]. As previously mentioned at the lower frequencies, a certain amount of the vibration is attenuated by the springs. The bushings, which connect the suspension members to the rest of the vehicle, have a dual purpose. They must be sufficiently rigid that the steering mechanism can properly control the direction of the vehicle, but they must also attenuate vibrations that appear at the top of the suspension system. As can be seen in Fig. 39, the bushings can provide an attenuation of as much as 20 to 1 in the lower frequency range, up to about 100 Hz, and their influence remains considerable until the break-even point is reached at about 400 Hz. In the lateral (side to side) and longitudinal (fore-aft) directions, the rubber bushings take on an even greater importance. This

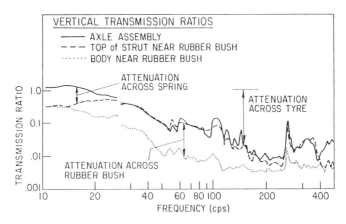

FIG. 39—*Vertical transmission ratios in vibration path through strut of strut-type suspension* [82].

occurs since the suspension system is considerably stiffer in the lateral and longitudinal directions than it is vertically, and essentially all the vibration attenuation must be provided by the bushings. And, as was true in the case of the vertical vibrations, resonances of the suspension components themselves can cause a large increase in the vibrations transmitted to the chassis.

The net result of all these various factors can be summarized (in an overly simplified fashion) as follows [81–83]. At frequencies below about 40 Hz, the transmissibility of vibrations from the tire tread to the chassis is greater in the vertical direction than in either the lateral or longitudinal directions (see Fig. 40). For higher frequencies, the situation is reversed. Bounce (wheel hop) and axle-roll resonances generally occur in a frequency range of 10 to 20 Hz, and the suspension members themselves can contribute additional resonances in the frequency range of 50 to 300 Hz.

Chassis Vibrations

As was true for the case of suspension vibrations, chassis vibrations have been studied both experimentally and analytically for many years [85, 94–102]. Modal analysis and finite-element methods have been used to evaluate existing chassis types and to design improved models. Such studies usually have a dual purpose: to evaluate the vibrational behavior of the chassis when subjected to external forces, and to insure that fatigue/failure problems do not arise as a result of the bending and flexing of the chassis. In this paper we will only be concerned with the vibrational behavior of the chassis.

There are two principal types of vehicle chassis. The older type, which is still utilized to some extent, is essentially a collection of beam-like elements of various types, connected together in some manner (usually welded) to form the "back-bone," or framework, of the vehicle. The types of elements used,

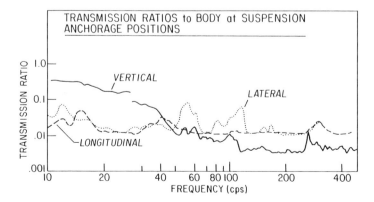

FIG. 40—*Comparison of overall transmission ratios to body anchorage positions of strut-type suspension* [82].

C-channel, box, solid members, and so forth, are determined by the need for structural integrity as well as the desire to minimize the overall weight of the chassis. This type of chassis interfaces with the suspension, drive train, and vehicle body through the bushings, motor mounts, and body mounts, respectively.

The other type of chassis is generically known as a "unibody," and it is a natural extension of the beam-type chassis. This type of chassis picks up where the beam-type of chassis leaves off in that the structural members of the body itself are integrally formed with, and attached to, the underlying backbone members. The net result is that essentially all of the structural members of the vehicle wind up in one compact component instead of being divided into two different components.

Unfortunately, unibody construction is not widely discussed in the literature. We have chosen, therefore, to discuss chassis vibrations from the point of view of the older beam-type chassis. This obviously simplifies the problem to a considerable extent, but the majority of what is said about beam-type chassis is likewise applicable to unibody chassis types. The principal difference is that the dynamic behavior of the unibody would be expected to be more complex, and the ordering of the vibrational modes as discussed below may not be accurate. A unibody chassis would also have a number of vibrational modes not found in beam-type chassis, principally many more lateral, twisting, and breathing modes. With this rather extensive caveat in hand, we proceed to discuss chassis vibrations.

A vehicle chassis may exhibit a very large number of vibrational modes, and they generally fall into one of three categories: vertical bending (or "beaming" motion in the z direction), lateral bending (y direction), and torsional modes (end-to-end twisting about the x axis). The frequency range begins at around 10 Hz and can extend out through several hundred Hertz for the higher order modes [85,96,97,99,102]. Figure 41, taken from Flanigan [99], shows a lateral mode shape for a chassis. In theory, there is really no upper limit to the frequency range, but as a practical matter the relative

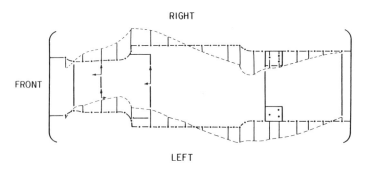

FIG. 41—*Lateral mode shape at 14.97 Hz* [99].

strength of the modes becomes quite weak above 100 Hz, and their influence on the overall vibrational behavior of the vehicle is quite minimal. For the lowest order vibrational modes the following is generally found:

1. For a free, bare chassis, the torsional mode usually exhibits the lowest frequency, followed by the vertical bending and then the lateral bending [96, 98, 99, 102]. The frequency range begins around 20 Hz.

2. For a fully dressed vehicle, the resonant frequencies are lower than for the free chassis, and the lowest modes are usually the vertical bending followed by the torsional and then the lateral modes [100, 102]. The frequency range usually begins around 10 Hz, although there are cases where the modes have been reported as low as 8 Hz [99, 100].

With regard to the higher order modes, one can really say very little aside from the obvious fact that the frequencies will be higher, and that as the mode number increases the overall responsiveness of the mode is generally, although not invariably, lower. This means that the transmission of vibrational energy is usually less efficient at the higher frequencies.

From the preceeding discussion, it should be clear that a vehicle chassis possesses a large number of different vibrational modes, some of which may have resonant frequencies in the range where wheel-hop (shake) and other low frequencies problems can occur. It is little wonder, therefore, that tire and vehicle designers strive mightly to avoid any situations where a chassis resonance might coincide with a tire/suspension resonance. Such a result would virtually guarantee a ride complaint. Similar comments might be made concerning chassis resonances matching up to the resonant frequency of body panel, the steering column, or anything else in proximity to the passengers.

And while it is beyond the scope of this paper, it is worth mentioning that vehicle designers must also be concerned about other possible vibration problems. The manner in which the engine and drive train interacts with the chassis can also be the source of customer complaints. The interested reader may wish to consult Refs 91 and 103-107 for additional information.

Vehicle Vibrations and the Passengers

There are a number of different vibrational sources that may disturb the passengers of a vehicle. For the sake of convenience, we will divide these sources into two categories: those that cause tactile (or touching) disturbances, and those that cause audible disturbances. There is a fairly natural frequency distinction between these two categories, albeit with some overlap. At a low frequency, 0.5 to about 30 Hz, we find vibrational sources that cause tactile disturbances, and from 20 Hz upwards we encounter vibrational sources that cause acoustic disturbances. The reader will find considerably more information on the response of the human body to acoustic and tactile disturbances in another section of this paper, but for the sake of this discussion we may state that

1. Human beings are most sensitive to tactile vibrations in the range of 4 to 8 Hz, and the sensitivity drops off rapidly as the frequency rises.
2. Human hearing comes into play around 20 Hz.

Below 20 Hz, most people will "feel" rather than hear an acoustic disturbance, although there are certain people with exceptional hearing that can actually "hear" sounds with a frequency as low as 13 to 15 Hz.

Tactile Sources

There are three main vibrational sources for tactile disturbances: seats, floorpans, and the steering column/wheel. The seats and floorpan are directly tied to the body of the vehicle, which, in turn, is connected to the chassis through the body mounts (obviously there are no body mounts in a unibody). The steering column interacts with the suspension through the steering gear, the steering box is often mounted on the chassis in the engine compartment, and the column itself is also usually bolted to the underside of the dashpanel.

Seats—The comfort of an automobile seat has both a static and a dynamic component. From a static point of view, a seat must adequately support the weight of the passengers and "feel right." Even load distribution, no hard spots, and support for the thighs and back are important considerations. Dynamically the seat is expected to isolate the passengers from vibrational inputs. As a practical matter, most seats are designed such that the vertical "bounce" of the passenger on the seat occurs at around 3 Hz (Fig. 42). The reason for this is to minimize the vibrational disturbances experienced by the passenger at his most sensitive frequency, 5.5 to 6.5 Hz, the principal resonance of the human torso in the vertical direction. Vibrations that occur at higher frequencies would be expected to be further attenuated. In addition, the total transfer of energy across the seat (the height of the peak) should be minimized as much as possible. Besides the vertical direction, an automobile seat obviously has two other directions of motion. It has been found, however, that the levels of vibrations in the vertical direction are usually about an order of magnitude greater than those in either the lateral or the horizontal directions [108]. Thus, if a seat provides good isolation to vibrations in the vertical direction, one can be reasonably sure that the vehicle seats will not be a source of ride complaints. There is one other concern, however. The peak at around 11 Hz is the result of the upright portion of the seat striking the back of the passenger. The vehicle designer must also insure that this vibrational disturbance does not become excessive.

Floorpans—The floorpan of a vehicle provides a vertical input to the feet of the passengers. The floorpan is usually a formed piece of metal that trans-

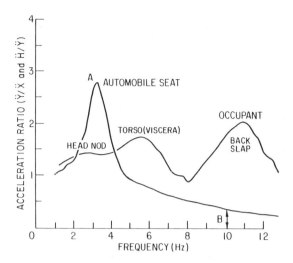

FIG. 42—*Relationship between a typical seat and occupant transfer function* [193].

verses the passenger compartment and extends forward and upward to where it joins the fire wall. Unfortunately, there is precious little in the literature regarding the dynamic behavior of floorpans, and no direct measures of the modes of vibration of a free floorpan. There is a certain amount of information available with regard to how the floorpan interacts with other body panel members [109–111], and some indirect measures of the response of a floorpan when subjected to external forces [108]. From this limited information we conclude that the resonant modes of vibration of a floorpan occur at frequencies in excess of 50 Hz. At lower frequencies, the motion of the floorpan is dominated by forced responses. The level of vibrations typically measured on the floorpan of a vehicle can be quite significant, often approaching those seen on the seat of the vehicle at frequencies less than 10 Hz, and usually exceeding the seat vibrations for frequencies above 10 Hz, often by an order of magnitude or more. Thus, floorpan vibrations are a nontrivial contributor to vehicle ride comfort. The theoretical background work is all intact. What is lacking is the real-world applications.

Steering Column/Wheel—The final vehicle/passenger interface we will consider is the steering wheel. If anything moves, the steering column will probably know about it, and so will the passengers! At the lowest frequencies, 0.5 to 20 Hz, the dynamic behavior of the steering wheel is one of forced response, it follows the vibrational energy provided to it by the suspension, chassis, or whatever. But even in forced response, the steering wheel can exhibit extremely large motions, amplitudes so large that they are easily visible to the human eye. Above 20 Hz, a number of wheel/column resonant modes of vibration can be found [68]. A steering wheel will usually exhibit three or

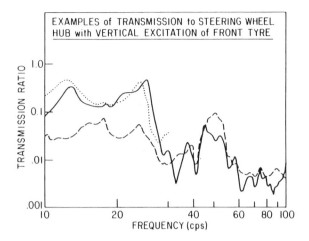

FIG. 43—*Three examples of steering wheel resonances* [82].

more vibrational modes between 20 and 50 Hz, and the relative strength (responsiveness) of the various modes will depend on the exact design of the wheel-column assembly. Figure 43 illustrates the transfer characteristics between the surface of the tire and three different steering wheels. The peak at about 12 Hz is the wheel hop response, and several steering wheel resonances can be seen at frequencies beginning about 18 Hz. Any or all of these resonances could contribute to tactile disturbances if the vibrational energy reaching the steering wheel has the appropriate spectral content.

Acoustic Disturbances

There are two primary paths of acoustic disturbance in the passenger compartment of a vehicle: direct airborne noise energy and structually transmitted energy. In this section, we will be concerned with the second category, but only to a very limited degree. This topic is covered more fully in a later section of this paper, as is the question of direct airborne sound energy.

There are two issues that must be addressed in order to put this topic into perspective: cavity resonances and body panel vibrations (and, of course, their interaction). These topics have been studied in considerable detail both experimentally and analytically for at least the last 20 years. The information that follows is based on Refs *109* through *114*.

Cavity Resonances—The term cavity resonance refers to the fact that in any enclosed space, it is possible to develop standing waves of acoustic energy. Examples included concert halls, organ pipes, and vehicle bodies. In the case of vehicle bodies, the expected frequency range of the standing waves is from 40 to 250 Hz. Why this occurs is discussed elsewhere in this paper. For now, it is sufficient to say that if some vibration source supplies energy in this frequency range, the passenger compartment will most likely act as a resonator, and a ride disturbance will result.

Panel Vibrations—The source of much of the interior noise in a vehicle is the result of vibrating body panels. This noise has been measured and analyzed by a number of different investigators. They have found that most panel fundamentals occur in the frequency range of 40 to 250 Hz. If subjected to external forces, these panels will vibrate and cause discomfort for the passengers, and particularily so if the panel resonances coincide with some cavity resonance.

Human Response to Acoustic and Tactile Vibrational Disturbances

In this section we will consider the manner in which the human body responds to acoustic or tactile vibrational disturbances. We will first examine what happens when a single disturbance is present, following which we will consider the effect of combined noise and vibration stimuli. Our goal here is to lay the groundwork so that in later sections of this paper we may pay particular concern to how acoustic or tactile vibrations disturb or fatigue the passengers of a vehicle, or those who may be otherwise affected because of their proximity to a passing vehicle.

Acoustical Response

The study of response of human beings to various types of sounds has a very long heritage. Beginning with Pythagoras' study of musical sounds in the 6th century BC, and continuing through to the present day, some of the finest minds of every age concerned themselves with how and what we hear (Galileo, Merseene, Newton, Sauveur, Helmholtz, Lagrange, Chladni, Savart, Rayleigh, Sabine, Fletcher, and Love, to name just a few) [115]. The common thread linking these investigators, and many others, has been the quest to understand four aspects of sound: creation, propagation, reception, and perception. The first two topics, creation and propagation, are covered in other portions of this paper. What happens after the sound waves reach our ears is our present concern. We will be principally concerned with WHAT we hear and our psychological response to the stimuli. The mechanical and neurological mechanisms which actually ALLOW us to hear will not be discussed. We begin with a definition of sound pressure level (SPL), the measure of the amplitude of a sound wave. The traditional unit of measurement of SPL is the decibel (dB), a logarithmic value referenced to the smallest amplitude of sound pressure that can normally be heard by a person with good hearing

$$SPL = 20 \log [P/20] \text{ dB } [20 \text{ } \mu\text{Pa reference pressure}] \qquad (7)$$

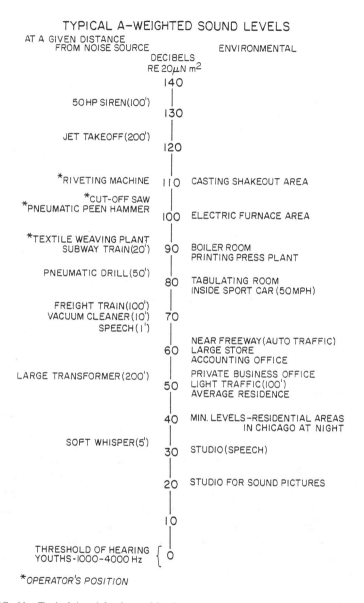

FIG. 44—*Typical A-weighted sound levels measured with a sound-level meter* [122].

where P is the root mean square sound pressure in micro Pascals for the sound in question.

The reader may wish to verify that if the amplitude of one sound wave is twice that of another, their SPLs will differ by 6 dB. Similarly, 40 dB represents a pressure ratio of 100 to 1. By way of illustration, Fig. 44 gives a comparison between some common sounds and their approximate SPLs (the A weightings mentioned on the chart will be discussed shortly). Notice that the human ear responds to SPL over a range of 10 million to one; a truly remarkable feat of engineering by mother nature! It is clear that as the SPL increases the overall loudness of the sound will also increase—incidentally, the threshold of pain is about 140 dB—and the degree by which we are annoyed or disturbed by noise is generally related to its amplitude. But SPL is not the whole story. In most situations we also need to know something about the way in which the sound energy is distributed at least within the frequency range from 20 to 15 000 Hz. (20 000 Hz for young people).

The apparent loudness of a sound varies not only with the SPL but also with the frequency (or pitch) of the sound. And while all the factors that influence noise disturbance and hearing loss are not yet known, in recent years psychoacoustical experiments have revealed many of the aspects of our response to sounds by asking subject listeners to rate the loudness of various types of sounds in laboratory situations. It must be emphasized that the findings that follow are the result of laboratory experiments, and the absolute numerical values may not apply to real-life situations if the test conditions are greatly different.

Robinson and Dadson [116] determined a set of equal loudness contour lines that relate the SPL of pure sinusoidal tones to a 1000-Hz reference tone with some specified SPL (Fig. 45). For example, a 1000-Hz tone with a SPL of 90 dB will have the same apparent loudness as a 60-Hz tone with a SPL of

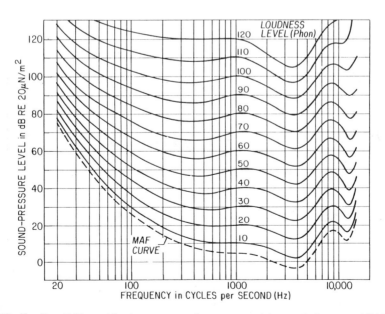

FIG. 45—*Free-field equal-loadness contours for pure tones (observer facing source)* [116].

100 dB. The numerical value shown on each curve is the SPL of the 1000-Hz tone used in calculating that curve and is defined as the "loudness level" in phons. Thus, a 100-Hz tone with a SPL of 70 dB has a loudness level of approximately 63 phons. (Similiar curves for narrow band random noise signals were found by Pollack [117]. Random noise has sound energy over a range of frequencies rather than being concentrated at one or a few distinct frequency components as in the case of pure tones.)

A set of curves similiar to those shown in Fig. 45 were also developed by Fletcher and Munson [118] and are the basis for the "A" and "B" weighting curves commonly found on sound level meters (Fig. 46). In essence, the A and B weighting curves are approximately the inverted 40- and 70-phon equal loudness contours, respectively. The reason for using a weighting curve, and the A-weighting curve in particular, is to simulate the manner in which the human ear attenuates the upper and lower frequencies of a noise signal. By multiplying a noise signal by the A-weighting curve, for example, we get a first approximation to what we actually hear. We shall meet some practical uses of this technique shortly, but let us first discuss a simpler situation, how we respond to pure sinusoidal sounds (or tones).

Let us consider the curves given in Fig. 45 and ask if it is possible to rate the relative loudness ratio of two sounds with the same frequency but different SPLs. That is, can we find a way to say that one sound is twice as loud as another, or four times as loud, or whatever. This has indeed been done and the results are given in Fig. 47. For pure tones with a SPL of 30 dB or greater, we find that the loudness in sones doubles each time the SPL increases by

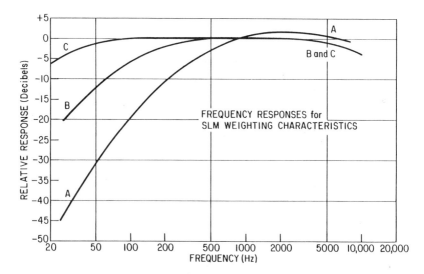

FIG. 46—*Frequency-response characteristics in the American National Standard Specification for sound-level meters, ANSI-S1.4-1971.*

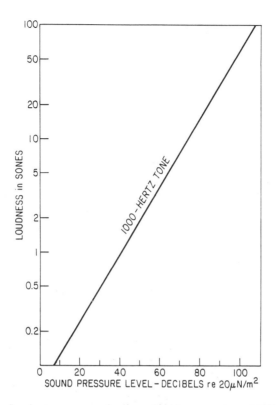

FIG. 47—*Loudness versus sound-pressure level for a pure tone of 1000 Hz* [122].

10 dB. And while this curve is plotted for a 1000-Hz tone, it works quite well for any pure tone or extremely narrow band of random noise within the frequency range of 200 Hz to 8 kHz. The reason this occurs in that over the specified frequency range, the equal loudness level contours are more or less uniformily separated by 10 dB. It is possible, therefore, to use this curve to determined the loudness ratio of two tones of different frequencies. For example, suppose Tone A has a frequency of 500 Hz and a SPL of 56 dB and Tone B has a frequency of 200 Hz and a SPL of 48 dB. Using the procedures discussed above and Fig. 45, Tones A and B will have loudness levels of 60 and 50 phons, respectively. By using Fig. 47, Tone A will have a loudness of 4 sones and Tone B will have a loudness of 2 sones. We can thus state that Tone A will appear approximately twice as loud as Tone B.

But what happens if we are not dealing with pure tones or very narrow bands of random noise? How can we determine the loudness level of a sound possessing energy at a number of different frequencies? A number of schemes have been suggested by different experimenters [*119–121*] to accomplish this mission. The details vary from study to study, but the usual approach is to first calculate the loudness level of the noise signal for a number of different frequency bands that cover the audible range and then sum these together in some manner to determine the overall preceived noise level. It is arguable, however, how much these elaborations significantly improve the estimation of the perceived loudness of a complex sound beyond what can be achieved through a simple weighting of the SPL data [122]. To date, no completely adequate measure of the manner in which people are disturbed or annoyed by noise has been developed, but certain generalities are possible:

1. Individual frequency components are usually more disturbing than a band of random noise energy. This is known as "tonality" [123].

2. The higher the SPL the more disturbing the noise. For pure tones, if the SPL increases by 10 dB the perceived loudness will double.

3. If one wishes to evaluate the subjective effect of a noise and reference it back to some pure tone or narrow band of random noise, then some type of calculation scheme is usually preferrable to a simple weighting of the data [124,125].

4. For rank ordering similiar noises, such as the noise level present in an automobile, the use of the A-weighting curve is usually adequate but not for tire noise [126].

5. Noises with a known source are usually less disturbing than a "sea of noise." This means that, for a given SPL, people are usually more comfortable if they can identify a particular object as the source of the noise than if they feel completely surrounded by the noise from unknown sources.

6. The longer the exposure time, the more disturbing the noise [127].

Tactile Disturbances

The subjective response of humans to tactile vibrations has been studied for slightly over 50 years (a mere infant by comparison to its acoustic cousin). The earliest investigators were primarily concerned with whole-body vibrations in the vertical direction, and by subjecting their volunteers to single frequency sinusoidal vibrations they attempted to determine three simple measures of subjective response: threshold of perception, an unpleasant level, and the limit of tolerance. But, as was true for acoustic disturbances, such studies are always prone to considerable variation dependent on the test conditions employed. There was some agreement, however, and eventually bands of reasonable consistent results could be determined [128]. Harris and Crede present an excellent review of these early studies (Fig. 48). As might be expected, correlation with real-world experience where the vibrations were usually more complex and the exposure time variable was, at best, problematical. But over the years the situation progressively improved as investigators became more astute in controlling experimental variables. By the early 1970s the data base had grown to the point where it was possible to develop reasonable guidelines to accomplish several purposes: to protect individuals against

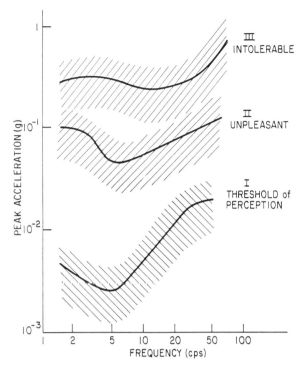

FIG. 48—*Average peak accelerations at various frequencies at which subjects* (I) *perceive vibration;* (II) *find it unpleasant; or* (III) *refuse to tolerate it further. Exposures of 5 to 20 min. Shaded areas are about one standard deviation on either side of mean. Data averaged from seven sources* [128].

physical injury (exposure limit), to preserve working efficiency (fatigue boundary), and to maintain comfort (comfort boundary). Figure 49 [129] shows the International Standards Organization (ISO) "fatigue boundary" curves for whole-body vertical vibrations. (The "exposure limit" curves are 6 dB higher, and the "reduced comfort" curves are 10 dB lower.) The boundaries are equal sensitivity contours for sinusoidal or one-third octave bands of random vibrations. For the case of wide band random vibrations, the rms value of the various octave bands should not exceed the limits shown. These curves imply that the human body is most sensitive to vibrations in the frequency range of 4 to 8 Hz. This result is due to the fact that primary torso resonance of the human body, the expansion/contraction of the spinal cord "spring," has a frequency of about 6 Hz. Similiar ISO curves exist for whole-body vibrations in the other directions. Subsequent investigations by many authors extended these initial findings to vibrations applied to the human hand [130,131], the effect of rotational degrees of freedom [132,133], and vibrational disturbances occurring in more than one direction at a time

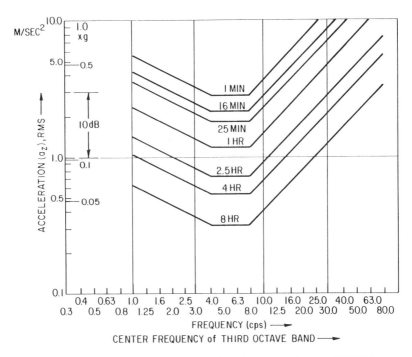

FIG. 49—*Fatigue boundaries for whole body vertical vibrations* [128,129].

[*133,134*]. The reader is cautioned to remember, however, that while these types of curves may appear rather fixed and immutable, such is not really the case. Any experiment that deals with the subjective response of human beings is subject to considerable variation. These curves, therefore, represent the average response for a large group of people, and the subjective response of any specific individual may diverge greatly.

A number of different investigators have looked specifically at the problem of maintaining the ride comfort of vehicle passengers. A number of schemes have been proposed that differ from the ISO curves in various respects. The ISO curves rely on rms-acceleration levels, but the use of absorbed power [*135*], power spectral density [*136*], and weighted rms-acceleration [*137*] has also been considered. In 1977, Smith and his associates [*138*] did an extensive one-on-one comparison between a number of different proposals for evaluating the ride comfort of passenger vehicles. They showed that all the various methods generally did a good job of predicting ride comfort, and there was very little to choose between the results. Their recommendation was that because of its inherent simplicity the use of unweighted rms acceleration data was the preferred method, and for the case of multi-directional inputs, the square root of the sum of squares of the individual rms accelerations should be used. For reference purposes, Fig. 50 is included as a typical example of

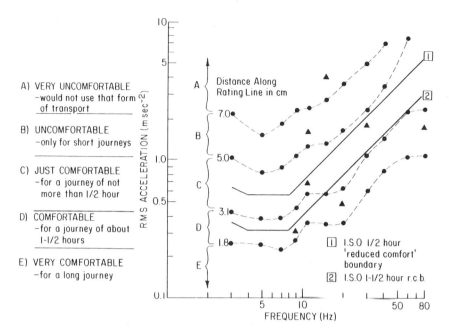

FIG. 50—*Equal comfort zones for subjects in Group 2. Stimuli that produced no agreement between subjects are indicated by* Δ [138].

what one might expect when dealing vertical vibrations experienced by vehicle passengers [*138*]. Similiar curves with different amplitudes can be used for vibrational inputs in other directions and to other parts of the anatomy [*108*].

Combined Acoustic and Tactile Disturbances

In recent years investigators have begun considering the manner in which human beings respond to combined acoustic and vibrational disturbances. As one might expect, this problem is considerably more difficult than the case of either disturbance applied separately since the physiological mechanisms involved are more complicated. Much of the early work in this area was undertaken because of concern about the high levels of both noise and vibrations commonly experienced by aircraft personnel. The usual approach is to evaluate either the tracking accuracy (tasks involving manual dexterity) or mental proficiency (tasks involving mental calculation or reasoning) of a subject when exposed to noise or vibrational disturbances or both. The results showed

1. *Tracking*—Tracking ability is adversely affected by 5-Hz vibrational inputs in the vertical direction with an amplitude greater than 0.20 *g* [*140*]. The addition of noise inputs can further affect performance, but only if the noise

level is quite high, greater than about 100 dB. Noise by itself has little effect on tracking [141].

2. *Mental*—Simple mental performance seems to be only minimally affected by either vibrational or noise disturbances [142,143], or even the combination of vibration and low level noise [144]. Mental ability is adversely affected, however, when vibrational inputs are combined with high noise levels (0.25 *g* at 5 Hz, plus 110-dB noise). Figure 51 shows the result of combined vibration and high noise levels on the ability of test subjects to perform a mathematical subtraction task [144].

More recently, a few investigations have been conducted to evaluate ride comfort in the presence of both acoustic and vibrational stimuli. One very extensive National Aeronautics and Space Administration (NASA) study by Leatherwood et al. [145] utilized over 2000 test subjects to develop an empirical model for passenger ride comfort. Ride comfort was modeled as a continuous function of the stimuli received by the passengers, namely, the amplitude and frequency of random or sinusoidal vibrations along any of five different axes, the effect of multiple-axis vibrations, and the correction factors to account for the duration of the vibrations and for the presence of noise within the vehicle. Figure 52 presents a schematic outline of the model. The model proceeds in a stepwise fashion by first transforming the measured peak accelerations in any direction into a "discomfort value" through the use of empirically determined equations. The discomfort caused by sinusoidal or random vibrations or both along each axis are calculated separately, and then com-

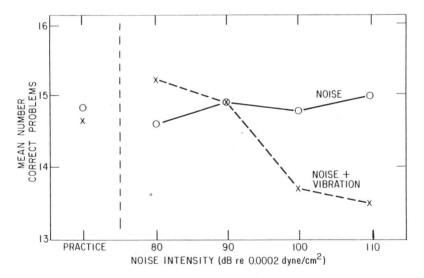

FIG. 51—*Mean number of correct problems for noise exposure group, and noise + vibration exposure group* [145].

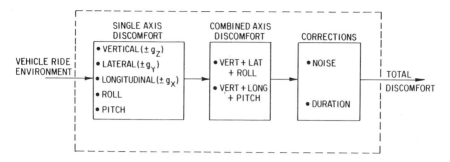

FIG. 52—*NASA ride comfort model concept* [145].

bined together into a single discomfort value by finding the square-root of the sum of the squares of the individual discomfort values. Other empirical equations are used to apply correction factors for the duration time of the vibrations and for the presence of noise within various octave bands. The final result of this model is a single number that describes the total discomfort experienced by the passengers for the ride environment. Figure 53 shows the discomfort scale used with this model. A total discomfort value of 1.0 corresponds to the situation where 50% of the passengers would complain about the ride (termed the "discomfort threshold" in this paper). To date, this work by NASA is by far the most ambitious attempt to relate perceived ride comfort to an environment containing both acoustic and vibrational disturbances. How well this approach will actually work for real-world situations will be proven over time.

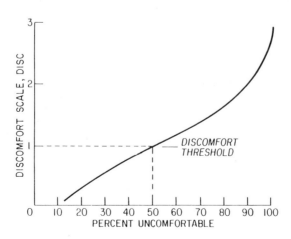

FIG. 53—*Discomfort (DISC) as a function of percent of passengers uncomfortable* [145].

The System In Action

The review to this point has made clear the complexities of the road, tire, vehicle, and human being. Each of these areas is a system in itself, but when noise or vibration problems or both occur, the engineer is forced to consider the total interaction of three or more of these separate systems. He must deal with the general system in action. It is sometimes hard to decide how to put the pieces together to solve a problem. To aid in learning how to look at the system in action, we will review five example cases where the literature provides reasonably complete information on the total system performance. Table 3 lists the example problems.

Shake

Shake is the name given to the vibration that occurs when a vehicle is traversing a smooth road, and the nonuniformity force variations of the tire in the vertical direction excite the vehicle suspension at or near its wheel hop frequency, typically 10 to 15 Hz for an automobile. A rough road can also induce shake, but this type of shake is not considered here.

It has long been recognized that excitation of wheel hop is quite undesirable since, as we have seen, humans are highly sensitive to vibrations in the 10- to 15-Hz frequency range (Figs. 48 through 50). Thus, if the tire provides strong excitation in the 10- to 15-Hz range, a ride discomfort problem is probable. The existence of various chassis and drive train modes within the same frequency range—beaming, twisting, and so forth—can further exacerbate the problem by additionally amplifying the vibrations provided by the wheel hop mode [83,94,146].

Figure 54 from Nordeen and Rasmussen [83] is a simple model representing tire/vehicle system response. Chiesa and Tangorra [36] used a similar but

TABLE 3—*System in action examples*

Topic	Road	Tire	Vehicle	Environment	Human
			Subsystem Involvement		
Shake	...	X	X	...	X
Roughness	...	X	X	...	X
Harshness	X	X	X	...	X
Tire/pavement Interaction Noise[a]	X	X	...	X	X
In car noise	X	X	X	...	X

[a]For other vehicle associated noises, the vehicle must be considered.

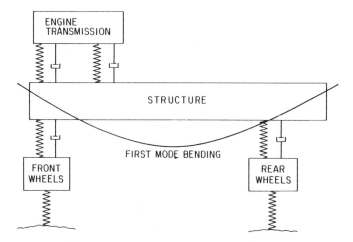

FIG. 54—*Two-dimensional vibrational model encompassing beaming shake, engine bounce and pitch, sprung mass bounce, and pitch and wheel motions* [83].

simpler model to demonstrate that the primary design parameters affecting wheel hop behavior are suspension mass, tire vertical rolling spring rate, and shock absorber damping. The chassis modes are determined by the chassis structural design. Every effort is made to keep transmissibility between the spindle and the passengers to a minimum during vehicle design, but this alone can not prevent shake complaints. It is necessary to control the amplitude of tire nonuniformity force inputs to the vehicle in order to obtain acceptable shake performance.

As shown earlier, Eq 6, any of the tire normal force variation harmonics can potentially excite wheel hop. Each harmonic would do so at one particular speed. In practice the first harmonic of normal force variation (Fig. 31) is usually the strongest source of excitation. Unfortunately, the first harmonic excites wheel hop at highway speeds where long periods of time are spent at a constant speed on a smooth surface. Thus, the first harmonic of normal force variation is the preeminent source of shake problems [83]. It is for this reason that reduction of the first harmonic of radial force variation has received intense attention. This reduction is effective in improving ride (Fig. 55) [64].

Supression of shake is produced by manipulating the vehicle sensitivity and the excitation level. Vehicle sensitivity is minimized by adjusting vehicle system parameters to minimize transmissibility. Excitation levels are reduced by controlling rotating assembly part runouts and improving tire uniformity. The effect of normal force variation on shake has been emphasized in this discussion because vehicle characteristics enhance response to wheel hop. However, if lateral force [83] or longitudinal force [47] first harmonics are quite large, they can also induce shake.

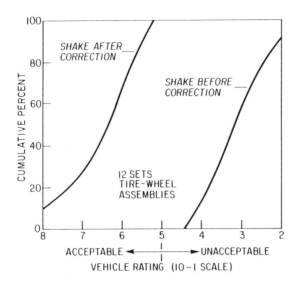

FIG. 55—*Change of vehicle ratings by servo-controlled correction. Population statistics expressed as cumulative percent* [64].

Tire Roughness

The term, "tire roughness," refers to a particular type of ride disturbance that is defined as follows [93]:

A vibration perceived tactilely and/or audibly, generated by a rolling tire on a smooth road surface and producing the sensation of driving on a coarse or irregular surface.

Tire roughness is thus a self-excited ride disturbance where some type of tire construction imperfection generates force or moment variations at the tire spindle. These, in turn, produce vibrations or noises that disturb the vehicle passengers, generally at a frequency above 20 Hz. In a physical sense, tire roughness is often described as a "tingling" or "buzzing" sensation in the drivers hands as he grasps the steering wheel. To a much lesser extent, tire roughness can also cause a disturbance to the passengers' feet. When the disturbance is perceived audibly it usually referred to as "boom."

An important characteristic of tire roughness is that it is a higher frequency, or higher order, ride disturbance. Tire roughness occurs at a frequency above 20 Hz, at a higher frequency than tire induced shake. By referring to the human response curves given earlier in this paper, we might logically guess that since tire roughness occurs at a higher frequency than tire shake, tire roughness should generally be of lesser importance than tire shake in disturbing the passengers (assuming, of course, that the same level of vibrational acceleration is present at each frequency). This indeed turns out to be the case. Hamburg and Horsch [64] found that when they force ground tires to near perfection (close to zero force variation level), the shake behavior of the vehicle improved dramatically, but the tire roughness performance changed very little (it actually got marginally worse, but not by a statistically significant amount) (see Fig. 35). This experiment revealed a couple of interesting facts about tire roughness:

1. Tire roughness is a second-level ride problem that can hide beneath a more prevalent problem, such as shake. In the vernacular of the psychoacoustic trade, this is usually called "masking." A primary or stronger effect may mask-off a secondary effect. The result being that the importance of the secondary effect may not be completely discernable until the stronger effect is virtually eliminated. This is what happened in the Hamburg and Horsch experiment.

2. After Hamburg and Horsch had reduced the radial force tire nonuniformity variations to a very low level, the tire roughness disturbance was still present. This is an important clue to the source of tire roughness, or at least an indication of what is not the problem. Namely, radial force variation is not the primary cause.

The discovery of the real source of the problem had to wait a few years and for the realization that tire roughness is a true systems problem. In order to determine the real cause of this ride disturbance it is necessary to understand the interaction between the tire and the vehicle. Most of the requisite pieces of information have already been discussed in this paper. What remains is for us to put the pieces together in the proper manner. The relevant references are 66, and 68–70.

In the section of this paper on tire uniformity we learned that machines exist that can measure the variation in the forces and moments that appear at the tire spindle. These are called high-speed uniformity machines (HISUM), and they are ideally suited to studying a problem such as tire roughness. As a tire rotates, any imperfections in the construction of the tire will cause force or moment variation or both to be generated at the tire/road interface. These are often referred to as "tire nonuniformities," and the first harmonic of any force or moment variation repeats once per tire revolution, the second harmonic repeats twice per tire revolution, and so on. At low speed, say 5 mph (8 km/h), tire nonuniformities excite the structure of the tire, which, in turn, will transfer these force and moment variations to the tire spindle. As the speed of the tire increases, the force and moment variations at the tire/road interface may increase in magnitude and excite the tire more strongly. In addition, the dynamic behavior of the tire will also come into play. If a tire resonance becomes excited the amplitude of the force and moment variations that will be generated at the tire spindle can be greatly increased. Since the axle of a HISUM is usually held at a fixed distance from the surface of the test machine (usually a roadwheel), the data recorded at the tire spindle are actually the "open circuit" force and moment variations that will excite the vehicle.

An example of this type of behavior is shown in Figs. 56 and 57. A belted

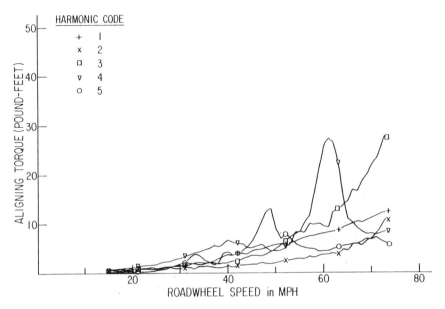

FIG. 56—*High-speed uniformity machine results on Tire 1, first five harmonics of aligning torque variation* [69].

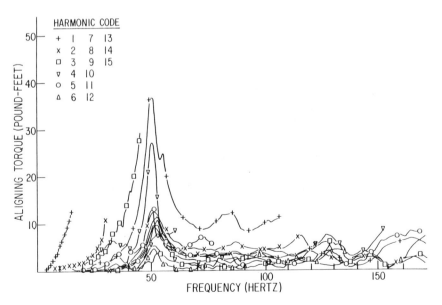

FIG. 57—*High-speed uniformity machine results on Tire 1, all harmonics of aligning torque variation* [69].

bias tire was run on a HSUM and the force and moment variations at the spindle were recorded over the speed range of 15 to 75 mph (24 to 121 km/h). For this particular tire the rotational rate was very nearly 1 rps for every 5 mph (8 km/h) speed increment. That is, at 50 mph (80 km/h) the tire was rotating at a rate of 10 Hz. The first harmonic of any force or moment variation would thus have a frequency of 10 Hz, the second harmonic a frequency of 20 Hz, the third harmonic 30 Hz, and so forth, at 50 mph (80 km/h). In Fig. 56, the first five harmonics of aligning torque variation are given as a function of speed. Note that the fourth harmonic peaks at 62 mph (100 km/h) and the fifth harmonic peaks at 48 mph (77 km/h). These peaks are an indication that a tire resonance was being excited by the third and fourth harmonics. (This type of behavior may also be due to a poorly designed HISUM having some spurious resonances in the frequency range of interest, but such is not the case here.) The tire resonance behavior is more clearly shown in Fig. 57. The strong peak at about 52 Hz is the first resonant mode of vibration of the tire in the aligning torque direction (essentially the moment about the steering axis of the tire). Note that aligning torque resonance is excited by each and every harmonic of the aligning torque variation (the speed was never sufficiently high to permit the first three harmonics to fully excite the resonance). Similiar data would normally be available for radial force, tractive force (longitudinal), lateral force, and camber moment variation.

As we saw in the previous section, tire shake is caused by the first harmonic of (usually) radial force variation, a force variation that occurs once per tire revolution. We might logically expect, therefore, that since tire roughness is a higher frequency ride disturbance it should be caused by some higher harmonic force or moment variation. If a vehicle is traveling at 60 mph (97 km/h), for the tires in this example, the second harmonic of any force or moment variation would exhibit a frequency of about 24 Hz (2 × 12 rps), the third harmonic a frequency of 36 Hz, and so forth. Since by definition tire roughness is a ride disturbance with a frequency greater than 20 Hz, harmonics of order two or greater would be likely candidates as the source of the problem. Combining this information with that from the previous paragraph, we may surmise that tire roughness will be particularly disturbing in certain speed ranges. Specifically, tire roughness will likely be most disturbing at or near those speeds where the harmonic of some force or moment variation is exciting some tire resonance and hence providing a lot of vibrational energy to the vehicle. But this still does not tell us exactly which force or moment variation (or all of them) is the real culprit. For the answer to this question we must consider the vibrational response of the vehicle.

Earlier in this paper we found that a vehicle can exhibit a lot of different types of vibrational behavior. For tire roughness, however, we are primarily interested in the vibrational behavior of the steering wheel since this is where a driver will normally detect the problem if it exists. The manner in which vibrational energy is transmitted from the spindle of the vehicle to the steering

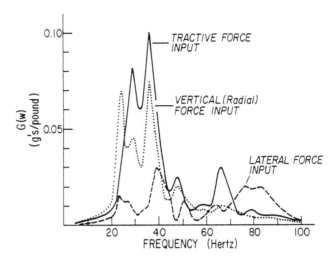

FIG. 58—*Transfer functions for test vehicle as determined by hydraulic exciter tests:* G(w) = *steering wheel acceleration/spindle axle force* [68].

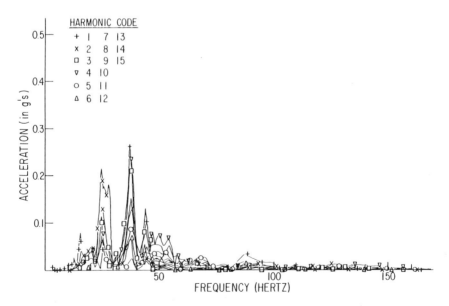

FIG. 59—*Instrumented vehicle results on Tire 1, vibration of steering wheel in fore-and-aft direction for Vehicle A* [69].

wheel and the modes of vibration of the steering wheel itself are the dominant factors involved. Figure 58 shows the transmissibility between the spindle and the steering wheel in the three principal directions for a particular test vehicle [68]. (There was no direct way to impose a pure moment to the spindle of the vehicle.) A number of different resonances can be seen in this figure. The peak that occurs in the vertical input curve at about 22 Hz is the wheel hop mode for this vehicle. This peak would be responsible for any tire shake ride disturbance and need not concern us here. The peaks at 28 and 38 Hz, and above, however, are related to tire roughness. These peaks are true resonances of the steering wheel and would be excited to a greater or lesser extent depending on the amplitude of the force and moment variations at the tire spindle. An example of the actual steering wheel vibrations is shown in Fig. 59.

Using HISUM data for a number of different tires and vehicle response curves similiar to that shown in Fig. 59, Marshall et al. [68,69] rigorously analyzed the complete tire/vehicle system. By performing a cross-correlation between the force variation data and the vehicle response curves they found that the predominant cause of tire roughness in bias-belted or radial tires was tractive force variation. The details of the mathematics employed are fairly complex and will not be dealt with here. It is possible, however, to obtain a "feeling" for why tractive force variation emerged as the most important cause of tire roughness.

In Figs. 60 through 62, the vehicle transmissibility data from Fig. 58 is plotted in overlay fashion with the force variation data from the HSUM for the radial tires [68]. The data for the variation in the moments are not shown since they had a negligible influence on tire roughness for the vehicle tested.

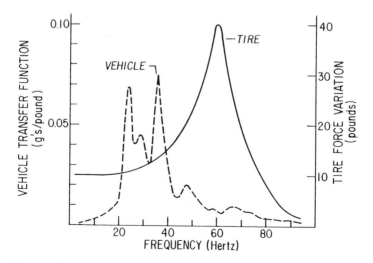

FIG. 60—*Vertical (radial) direction, tire input and vehicle transfer function* [68].

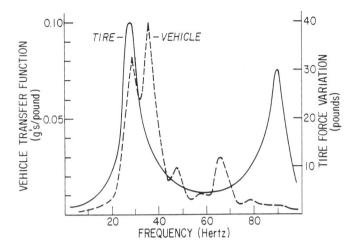

FIG. 61—*Tractive (fore and aft) direction, tire input and vehicle transfer function* [68].

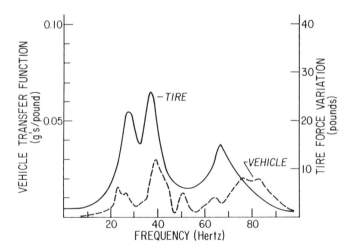

FIG. 62—*Lateral (side to side) direction, tire input and vehicle transfer function* [68].

The curves shown for the tire in each graph are "typical," in that they are representative of the actual test tires with respect to resonant frequency and force amplitude. An approximate measure of the contribution of each force variation to tire roughness can be obtained by multiplying the vehicle transfer function by the tire force variation at each frequency. The results of this multiplication are given in Fig. 63. The reader is cautioned that this calculation is not a rigorous treatment of the problem. By directly multiplying the tire force

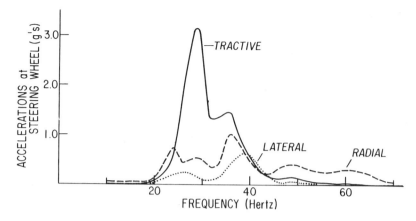

FIG. 63—*Predicted steering wheel accelerations, contribution of tractive, radial and lateral force variations are shown separately* [68].

by the vehicle transmissibility we are essentially assuming that there is a perfect impedance match between the tire and the vehicle in every direction. That is, we are assuming that all the energy from the tire would be transferred to the vehicle without any attenuation or distortion. This is certainly not true, but the results are directionally correct and quite illuminating. Most importantly, Fig. 63 predicts that tractive force variation is the most important contributor to tire roughness, a result identical to that found by the more accurate cross-correlation method discussed in the preceding paragraph.

An examination of Figs. 60 through 62 reveals the basic mechanism of tire roughness. For those situations where the tire and the vehicle have resonances that are closely aligned, the energy generated by the tire will be easily transmitted into the vehicle and cause tire roughness. This situation is most prevalent in the tractive direction since the tire and vehicle resonances are essentially superimposed at 28 Hz. We would be quite justified, therefore, in believing that this should be a major cause of tire roughness, and indeed it is. For the radial direction case the resonances are separated by a considerable margin, thus minimizing the tendency for energy transmission. In the lateral direction there is a coincidence of tire and vehicle resonances at 38 Hz, but two factors serve to minimize the importance of these lateral inputs. First, the lateral force variation level and the vehicle transmissibility are both quite low, at least when compared to those in the tractive direction. And second, if we refer back to human sensitivity curves given earlier in this report, we can see that, all other things being equal, the tractive input at 28 Hz would be more disturbing to the vehicle passengers than the lateral input at 38 Hz. The lateral direction is thus of considerably less importance to tire roughness than is the tractive direction. Turning once again to Fig. 63, we can now fully understand why tractive force variation is the primary cause of tire roughness, an understanding that could only be achieved by performing a complete analysis of the tire/vehicle system. That is, the coincidence of a tire and a vehicle resonance is a prescription for disaster, a virtual guarantee that a ride complaint will be forthcoming. And finally, if we recall (see Ref *68*) that essentially every vehicle exhibits steering wheel/column resonances in the frequency range of 20 to 40 Hz, we may conclude that tractive force variation will be the primary cause of tire roughness in all vehicles.

Tire Harshness

The term, tire harshness, refers to a ride disturbance that is defined as [*93*]:

Vibrations (15-100 Hz.) perceived tactily and/or audibly, produced by the interaction of the tire and road irregularities.

If a vehicle tire encounters a road irregularity, such as a tar strip or a pavement discontinuity, vibrations will be generated at the tire/road interface, transmitted into the vehicle, and possibly disturb the passengers. If the disturbance is detected tactily it is called tire harshness. If the disturbance is perceived audibly it is usually called "impact boom" (or some similar term). The topic of this section of the paper is tire harshness.

From a dynamics point of view, tire roughness and tire harshness have more commonalities than differences. As a matter of fact, the only really significant difference between them is the source of the excitation and character of the response produced in the vehicle. Roughness is caused by imperfections in the structure of the tire and is subjectively perceived to be a steady state ride disturbance (at least if one is driving at a constant speed where the problem is significant). Harshness, on the other hand, is caused by road irregularities and is perceived to be a transient or impulsive burst of vibrational energy, usually felt in the steering wheel, but also occasionally on the floorpan of the vehicle. This transient disturbance has a very rapid rise time (nearly instantaneous) and decays away to an undetectable level after a few tenths of a second. Aside from these differences, however, roughness and harshness are one and the same problem. The tire resonances, the vehicle resonances, and the tire/vehicle interaction are identical in both cases. When viewed from this perspective, we can discuss and understand tire harshness with little difficulty. The relevant references are *50, 68*, and *147-149*. We begin with a short summarization of some pertinent information.

1. In the section of this paper on tire enveloping we found that for the case of a short bump, for example, a tar strip or a pavement discontinuity:

(a) The enveloping of a bump by a tire is a nonlinear process. The forces generated at the axle are not related in any simple way to the physical dimensions of the bump.

(b) The principal vibrational frequencies observed were the first mode of vibration in the radial or tractive direction. For a radial tire, depending on type and size, this implies 60 to 90 Hz in the vertical (radial) direction, and 24 to 30 Hz in the tractive direction.

2. In the section of this paper on tire roughness we found:

(a) The primary cause of tire roughness was tractive force variation, principally because the resonance of the tire in the tractive direction coincided with resonances of the steering wheel.

(b) Virtually all vehicles will possess steering wheel/column resonances in the frequency range of 20 to 40 Hz.

There is one other piece of information that is required before we can completely understand tire harshness. And that is how tire harshness varies as a function of vehicle speed. Figure 64 [50] shows how the longitudinal (or tractive) and vertical spindle forces vary as a function of speed when a tire encounters a small bump (cleat) attached to a roadwheel, with the tire axle held at a fixed distance from the roadwheel. The data plotted at each speed are the maximum transient force level detected during the passage of the bump through contact. Note that in the vertical direction the maximum force is realized at a speed of about 50 km/h (31 mph), and in the tractive direction at about 40 km/h (25 mph). We can gain an understanding of these results by referring to Figs. 28 and 29 from the enveloping part of this paper. These figures show that at a speed of 35 km/h the passage of the bump through tire

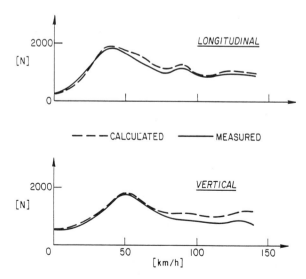

FIG. 64—*Maximum force peak for roadwheel cleat impact tests* [50].

contact is exciting the vertical and tractive resonances of the tire. But since a small bump approximates the application of an impulsive force to the tire, there is a certain amount of excitation supplied to the tire at its resonant frequencies for any speed. At some speed, however, the spectral content of the bump will provide maximum excitation at the resonant frequency of the tire, and the tire will respond most strongly. The peaks of the curves in Fig. 64 are an indication of this situation.

This is all well and good, but we still have not really shown that what we measure on the roadwheel is definitely the source of the problem. "Are these roadwheel forces really what causes tire harshness?" To do this we must take a look at the vehicle. In Fig. 65 we show some results from actual vehicle studies [147]. The vehicle was driven on a test track such that the wheels on the left side of the vehicle encountered a small bump embedded in the track surface. The vibrations observed on the steering wheel at various speeds are given in Fig. 65. Note that the steering wheel vibrations reached a maximum value at about 20 mph (32 km/h) (suspiciously close to the speed range where the roadwheel forces peaked in the paragraph above, albeit for experiments carried out by different experimenters many years apart). Roadwheel tests were also conducted during these experiments, and the results are shown in Fig. 66. Note that the tire forces peak at about 20 mph (32 km/h), a perfect match for the vehicle results (the upward slope in the roadwheel data above 30 mph [48 km/h] was the result of a test machine resonance at approximately 140 Hz). The final piece of evidence is given in Fig. 67. Here the subjective perception of the harshness is plotted against the steering wheel vibrations at 20 mph (32 km/h). The worst harshness disturbance invariably occurred at this speed for the test vehicle. Clearly, the passage of the bump through contact excited various tire resonances, and these produced the maximum harshness disturbance at a speed of 20 mph (32 km/h). For other tires

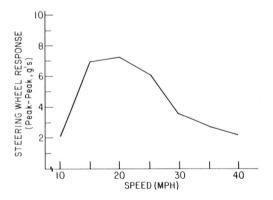

FIG. 65—*Steering wheel response to ¹/₂-in. (1.27-cm) cleat impact* [147].

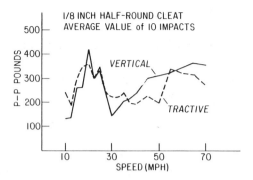

FIG. 66—*Roadwheel cleat impact, ⅛ in. (0.318 cm) half-round cleat* [147].

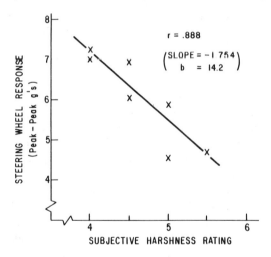

FIG. 67—*Subjective evaluation versus vehicle response, 20 mph (32 km/h)* [147].

and vehicles, the maximum harshness disturbance could occur for speeds from 20 to 30 mph (32 to 48 km/h).

Putting toegther all these various bits of information, we may state the following about tire harshness. Tire harshness is the result of a vehicle tire enveloping a small road irregularity such as a tar strip or a pavement discontinuity. The road irregularity transiently excites certain tire resonances that result in transient vibrational force inputs at the spindle of the vehicle. These spindle vibrations subsequently excite resonances of the steering wheel which disturbs the passengers. The maximum harshness disturbance will normally occur in the speed range of 20 to 30 mph (32 to 48 km/h).

Exterior Noise from Tire/Pavement Interaction

In this section particular attention is paid to work on the mechanisms responsible for generating tire/pavement interaction as observed at the roadside. This is a systems problem within the overall systems problem of environmental noise. The environmental and human response aspects of this topic are not emphasized. This was done for brevity, not because we wished to ignore the importance of the many field investigations of vehicle coastbys that have been conducted. These on-road experiments have provided us with an evaluation of where tire/pavement interaction noise stands relative to overall vehicle noise from various highway vehicles [*150*], and showed us, furthermore, what a wide variability to expect as a function of pavement type [*151*]. These matters have been fairly well established, however, and the more pressing questions now have to do with what makes the noise and what can be done about it from the standpoints of the pavement engineer and the designers of tires and vehicles. Several investigations have been undertaken over the past 15 years or more to explore the noise generating mechanisms in tire/pavement interaction.

It has been recognized (and was stated explicitly by Heckl [*152*]) that noise is a second order byproduct of tire/pavement interaction processes involving transfers of amounts of energy several orders of magnitude larger than the acoustic energy produced. It is not surprising, therefore, that changes in parameters of the tire and pavement that mean only a few percentage points difference in, say, rolling resistance or traction, can dramatically change the amount of noise produced. The wide variability of noise as pavement texture is changed [*151*] is an obvious example.

Some part of the first order energy transfer is probably present as pseudo-sound. Air flow caused by vehicle motion and tire rotation will produce local turbulent pressure variations that radiate little sound at typical vehicle speeds. Nonetheless, this pseudo-sound is sensed by microphones placed too close to the moving vehicle or, in laboratory installations, to the tire. At low frequencies even some of the vibration-induced and air-pumping-induced pressure fluctuations may be pseudo-sound. Heckl [*153*] talks about the pair of opposing monopoles (simple radiating points, radiating spherical waves), one delayed from the other, accounting for the air squeeze and suction as a tire cavity enters and then leaves the contact patch. Some nonradiating cross flow must be present here.

The air pumping mechanism in tire/pavement interaction noise was among the earliest to have been modeled [*154*]. Its manifestations have been discussed and debated ever since. As a starting point we call attention to the work of Wilken et al. [*155*], at the General Motors Research Laboratory (GMRL). These investigators ran careful experiments with a single-wheel trailer in order to assess both the aerodynamic noise generation (turbulence and vortex shedding) and the air pumping process at the tire/pavement interface. Their investigation showed that tire aerodynamic sources are insignificant in highway noise considerations. With a flow visualization technique (an array of tufts suspended from a screen in the wake of the test tire), they showed that vortex shedding did not appear in any pronounced way.

With regard to air pumping mechanisms, Wilken et al. demonstrated significant effects. The sound pressure field 0.6 m from the contact patch showed definite impulses when the specially cut single cross-cavity of the test tire entered and left the contact patch. Furthermore, just following the entry impulse, a damped-resonant-like ringing was observed. When the cavity was filled with foam rubber, other things remaining the same, the ringing was no longer observed, and the entrance impulse itself was somewhat reduced.

Their investigation showed a very considerable variation in the height and shape of the entrance and exit impulses as a function of microphone position, from behind, to opposite, to in front of the tire at comparable (0.6 m) distance. The effect of the foam in quenching the ringing was tested on a commercial 10.00-20 crossbar tire (all cavities were filled). A dramatic (5 to 10 dB) reduction in far field noise spectrum levels resulted over a band from about 600 to about 1750 Hz (microphone $\approx$ 3 m out and 1 m up from the contact patch). Unfortunately, this is not a practical addition to a real tire because it would interfer with wet traction performance and not endure.

In discussing air pumping mechanisms for a lug tire, there is a tendency to consider the volume change as if it occurred at constant cavity width. Since the lug elements must experience radial compressive stress and since rubber is nearly incompressible, there must be a circumferential squeezing or flattening of the lugs, thus reducing cavity volumes. In addition, of course, there will be a radial "rigid body" component of lug displacement that is countered by sidewall yielding. This is shown clearly in the simultaneous lug and sidewall acceleration record taken by Eberhardt in his investigations [156].

Eberhardt is a proponent of the thesis that most tire/pavement interaction noise is explainable by tire vibrations excited by pavement texture. He has shown that tire vibrations decay almost completely over the first 10 to 20 cm of tire circumference after the exit point on the contact patch. He models the vibration process as the vibration of a semi-infinite beam, excited near one end with a rapidly decaying excitation. His beam is in tension and is resiliently supported in order to account for pneumatic pressure and sidewall constraints, respectively. In the discussion of his paper [156] some question was raised about his choice of beam solutions and particularly about matching the boundary condition of zero bending wave velocity in the contact patch. It appears that he may need a reflected wave there, perhaps of both the traveling wave part of his solution and the bending wave near field.

Nilsson et al. [157] have summarized interpretations of observations made by various IFM Akoustikbyran investigators over several years [158–161] in the following way. First, they distinguish two frequency regimes, one below about 800 Hz, the other above, say 1000 Hz. The noise mechanism descriptors they have identified differ in these two regimes. In the lower frequency regime they show there is a pavement-to-pavement variation in noise spectrum levels that may be predicted reasonably well from the road roughness wave number spectra [33] of these pavements. The actual portion of the wave number spectra that is important depends on the vehicle speed. Predictions are improved when the shape of the wave number spectrum is adjusted by two filter functions, one to account for the enveloping action of the finite contact patch length, and one to account for the transfer function between tread forcing and sidewall velocity. The first filter function is an arbitrary but effective construction based on geometrical considerations. The second filter function was derived from imposing a footprint excitation on a stationary tire as Potts and Csora did [45]. They claim that in this frequency range, a considerable portion of the carcass vibrates. Moreover, they find that the observed sound pressure is coherent with the vibrations. As further evidence supporting their point of view, they cite the result of filling the test tire with soft rubber instead of air. The measured noise spectrum levels are reduced by doing so by some 8 dB over a frequency range from about 400 to about 1100 Hz. The reduction is attributed to reduced vibration levels. Sandberg [162,163] too, discusses the texture-to-noise relationship in the low frequency range and supports the vibration source argument.

At frequencies about 1000 Hz or so, Nilsson et al. [157] found that the noise processes at contact patch entry and contact patch exit became independent of one another. Different generating mechanisms come into play at the two different locations.

At the exit location they find that the noise spectrum above 1 kHz is dominated by a chirp-like (frequency varying) resonant burst. They postulate a Helmholz resonance effect with varying compliance and air mass elements. The compliance, they say, is that of the cavity comprising their specially cut lateral groove (curved to match the rear shape of the contact patch). The "neck" of the resonator, they say, is the restricted (and opening) access passage to the cavity as it moves out of the contact patch. Both the compliance and the air mass in the restriction are time varying, so the resonant ringdown is frequency varying (much the same as the oscillations of a swing whose ropes are continuously shortened).

A microphone placed near the rear of the contact patch shows a frequency varying ringdown in accord with calculations on the investigators model. Initial excitation for the resonance, according to Nilsson et al. [157] is the tangential tread snap, as the tread surface is released by the pavement on exit from the contact patch. As supporting arguments, they cite observations that noise spectrum levels are reduced in the chirp frequency range when talc is injected into the contact patch, thus reducing adhesion forces, while braking action, with increased tangential stress, increases noise. Also, in support of the air-resonant model as the cause of the chirp, they cite the observed quenching of the chirp noise when helium is flooded into the exit region.

The entrance area noise mechanism, according to Nilsson et al. [157], is a tread slap-down effect, wherein air is quickly driven out from beneath successive tread elements. To support the hypothesis the investigators demonstrated that high-frequency spectrum levels were higher on concrete than on asphalt pavement in the same proportion as were spectrum levels of noise from rubber hammer blows to the same surfaces.

The IFM investigations gave considerable emphasis to the concept of synchronous triggering and the separation of so-called tire-periodic effects from pavement-periodic effects. These designations were first enunciated by Pope and Reynolds [164]. The latter authors, incidently, caution that each of the periodic effects mentioned may depend on both the road and the tire characteristics. Nevertheless, there is a tendency to say that what shows up as "road-periodic" on a drum test depends only on the road, while that which is "tire-periodic" depends only on the tire. These are inferences to be examined carefully. Moreover, one is generally interested in noise in a frequency range containing high order harmonics of tire or drum rotation rates. Even small triggering errors from rotation to rotation can spoil the correct rendition of harmonic amplitudes in this region.

It should be noted that the cavity resonance effect discussed by Nilsson et al. of IFM [157] is a different effect from that noted by Wilken et al. [155] at GMRL and discussed earlier. The GMRL observation was a ringdown following entrance of the cavity into the contact patch. The ringdown actually decayed almost fully before the cavity exited the contact patch. Foam filling, which had been successful in reducing noise from the GMRL experiment, was unsuccessful in the IFM experiment (the IFM investigators say that the reason for the lack of effect is that in the exit phenomenon the cavity is just the compliance in the Helmholz resonator, so that impeding air particle velocity there is not effective. In a quarter wave resonator, on the other hand, particle velocity in at least the outer part of the resonator is high).

It should be especially noted that all IFM observations pertain to tires of passenger car size while the GMRL tests pertained to truck tires.

While much of the discussion of air-pumping and cavity resonating phenomena has pertained to the cross lug tire, some mention has been made of the contact-patch-entrapped portion of the longitudinal groove as a resonant "groove-pipe" cavity. The existence of such resonances seems plausible in view of Pope and Reynold's ability to quench a broad, speed-independent, noise peak around 1500 Hz in their rib tire just by wrapping ordinary knitting yarn in the circumferential grooves [164]. Plotkin et al. have made a (static) measurement of cavity volume change of rib cavities within the contact patch. They do not discuss "groove-pipe resonance" phenomenon in these terms, but they suggest that constricted flow through the groove may be an excitation function for it [165].

The belief that pavement texture is responsible for tire vibrations, which, in turn, generate noise, has increasingly aroused interest in texture characterization and in the development of some "standard" test textures that may be meaningful in a broad range of tire testing. Sandberg and Eismont [166] report, vis-a-vis, the current status of the European community's efforts in this direction, that two surfaces are under serious consideration as standard surfaces at this time, characterized by differences in their wave number spectra in the 2- to 200-mm wavelength regimes.

The acoustic and mechanical properties of pavement surfaces have been studied, and it has been argued [167] that when the mechanical impedance (or the mechanical mobility) of the pavement beneath the contact patch is comparable to that of the tire itself, the pavement will partake of the vibrations and exact vibrational energy from the tire. IFM (A. Koustikbyran) has actually patented a special pavement surface design incorporating this feature [168]. The design also embodies a porosity that allows acoustic absorption of sound radiation and reduces air-resonant effects in the tire cavities. Such quiet pavement designs have been advocated by Walker and others as well [169].

The acoustic absorption of pavement surfaces influences tire/pavement noise not only in the generation processes, but in propagation to far field microphones. Especially for sources as close to ground level as tire/pavement interaction sources, the sound reflections from absorptive pavement, and even more, from any absorptive terrain adjacent to the pavement, well modify the direct source-to-receive propagation by partially destructive interference [170]. Generally, the effect is felt at frequencies above about 500 Hz. In some instances, the effect is as large as that of a noise barrier erected between the receiver and the highway.

Although special pavement designs as well as special tire designs have been suggested as methods for reducing exterior vehicle noise, the trade-offs in following such suggestions have not been fully weighed. The designs seem to be in part based on intuition, bolstered by observations such as have been reported above. The modeling of tire/pavement interaction noise processes has clearly been advanced in the last 15 years, but findings still seem rather fragmented and controversy still remains.

A report on tire/pavement interaction noise would be remiss if it did not call attention to the resourceful experimental setups that have been developed by the investigators in the area. The use of helium injection to change the sound velocity and the use of talc on the pavement surface to reduce adhesive forces have been mentioned above, as have the experiments with foam-filled cavities and rubber-filled tires (see also M. Richards' paper [171] for a note on runs on a water-filled tire). Not mentioned specifically have been the various investigators' use of special hand-cut treads to isolate one effect or another. There may be danger in concluding too much about real tires from tires with such specially cut treads, but they serve as an excellent means of testing the predictions of models of the processes they seek to enhance.

The IFM Akoustikhyran use of the textured internal drum at the Bundes-anstalt fur Strassenwesen, in Rodenkirchen, and their use, there, of the laser doppler velocemeter (LDV) for tire vibrational velocity measurements [158] deserves special mention. The LDV measures vibrational velocity in an Euler-ian reference frame, unlike that characterizing velocities deduced from accel-erometers moving with the tire. It is not clear how easy it is to change the spot at which the LDV "looks," so as to map the velocity field. If this can be done readily, the results should be useful in further testing the theory of the vibra-tion mechanisms.

Expectations have been raised that it may be possible, soon, if not already, to reconstruct the sound field close to and even on the tire, or test vehicle, as well as the radiated sound field, all just from measurements over a dense area of microphones placed in a plane a short distance from the tire [172]. This would be very useful indeed.

There have been some ingenious accelerometer setups, in vibration testing, too. Eberhardt's telemetering system [156], which avoids the need for slip rings, is noteworthy, and the hub mounted preamplification of accelerometer outputs before delivery of the signals to the slip rings is an essential feature of other experiments [173]. Finally, attention should be drawn to the way that the various investigators avoided noise reflections from their own apparatus and, in the laboratory experiments, from the walls of the test room. This iso-lation is necessary, and its demonstrated satisfactory performance should be part of any investigation.

In-Car Noise

This section of the review discusses the part of the vehicle interior noise that is generated by the tire/pavement interaction. It does not include noise gener-ated by the engine, driveline, wind, and so forth. Unfortunately, the litera-ture on interior vehicle noise is not abundant, and further, the number of "clean" experiments (those where tire/pavement noise is the only stimuli present) is even smaller.

It will be shown later that the loudest sounds induced in the car by the tire/pavement interaction are due to the excitation of the interior cavity by struc-ture-borne energy. Thus, while the principals of vehicle cavity acoustics are not part of this review, the physics of enclosed spaces cannot be completely ignored. Therefore, we will begin with a brief discussion of vehicle cavity characteristics such as resonant frequencies.

Resonant frequencies of an enclosed space are usually difficult to calculate. However, for a rectangular room having smooth, hard walls, the computa-tions are relatively simple. If L, W, and H are the length, width, and height of a rectangular room, the room resonant frequencies f can be obtained from the following formula

$$f = \frac{c}{2}\left[\left(\frac{p}{L}\right)^2 + \left(\frac{q}{W}\right)^2 + \left(\frac{r}{H}\right)^2\right]^{1/2} \quad \text{cycles/s} \quad (8)$$

where p, q, and r are integers and specify the mode of vibration, and c is the velocity of sound.

Clearly, one would not want, for instance, a cubic shaped vehicle cavity because the resonant frequencies would fall on top of each other. The shape of the vehicle cavity should ideally be such that there is a uniform distribution of the natural frequencies. However, vehicle designers are constrained from using ideal shapes by many factors. Design considerations for acceptable cavity shapes can be found in books on architectural acoustics [174]. If the wavelengths of the sounds occurring in the low-frequency audible part of the spectrum are comparable to or even less than the interior dimensions of a typical vehicle, it can be shown that the cavity will have clearly defined resonances and standing wave patterns.

Generally speaking, the simple axial modes formed by the reflection from two parallel surfaces are responsible for the "boom" phenomena in the vehicle cavity [93]. Boom can be excited in the vehicle by engine noise, powertrain vibration, road roughness, tire roughness or all of these. Whether axial modes, tangential, or oblique modes, are a problem or not will depend on the degree of excitation of the mode, the location of the listener, the frequency content of the noise sources, and the band width of the mode. Tangential modes are those that have only one zero (that is, p, q, or r) in Eq 8 whereas the oblique modes have no zeros [175].

Equation 8 is for calculating resonant frequencies of a hard walled rectangular cavity. However, a change in shape or boundary conditions of the cavity from a simple rectangular hard walled cavity will shift the resonant frequencies of the normal modes and their mode shape making computations very difficult. However, even though an analytical solution is impossible for an arbitrary shaped vehicle cavity with complex boundary conditions, the modes can be calculated by using the finite-element method.

Wolf et al. [176] calculated the natural frequencies and mode shapes for a station wagon (Figs. 68 and 69). Wolf's excellent paper was followed by a series of papers on finite-element modeling of cavity resonances [111,

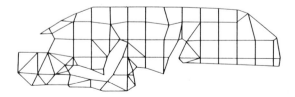

FIG. 68—*Finite-element model of station wagon passenger compartment* [176].

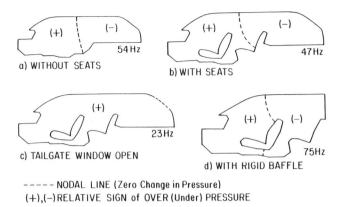

a) WITHOUT SEATS   54 Hz

b) WITH SEATS   47 Hz

c) TAILGATE WINDOW OPEN   23 Hz

d) WITH RIGID BAFFLE   75 Hz

```
----- NODAL LINE (Zero Change in Pressure)
(+),(-)RELATIVE SIGN of OVER (Under) PRESSURE
```

FIG. 69—*Acoustic mode shapes for four configurations of a station wagon* [176].

113,177–179]. Bearing in mind the importance of cavity resonances to the whole problem of in the car noise, we plan to begin our review with a discussion of road roar.

In 1957, Apps authored Chapter 13 of Ref *180*. Apps' discussion of road rumble or roar is the starting point of our discussion. It is part of his discussion of many topics, some of which we will not discuss, and is particularly germane to problems observed when bias tires are fitted. Only bias tires were in use in the United States at the time Apps wrote, and most automobiles he discussed had frames.

According to Apps [*180*] road roar started to become a serious problem in the 1930s. This noise results from vibration of the tire that is excited by a roughened road surface. The vibration is transmitted through the tire, spindle, and suspension system to the vehicle body, which in turn radiates noise into the passenger compartment. Road roar is a particular part of road roughness induced noise.

Weiner [*181*] indicated how significant road roughness induced noise could be (Fig. 70). Apps [*180*] stated road roar, a limited part of the problem indicated by Weiner [*181*], has a frequency range limited to 100 to 200 Hz, and the frequency range is independent of road speed. Phillips [*38*] also observed that the frequency was independent of road speed. However, Phillips indicated that the dominant frequency range is 30 to 300 Hz (Fig. 71). This broader range may reflect both the coming of the radial tire with its lower resonance frequencies and changes in the vehicle structure.

The reduction of road noise inside the passenger compartment to acceptable levels is difficult. There are a number of components (tire, suspension, bushings, and so forth) in the vibration path from the road to the passenger, and all of these including the body structure can require adjustment. Some control is possible in framed cars by use of rubber body mounts. For all cars

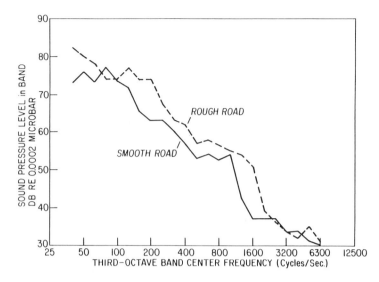

FIG. 70—*Noise spectra inside an automobile at 60 mph (97 km/h) with windows closed* [181].

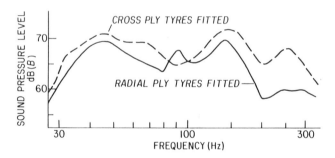

FIG. 71— *Vehicle interior noise* [38].

both framed and unibodied isolation by suspension bushings is crucial (Fig. 39). However, as previously mentioned, only limited isolation by suspension bushings is possible because handling and stability characteristics of the car must be maintained. Damping materials can be applied to the body with some degree of success (Fig. 72). Sound absorbing materials can also be applied to the interior of the car and a small amount of road noise reduction can be achieved. Equation 9 allows one to estimate the reduction

$$\text{dB reduction} = 10 \log A_2/A_1 \qquad (9)$$

where A_1 is the number of absorption units before treatment, and A_2 is the number after treatment.

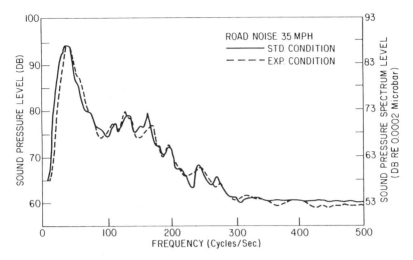

FIG. 72—*Road noise: frequency analyses showing effect of spray-on damping material applied to certain sheet metal areas of 1954 sedan (see text). Flat weighting network. Microphone in right front seat. Speed 35 mph (56 km/h) on coarse-textured road, 5 cps passband* [180].

In 1972, Phillips [38] proposed that mathematical models be constructed to represent the various components in the transmission path (tire → body). These models would allow parametric design studies showing the expected improvement in the suppression of road noise caused by design modifications. However, in spite of the progress in modeling, road noise continues to be a problem today. And even with considerable system design and analysis, considerable experimentation is still required to obtain a satisfactory suppression of road texture induced noise in individual vehicle designs.

Tire roughness, like road roughness, is also a source of vehicle interior noise. Tire roughness has its source in the tire nonuniformities discussed earlier. The frequency range associated with tire roughness is from 15 to 100 Hz, so that it usually causes boom. According to Apps [180], tire roughness began to be a problem in some cars around 1950. Tire roughness is both heard and felt. The roughness effects we feel were discussed in detail earlier.

Tire roughness as a source of boom is discussed in Refs 66 and 67. Audible manifestations caused by tire roughness are associated with higher order tire nonuniformities (usually 3rd, 4th, and 5th harmonics). The same comments as those about the need to use experimentation to suppress pavement roughness induced noise apply to the problem of tire roughness induced noise. Reliable measurement techniques are crucial to the required experiments. Unfortunately, measures of noisiness, which correlate very well with subjective annoyance caused by noise, are not available. This greatly complicates experimental studies that are intended to produce an automobile interior in which conversation or radio listening can be accomplished comfortably [182].

Ford et al. [*182*] set out to establish a measurement procedure that would determine the noisiness (a single-number rating system) for the interior noise of a vehicle. They did not try to compare different vehicles or establish that a particular noise level would be unacceptable. They used six different brands of vehicles of varying age and condition in a combined subjective and objective experiment. Ford et al. compared various measures of the total interior noise (not just tire/pavement interaction generated noise) in the vehicles with the subjective ratings of 12 ride jurors. Since they were not making comparisons between cars, it was not necessary for them to use the same tires on each vehicle, and it was not necessary to have the cars in the same mechanical condition. The measured noise data were operated on to prepare graphs of noise level in Steven's phons, Zwicker phons, dB(A), dB(B), noise criterion curves (NC), speech interference level (SIL), and noise rating number R arranged in order of subjective preference from quiet to noisy. Figure 73 is a

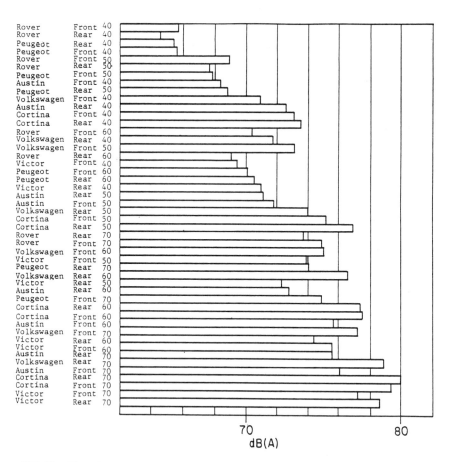

FIG. 73—*The noise levels in dB(A) in order of subjective preference from quiet to noisy* [182].

typical example of the type of correlation obtained. It shows dB(A) as a function of subjective ranking. Similar jaggedness is seen using the other measures. The smoothness of the plot is an indication of the degree of correlation.

Table 4 shows the Spearman rank correlation coefficient for each objective measure. Ford et al. applied the Fisher test [183] to the correlation coefficients, and there is no meaningful difference between the Zwicker phons, the Stevens phons, dB(A), and dB(B), nor is there a meaningful difference between NC, SIL, and R numbers. These results indicate a number of different objective measures can be used to rate noisiness in vehicles but that there is considerable uncertainty in the correlation to subjective opinion for any of the measures they tried. Zwicker phons, Stevens phons, dB(A), and dB(B) appear to all be acceptable for use as measures of noisiness. However, acceptability criteria would have to be established if one wished to use any of the above measures for rating noisiness.

Underwood and Solomon [184], obtained some interesting data on interior noise for ten different cars. Their data agree qualitatively and to some degree quantitatively with that of Apps [180]. Unfortunately, again there are no pure tire/pavement interaction noise data in the experiments that consider idling automobiles in an open space, automobiles driving a constant 15 mph (24 km/h) on a gravel road, automobiles driving a constant 35 mph (56 km/h) on a smooth asphalt street in a residential area, and automobiles driving a constant 70 mph (113 km/h) on a smooth concrete expressway. All measurements were taken with the microphone situated at ear level in the center of the front seat and at the same location along the different test roads.

Figure 74 represents the dB(A) level for each car under the four different test conditions: (a) idling, (b) traveling at 15 mph (24 km/h) on a gravel road, (c) traveling at 35 mph (56 km/h) on an asphalt road, and (d) traveling at 70 mph (113 km/h) on the expressway. The average of the sound pressure level for each test condition is plotted against speed in Fig. 75. Clearly, the noise level inside the vehicles increases linearly with speed. Figure 76 presents the spectral analysis for each vehicle in the residential street test. The spectra from all tests appear similar to those in Fig. 76 and resemble the equal loud-

TABLE 4—*Correlation between subjective ratings and objective units* [182].

Objective Unit	Spearman Rank Correlation Coefficient
Zwicker phons	0.89
Stevens phons	0.86
dB(A)	0.86
dB(B)	0.86
Noise criterion	0.79
Speech interference level	0.78
Noise rating number	0.77

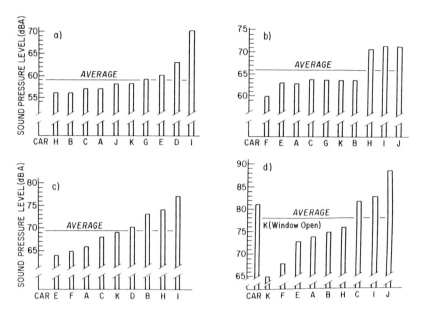

FIG. 74—*SPL of automobiles* (a) *idling;* (b) *traveling at 15 mph (24 km/h) on a gravel road;* (c) *traveling at 35 mph (56 km/h) on an asphalt road;* (d) *traveling at 70 mph (113 km/h) on an expressway. A-scale-frequency weighting was used for all* [184].

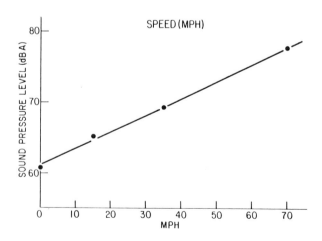

FIG. 75—*Average SPLs for all test conditions shown in Fig. 74* [184].

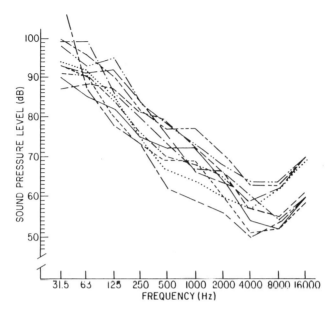

FIG. 76—*SPL of automobiles at preferred frequencies traveling over an asphalt road at 35 mph (56 km/h)* [184].

ness contours (Fig. 45) and the noise criteria curves that are commonly seen in the acoustics field. The loudness for each test was computed and is compared with equal loudness contours shown in Fig. 77. The perceived noise level in phons shown in Fig. 77 would seem to indicate that to a human being, all interior automobile noise would appear to be roughly broad band. Loudness ranges from 50 phons at idling, 55 phons on the gravel, 59 phons on the asphalt, and 76 phons on the expressway. As a point of clarification, the phon level at 1000 cycles is equal to the decibel (dB) level. Viewed on the basis of sones, the relative loudness of the test conditions were idling (1), gravel at 15 mph (24 km/h) (2), asphalt at 35 mph (56 km/h) (2), and expressway (6). Sixty to seventy-five percent of the energy in the interior was below 250 Hz.

Bryan [185] notes that there was apparently no criterion for what noise levels were acceptable inside the vehicle. He reports on a small survey of the noise climate inside 1-L, 2¼-L, 3-L, and 4-L automobiles. Bryan attempted to find a measure of subjective response to interior vehicle noise measurements made in the front and rear seats during smooth road operation at 40, 50, 60, and 70 mph (64, 80, 97, and 113 km/h). His study is similar to that of Ford et al. [182]. Bryan's data (Table 5) suggests that there is a poor relationship between annoyance within a vehicle and dB(A), NR, or perceived level (PLdB). However, Bryan indicates that a somewhat more reasonable subjective versus objective relationship exists between vehicles, especially with a dB(A) numeric measure.

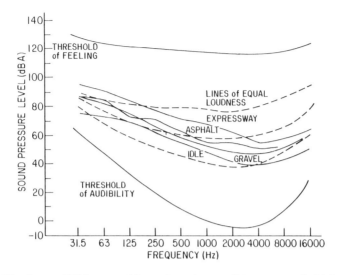

FIG. 77—*Average SPL in automobiles under various conditions compared with human hearing thresholds (flat-frequency weighting)* [184].

Table 6 shows Bryan's recommendation for acceptable criterion for annoyance inside passenger vehicles, and his point of view, in part, is reinforced by the data previously discussed by Ford et al. [*182*].

Although the relationship between objective and subjective is relatively poor within cars, it is reasonable between vehicles, and Bryan feels that this is a result of the small differences in sound level at the middle and high frequencies.

Hillquist and Scott [*186*] present limited but useful data on interior vehicle noise as part of a much larger general review of motor vehicle noise. Curtis [*187*] presents good arguments for the formulation of a special purpose scale to evaluate the interior noise levels in automobiles.

It appears that the important question of finding objective measures of interior noise that correlate well with subjective opinions is still unanswered. In spite of these difficulties, very practical use of measurements is made in solving tire/pavement interaction induced noise problems.

Lippmann and Oblizajek [*188*] is an example of how to deal with interior noise problems in spite of the scientific deficiencies we face. They are concerned with the effect of tire design on sounds heard in the passenger compartment since, as they say, the occupant's concept of automobile quality is partially based on sounds heard in the passenger compartment. According to Lippmann and Oblizajek, the tire associated acoustical energy in the interior of the vehicle is made up of structure-borne and airborne parts. The structure-borne path is from the tire to the wheel, to the spindle, and on through the suspension linkages to the body until it finally appears as acoustic energy

TABLE 5—*Actual and predicted annoyance inside four passenger vehicles, in descending order of acceptability for speeds of 40, 50, and 60 mph (64, 80, and 97 km/h), windows closed; Lin = SPL on linear scale of sound level meter* [185].

Vehicle	NR	dB(A)	PLdB	Lin	Rating
			40 MPH		
4-L saloon	60	63	72	101	1
3-L saloon	70	69	80	97	1
1-L saloon	78	76	84	101	2
2¼-L vehicle	93	90	101	108	4
			50 MPH		
4-L saloon	65	66	67	101	1
3-L saloon	82	74	87	98	2
1-L saloon	80	78	86	104	2
2¼-L vehicle	93	95	100	109	5
			60 MPH		
4-L saloon	71	67	78	106	¹/₂
3-L saloon	81	77	87	103	3
1-L saloon	90	85	92	107	4
2¼-L vehicle	93	97	101	107	6

RATING VALUES: 1 = quiet, 2 = noticeable, 3 = intrusive, 4 = annoying, 5 = very annoying, 6 = unbearable.

TABLE 6—*Salford criterion for noise in vehicles* [185].

Subjective Rating	Noise Level Not Exceeding, dB(A)
Quiet	67
Noticeable	73
Intrusive	79
Annoying	85
Very annoying	91
Unbearable	97

in the interior. The airborne part is the acoustic radiation from the tire into the surrounding air that in turn impinges on the panels of the vehicle, and they in turn radiate acoustical energy into the interior of the car. Tire noise is repetitive and the sounds generated are synchronous with the tire's rotation. The nature of this sound is tonal and the degree of tonality can be controlled by varying the tread pattern element size around the tire in some manner. The noise generating mechanisms of tire road noise are not well understood as discussed in the previous section.

At present, however, it is not possible to get quantitative results derived from theory for any of the proposed mechanisms and further, which of the mechanisms are dominant. What is clear, though, is that the tread design is fundamentally a significant source of the noise problem, and the tread pattern is absolutely necessary to the functioning of the tire. Lippmann obtained a measure of the tire's tread pattern contribution to interior sound by measuring the differences in sound in a vehicle alternatively equipped with smooth tread and conventional tires on the same piece of smooth asphalt road. Figure 78 shows the A-weighted power spectra for these tires. The carrier frequency or mean frequency, as Lippmann calls it, is indicated by the arrowhead. The arrowhead shifts to higher frequency as the car speeds up, as one would expect. This subject of carrier frequency and side bands is discussed at length by Varterasian [189].

Another point is that in Fig. 78 for speeds less than 100 km/h, there are two frequencies, 640 and 860 Hz, at which the acoustic energy has peaks. The peaks are there for all speeds at the same frequency. This suggests that these two frequencies are resonant frequencies and can be attributed to the natural frequencies of the individual tread elements. They could be radial, drag, or lateral vibrations of these tread elements. Our own work (unpublished) on making acceleration measurements on individual blocks when operating under normal load and speed conditions, shows similar resonant frequencies for the individual blocks.

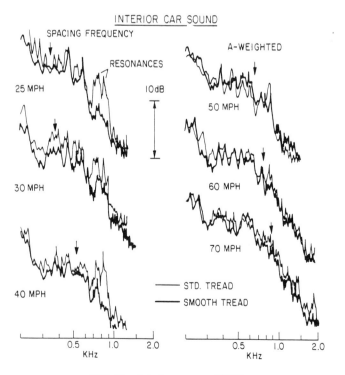

FIG. 78—*Interior car sound* [188].

Figure 79 shows the difference in sound power in the 200- to 1400-Hz band as a function of speed between the standard tire and a smooth tire on an arbitrary scale. The sound power in the same band caused by the tread pattern can be calculated in a straightforward way from this information. It is plotted as well in Fig. 79 as a function of speed. The data show that the energy caused by the tread pattern alone is less than the background energy, that is, the smooth tire energy. Since arbitrary scales are used, the absolute dB(A) levels for this car and set of tires are not known. Also the precise answer depends on the individual road surface used.

In previous sections, road texture was discussed. It is a part of the system that has a strong influence on interior noise, and the practical answers obtained [188] are dependent on the test surface used. Young and Jordan [190] discuss the effect of texture on interior noise.

Young and Jordan's measurements were made on eleven different surfaces. These surfaces ranged from a fine cold asphalt through a range of surface textures up to a very coarsely grooved concrete. Test Surface 11, which is a fine cold asphalt section, is the control surface. The interior noise was measured in four different cars. Measurements were made at a constant speed in the range of 20 to 95 km/h in 15-km/h increments. To distinguish the road noise from that of the engine, exhaust, mechanical components, and aerodynamic effects, the noise level from the test surfaces was computed relative to that of the control surface, Surface 11. Thus, the road noise contribution was effectively isolated.

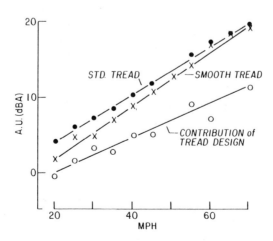

FIG. 79—*Interior sound* [188].

The range of the linear and A-weighted spectra of their investigation are shown in Fig. 80. Most of the energy is at the low end of the frequency spectra. There is little energy above 5 kHz.

Figure 81 shows that overall interior noise level decreases markedly as car size increases. In Fig. 82, the average road noise component in dB(A) averaged over all speeds relative to the control surface is plotted against the various road surfaces. Surfaces 2 (pervious macadam) and 10 (spray grip) give the lowest road noise component, whereas Surface 9 (coarsely grooved concrete) gave the largest. The differences are quite significant. Again, the largest vehicle is the quietest.

Figure 83 shows the overall interior noise level in dB(A) as a function of speed in kilometres per hour for the various road surfaces. The average increase in interior noise level is about 1.5 dBa per 10 km/h. Clearly, the rate of increase in road noise with speed within the speed range examined is independent of the type of road surface on which the vehicle is traveling. Figure 84 shows the road noise component, decibels (dB) relative to the control, as a function of speed in km/h. In the speed range from 30 to 80 km/h, the road noise component is invariant with speed for all the surfaces tested.

Does the noise component in the car come primarily through the structural or airborne path? Jha provides a partial answer [191].

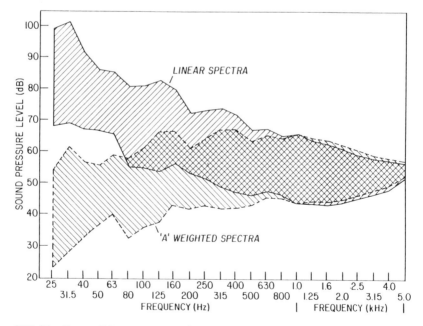

FIG. 80—*Range of ⅓-octave spectra obtained in test vehicles traveling over a variety of bituminous and concrete surfacings at speeds in the range 20 to 95 km/h* [190].

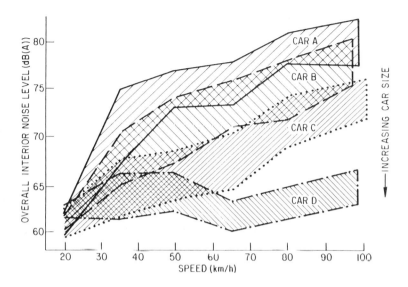

FIG. 81—*Rate of increase with speed of overall noise levels from different surfacings for each test car* [190].

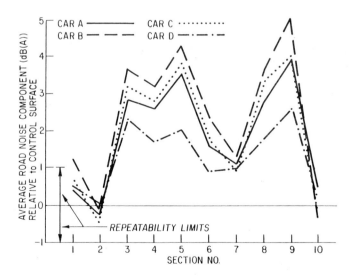

FIG. 82—*Overall noise levels and road noise components for the different test cars and surfacings* [190].

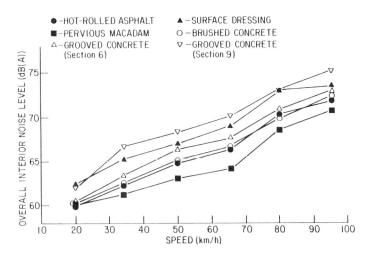

FIG. 83— *The effect of speed on overall noise level* [190].

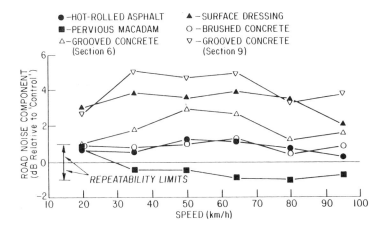

FIG. 84— *The effect of speed on road noise component for test C* [190].

Jha used coherence function (ordinary, multiple, and partial) analysis techniques to rank order the road/tire induced noise transmission path in a vehicle. For a review of these techniques, see Bendat and Piersol [*192*].

Jha's experimental vehicle was a front wheel drive car. In his first set of experiments, he mounted two accelerometers on the right front wheel and two on the left rear wheel. One measured the vertical acceleration and the other measured the fore/aft acceleration. The interior noise was measured in the driver's left and right ear positions. All data were recorded simultaneously on the highway with the vehicle coasting at an approximately constant speed. Figure 85 shows the model of the noise transmission path Jha used.

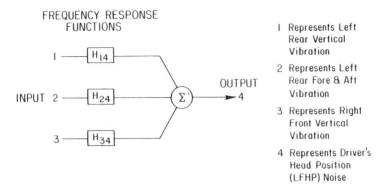

FREQUENCY RESPONSE
FUNCTIONS

1 Represents Left
Rear Vertical
Vibration

2 Represents Left
Rear Fore & Aft
Vibration

3 Represents Right
Front Vertical
Vibration

4 Represents Driver's
Head Position
(LFHP) Noise

FIG. 85—*3-input/1-output model representing road tire road tire induced noise transmission paths in a vehicle* [191].

From his analysis of the data from the coasting experiments, Jha concludes that at peaks in the low-frequency noise spectrum (Fig. 86) the structural transmission path from the tire/road interface is most important to in the car noise. This is a case where engine noise is not present but aerodynamic noise is.

Next, Jha presents some experimental data on structural borne noise that he derived from a two-part experiment, free of both aerodynamic and engine noise. First, he measured the total noise in a vehicle, airborne plus structural borne, to get this data. The four wheels of the vehicle were run on four roadwheels. Next, he obtained a measure of the airborne noise by disconnecting the body from the wheel assembly. The body was supported in a normal position. The wheels were mounted on external frames and were run in situ, that is, at the same relative position with respect to the vehicle. The airborne noise was subtracted from the total noise, leaving only the structural borne

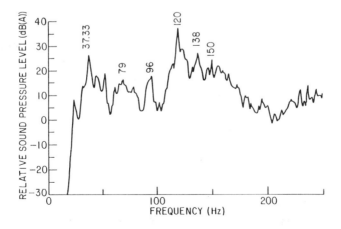

FIG. 86—*Noise spectrum inside a vehicle coasting at 32 mph (51 km/h)* [191].

noise. Figure 87 shows a comparison between the total structural-borne and airborne as a function of speed. The structure-borne noise dominates throughout the speed range. Figure 88 shows the percent of sound energy versus speed and at 48 km/h (30 mph), approximately 89% of the energy is structure borne. If we now go back to the analysis using the coherence function technique and make some assumptions taking advantage of symmetry and interpolation, it can be shown that approximately 83% of the noise is structure borne, which is in fairly close agreement with the derived 89%.

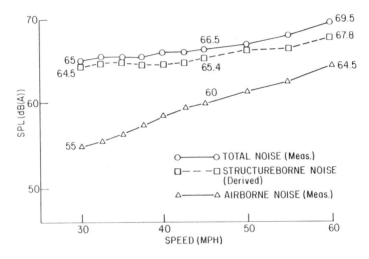

FIG. 87—*Parts of noise level caused by each path* [191].

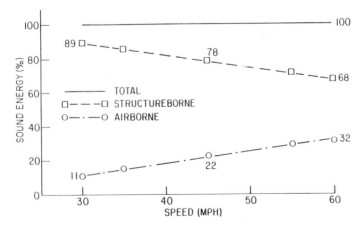

FIG. 88—*Noise from each transmission path* [191].

This discussion has demonstrated that in-car noise is affected in a very major way by tire/pavement interaction induced effects, structure-borne noise is highly important, there is no way to fully assess annoyance on the basis of instrumented measurements, road surface texture is crucially important, and the total body of data is not large.

Summary

A systematic review of tire-pavement interaction generated noise and vibration has been presented. In this review, we have emphasized a systems approach involving: pavement surface characteristics, tire effects, vehicle vibrational response, and human response. To illustrate how all these factors play a part, we have considered five examples of the system in action: shake, tire roughness, tire harshness, exterior noise, and in-car noise.

These problems are complex, and as we have shown, the systems approach is crucial. However, much work remains to be done. We particularly believe that much valuable work remains to be done on these topics: tire and vehicle transmissibility, and the systemization of knowledge in design models.

Acknowledgments

The authors would like to thank the Uniroyal-Goodrich Tire Company for the opportunity to prepare and present this paper.

We owe a very special debt of gratitude to two people without whom this paper could not have been produced. Linda J. Albert did all the typing and thoroughly checked our spelling. Arthur R. Canterbury prepared all the illustrations.

APPENDIX A

Glossary of Terms

Where possible, the definitions given follow SAE J670e, "Vehicle Dynamics Terminology," [93].

Boom—a high intensity vibration (25 to 100 Hz) perceived audibly and characterized as a sensation of pressure by the ear. Usually, there is a coincidence of a tire modal natural frequency, a panel natural frequency, and a body cavity resonance frequency at predominant boom frequencies.

- *Impact Boom*—boom excited by the tire impacting abrupt but modest changes in pavement elevation, such as tar strips, slab edges, and areas of spalled pavement.
- *Rolling Boom*—boom excited by higher harmonics of tire uniformity. It occurs on a smooth pavement.

Conicity—the component of lateral force offset that changes sign (with respect to the tire axis system) with a change in direction of rotation (positive away from the serial number or toward the whitewall). Conicity is always directed towards the same side of the tire regardless of rotation direction. Conicity is camber-like.

Harshness—vibrations (15 to 100 Hz) perceived tactily or audibly or both, produced by interaction of the tire and road irregularities. Pavement roughness is the excitation source.

Lateral Force Offset—the average lateral force of a free rolling tire rolling at a zero steer angle and at a zero camber angle.

Nibbling—a lateral transient generated when a tire climbs on to or off of a pavement edge running nearly parallel to the vehicle direction of motion.

Plysteer—the component of lateral force offset that does not change sign (with respect to the tire axis system) with a change in direction of rotation (positive is along the SAE positive Y axis). Plysteer is like a slip angle generated force.

Road Roar—a high intensity vibration (100 to 300 Hz) perceived audibly and excited by pavement texture such as pebbly surfaces.

Tire Roughness—vibration (15 to 100 Hz) perceived tactily or audibly, generated by a rolling, nonuniform, tire on a smooth road surface and producing the sensation of driving on a coarse or irregular surface.

Shake—the intermediate frequency (5 to 25 Hz) vibrations of the sprung mass as a flexible body. This is associated with beaming, wheel hop, and power train rigid body vibration.

- *Beaming*—a mode of vibration involving predominantly bending deformations of the sprung mass about the vehicle Y axis.
- *Hop*—the vertical oscillatory motion of a wheel between the road surface and the sprung mass.

Thump—a periodic vibration or audible sound generated by the tire or both and producing a pounding sensation that is synchronous with wheel rotation.

Tire/Pavement Interaction Noise—airborne sound induced because of excitation of the rolling tire.

- *Pavement Induced*—the excitation is due to the pavement texture.
- *Tire Induced*—the excitation is due to the tire surface texture, the tread pattern.

Waddle—low-frequency (<5 Hz) sprung mass rigid body vibrations. These may be excited by the first harmonic of tire normal force nonuniformity at low speeds (<30 km/h) or at any speed by appropriate wavelength highway undulations.

Wiggle—small low frequency (≈ 2 Hz) vehicle oscillations induced by interaction between the tire tread pattern and longitudinal road grooving.

APPENDIX B

Author Responsibilities

To aid readers who may wish to ask a specific question about some part of the paper, the authors split the responsibility for the various sections in this way.

J. M. Lawther

- Pavement Surface Undulations
- Exterior Noise from Tire/Pavement Interaction

K. D. Marshall

- Vehicle Vibrational Response
- Human Response to Acoustic and Tactile Vibration
- Tire Roughness
- Tire Harshness

M. G. Pottinger

- Introduction
- Tire Effects
- Shake
- Organization and Editing

D. B. Thrasher

- In-Car Noise

References

[1] U.S. Department of Transportation, Federal Highway Administration. *Standard Specifications for Construction of Roads and Bridges of Federal Highway Projects,* Report FP-79, Washington, DC, 1981 revision.

[2] Buchanan, J. A. and Catudal, A. L., "Standardizable Equipment for Evaluating Road Surface Roughness," *Public Roads,* Feb. 1941.

[3] Brokaw, M. P., "Development of the PCA Roadmeter: A Rapid Method for Measuring Slope Variance," HRB Highway Research Record 189, Washington, DC, 1967, pp. 137–149.

[4] Anonymous, "The Incomparable Mays Ride Meter for Pavement Surveillance," The Rainhart Co., Austin, TX, Jan. 1972.

[5] Wambold, J. C., Defrain, L. E., Hegmon, R. R., McGhee, K., Reichert, J., and Spangler, E. B., "State of the Art of Measurement and Analysis of Road Roughness," TRB Transportation Research Record 836, Washington, DC, 1981, pp. 21–29.

[6] "The AASHO Road Test, Report 5, Pavement Research," Highway Research Board Special Report 61E, 1962.

[7] "CHLOE Profilometer Operating and Servicing Instructions," Federal Highway Administration Internal Report, Washington, DC, 1967.

[8] Spangler, E. B. and Kelley, W. J., "GMR Road Profilometer—A Method for Measuring Road Profile," HRB Research Record 121, Washington, DC, 1966, pp. 27–54.

[9] Spangler, E. B. and Kelly, W. J., "GMR Profilometer Method for Measuring Road Profile," GM Publication GMR-452, Warren, MI, 1964.

[10] Gillespie, T. D., Sayers, M. W., and Segel, L., "Calibration of Response Type Road Roughness Measuring Systems," NCHRP Report 228, Transportation Research Buletin, Washington, DC, 1980.

[11] Spangler, E. B., "Inertial Profilometer Uses in the Pavement Management Process," Transportation Research Record 893, Washington, DC, 1982, pp. 20–27.

[12] Baum, N. P. and Stough, T. A., "Evaluation of Inertial and Laser Profilometer Systems," Report AFWL-TR-74-289, Air Force Weapons Laboratory, Dayton, OH, April 1975.

[13] Wambold, J. C., "A Preliminary Evaluation of the System for Inventorying Road Surface Topography (SIRST)," FHWA RD-81-089, Federal Highway Administration, Washington, DC, July 1981.

[14] Joyce, R. P., "Development of Noncontacting Profiling System," Federal Highway Administration Contract Report, FHWA-RD-75-36, Jan. 1975, Illinois Institute of Technology Research Institute.

[15] Lawther, J. M., "Feasibility Study for an Improved Acoustic Probe for Road Roughness Profiling," Report FHWA RD-80-171, Washington, DC, July 1981.

[16] Swift, G., "Apparatus for Testing Road Surfaces, and Method," U.S. Patent 3,353,404, November 21, 1967.

[17] Riesz, F. and Sz.-Nagy, B., *Functional Analysis,* Ungar, New York City, 1955.

[18] Quinn, B. E. and Smeyak, L. M., "Measuring Pavement Roughness Spectra Using the Modified BPR Roughometer with Additional Refinement," Report FHWA RD-72-27, Federal Highway Administration, Washington, DC, Nov. 1972.

[19] Walls, J. H., Houbolt, J. C., and Press, H., "Some Measurements and Power Spectra of Runway Roughness," NACA Technical Note 3305, Washington, DC, Nov. 1954.

[20] Thompson, W. C., "Measurements and Power Spectra of Runway Roughness at Airports in Countries of the North Atlantic Treaty Organization," NACA Technical Note 4303, Washington, DC, July 1958.

[21] Quinn, B. E., "Establishing Acceptable Limits for Guideway Roughness," *Highspeed Ground Transportation Journal,* Vol. 10, No. 3, 1976, pp. 255-265.

[22] Nefski, D. J., Wolf, J. H., Jr., and Howell, L. J., "Structural Acoustic Finite Element Analysis of the Automobile Passenger Compartment: A Review of Current Practice," *Journal of Sound and Vibration,* Vol. 80, No. 2, 1982, pp. 247-266.

[23] Dodds, C. J. and Robson, J. D., "The Description of Road Surface Roughness," *Journal of Sound and Vibration,* Vol. 31, No. 2, 1973, pp. 175-183.

[24] LaBarre, R. P. et al., "The Measurement and Analysis of Road Surface Roughness," Report #1970/5, The Motor Industry Research Association (MIRA), Lindley, Warwickshire, England, Dec. 1969.

[25] Longuet-Higgins, M. S., "Statistical Properties of a Random Moving Surface," *Proceedings of the Royal Society,* Vol. 249, No. A966, 21 Feb. 1957.

[26] Rice, S. O., "The Mathematical Analysis of Random Noise," *Bell System Technical Journal,* Vol. 23.

[27] Robson, D. J., "Road Surface Descriptions and Vehicle Response," *International Journal of Vehicle Design,* Vol 1, No. 1, 1979, pp. 25-35.

[28] VanDeusen, B. D., "A Study of the Vehicle Ride Dynamics Aspect of Ground Mobility," *Vol. I—Summary, Vol II—Human Response to Vehicle Vibration, Vol. III—Theoretical Dynamics Aspects of Vehicle Systems, Vol. IV—Field Measurements* (coauthored by C. H. Hoppe), Chrysler Corp. Contract Report 3-114 for U.S. Army Waterways Experimental Station, Vicksburg, MI, 1965.

[29] Helms, H., "Vibrations of Four Wheel Motor Vehicles Due to Uneven road Surface." *Proceedings of 7th Symposium on the Dynamics of Vehicles on Roads and Tracks,* Cambridge, England, 7-11 Sept. 1981.

[30] Hegmon, R. R. and Mizoguchi, M., "Pavement Texture Measurement by the Sand Patch and Outflow Meter Methods," Automotive Safety Research Program Report S40, Study No. 67-11, Pennsylvania State University, University Park, PA, Jan. 1970.

[31] *Annual Book of ASTM Standards,* Vol. 04.03, American Society for Testing and Material, Philadelphia.

[32] Schonfeld, R., "Photo Interpretations of Pavement Skid Resistance in Practice," TRB Transportation Research Record 523, Washington, DC, 1974, pp. 65-75.

[33] Lawther, J. M. and Henry, J. J., "Characterization of Pavement Macrotexture by Profile Spectral Analysis," Pennsylvania State University, University Park, PA, June 1974.

[34] Pottinger, M. G., Thomas, R. A., and Naghshineh, K., "Stiffness Properties of Agricultural Tires," *International Conference on Soil Dynamics,* Auburn, AL, 16-21 June 1985.

[35] Rasmussen, R. E. and Cortese, A. D., "Dynamic Spring Rate Performance of Rolling Tires," SAE 680408, Society of Automotive Engineers, Detroit, MI, 1968.

[36] Chiesa, A. and Tangorra, G., "The Dynamic Stiffness of Tyres," *Revue General de Caoutchoucs,* Vol. 36, No. 10, 1959, pp. 1329-1339.

[37] Thomson, W. T., *Theory of Vibration with Applications,* Prentice-Hall, Englewood Cliffs, NJ, 1972.

[38] Phillips, A. V., "A Study of Road Noise," *Vibration and Noise in Motor Vehicles,* Institution of Mechanical Engineers, 1972, pp. 70-81.

[39] Pottinger, M. G., "The Effect of Belt Materials on Performance of Radial Passenger Tires," SAE 750405, Society of Automotive Engineers, Detroit, MI, 1975.

[40] Tielking, J. T., "Plane Vibration Characteristics of a Pneumatic Tire Model," SAE 650492, Society of Automotive Engineers, Detroit, MI, 1965.

[41] Bohm, F., "Mechanics of the Belted Tire," *Ingeniur-Archiv,* Vol. XXXV, 1966.

[42] Fiala, E. and Willumeit, H. P., "Radial Vibrations of Belted Tires," *Automobiltechnische Zeitschrift,* No. 2, Feb. 1966.

[43] Chiesa, A., Oberto, L., and Tamburni, L., "Transmission of Tyre Vibrations," *Automobile Engineer,* Dec. 1964, pp. 520-530.

[44] Potts, G. R., Bell, C. A., Charek, L. T., and Roy, T. K., "Tire Vibrations," *Tire Science and Technology,* Vol. 5, No. 4, Nov. 1977, pp. 202-225.

[45] Potts, G. R. and Csora, T. T., "Tire Vibration Studies 'The State-of-the-Art'," *Tire Science and Technology,* Vol. 3, No. 3, Aug. 1975, pp. 196-210.

[46] Soedel, W. and Prasad, M. G., "Calculation of Natural Frequencies and Modes of Tires in Road Contact by Utilizing Eigenvalues of the Axisymmetric Non-Contacting Tire," *Journal of Sound and Vibration,* Vol. 70, No. 4, 1980, pp. 573-584.

[47] Barson, C. W. and Dodd, A. M., "Vibrational Characteristics of Tyres," *Vibration and Noise in Motor Vehicles,* Institution of Mechanical Engineers, London, England, 1972, pp. 1-12.

[48] Barson, C. W., Gough, V. E., Hutchinson, J. C., and James, D. H., "Tyre and Vehicle Vibration," *Proceedings of Institution of Mechanical Engineers,* Vol. 179, No. 7, Part 2A, 1964-65.

[49] Mills, B. and Dunn, J. W., "The Mechanical Mobility of Rolling Tyres," *Vibration and Noise in Motor Vehicles,* Institution of Mechanical Engineers, London, England, 1972, pp. 90-101.

[50] Bandel, P. and Monguzzi, C., "Simulation Model of the Dynamic Behavior of a Tyre Running Over on Obstacle," Second Meeting of the Tire Society, Akron, OH, 1983.

[51] Julien, M. A. and Paulsen, J. F., "The Absorptive Power of the Pneumatic Tire, Experimental Method of Measurement and Definition," *IV International Technical Congress on Automobiles,* Madrid, Spain, 20-26 Oct. 1952.

[52] Lippmann, S. A. and Nanny, J. D., "A Quantitative Analysis of the Enveloping Forces of Passenger Tires," SAE 670174, Society of Automotive Engineers, Detroit, MI 1967.

[53] Lippmann, S. A., Piccin, W. A., and Baker, T. P., "Enveloping Characteristics of Truck Tires, A Lab Evaluation," *1966 SAE Transactions,* Vol. 74, Society of Automotive Engineers, Detroit, MI.

[54] Barone, M. R., "Impact Vibrations of Rolling Tires," SAE 770612, Society of Automotive Engineers, Detroit, MI 1977.

[55] Davis, D. C., "A Radial-Spring Terrain-Enveloping Tire Model," *Vehicle Systems Dynamics,* Vol. 3, 1974, pp. 55-69.

[56] Lessem, A. S. and Green, A. J., "A Mathematical Model for Traversal of Rigid Obstacles by a Pneumatic Tire," AD 837142, U.S. Army Waterways Experimental Station, 1968.

[57] Captain, K. M., Wormley, D. N., and Grande, E., "The Development and Comparative Evaluation of Analytical Tire Models for Dynamic Vehicle Simulation," AD-A 005 415, Army Tank-Automotive Command, 1974.

[58] Walter, J. D., Augeropoulos, G. N., Janssen, M. L., and Potts, G. R., "Advances in Tire Composite Theory," *Tire Science and Technology,* Vol. 1, No. 2, May 1973, pp. 210-250.

[59] Caulfield, R. J. and Higgins, R. J., "On-Car Tire Grinder for Improved Ride Smoothness," SAE 720465, Society of Automotive Engineers, Detroit, MI, 1972.

[60] Herzegh, F., "A Method of Measuring Thump and Roughness for Quality Control of Passenger Car Tire Production," SAE 124, Society of Automotive Engineers, Detroit, MI, 1957.

[61] Morrish, L. M. and Haist, R. R., "The Effect of Loaded Radial Runout on Tire Roughness and Shake," SAE 322E, Society of Automotive Engineers, Detroit, MI, 1961.

[62] Anderson, M. G., "Tire Uniformity," SAE 322B, Society of Automotive Engineers, Detroit, MI, 1961.

[63] Gough, V. E., Barson, C. W., Gough, S. W., and Benett, W. D., "Tire Uniformity Grading Machine," SAE 322A, Society of Automotive Engineers, Detroit, MI, 1961.

[64] Hamburg, J. and Horsch, J., "Reduction of Tire Nonuniformities by Machining Techniques," SAE 710089, Society of Automotive Engineers, Detroit, MI, 1971.

[65] Gursky, L. A., "Tire Uniformity and Correlation of Vehicle Ride," SAE 710086, Society of Automotive Engineers, Detroit, MI, 1971.

[66] Klamp, W. K. and J. Meingast, "Higher Orders of Tire Force Variations and Their Sig-

nificance," SAE 720463, Society of Automotive Engineers, Detroit, MI, 1972.

[67] Lippmann, S. A., "Forces and Torques Associated with Roughness in Tires," SAE 322D, Society of Automotive Engineers, Detroit, MI, 1961.

[68] Marshall, K. D. and St. John, N. W., "Roughness in Steel-Belted Radial Tires—Measurement and Analysis," SAE 750456, Society of Automotive Engineers, Detroit, MI, 1975.

[69] Marshall, K. D., Wik, T. R., Miller, R. F., and Iden, R. W., "Tire Roughness—Which Tire Nonuniformities Are Responsible," SAE 740066, Society of Automotive Engineers, Detroit, MI, 1974.

[70] Walker, J. C. and Reeves, N. H., "Uniformity of Tires at Vehicle Operating Speeds," *Tire Science and Technology*, Vol. 2, No. 3, 1974, pp. 163-178.

[71] Wylie, C. R., Jr., *Advanced Engineering Mathematics*, McGraw Hill, New York, 1960, Chapter 7.

[72] Daberkoe, C. W., "Vehicle Application of Tire/Wheel Rolling Smoothness Controls," SAE 710088, Society of Automotive Engineers, Detroit, MI, 1971.

[73] Davisson, J. A., "Factors of Tire Design and Manufacture Affecting Uniformity," SAE 650521, Society of Automotive Engineers, Detroit, MI, 1965.

[74] Nedley, Q. L. and Gearig, D. M., "Radical Improvements in Tire and Wheel Manufacture—Their Effects Upon Radial Force Variation of the Assembly," SAE 700089, Society of Automotive Engineers, Detroit, MI, 1970.

[75] Hofelt, C., Jr., "Uniformity Control of Cured Tires," SAE 690076, Society of Automotive Engineers, Detroit, MI, 1969.

[76] Topping, R. W., "Tire Induced Steering Pull," SAE 750406, Society of Automotive Engineers, Detroit, MI, 1975.

[77] Pottinger, M. G., "Ply Steer in Radical Carcass Tires," SAE 760731, Society of Automotive Engineers, Detroit, MI, 1976.

[78] Chiesa, A. and Tangorra G., "Effect of the Mechanical Properties of Pneumatic Tires on the Vertical Vibrations of the Vehicle," translation of article from Verein DeutscherIngenieure, Report 35, Düsseldorf, West Germany, 1958.

[79] "Dynamic Rigidity of Tires and the Vertical Vibrations of the Car," ATZ, Vol 63, No. 2, 1961, pp 47-51.

[80] Chiesa, A., "Vehicle Vertical Vibration and Tire Performance," SAE Paper 490C, Society of Automotive Engineers, Detroit, MI, 1962.

[81] Chiesa, A. and Oberto, L., "Influence of Tyres and Car Vibration Studied with a New Classification Method," Rubber Laboratories, Pirelli S.p.A., Milano, Italy, 1964.

[82] Gough, V. E., et al., "Tyre and Vehicle Vibrations," Proceedings of the Institute of Mechanical Engineers, 1964.

[83] Nordeen, D. L. and Rasmussen, R. E., "When a Vehicle gets the Shakes the Tires May Be the Culprit," *SAE Journal*, Vol. 74, No. 5, 1966.

[84] Skattum, K. S., Harris, J. F., and Howell, L. J., "Preliminary Vehicle Structural Design for Comparison with Quantitative Criteria," SAE Paper 750136, Society of Automotive Engineers, Detroit, MI, 1975.

[85] Vail, C. F., "Dynamic Modeling of Automobile Structures from Test Data," American Society of Mechanical Engineers, Winter Meeting on System Identification of Vibrational Structures, New York, 1972.

[86] Davis, R. L., "Suspension System Modeling and Structural Loading," SAE Paper 750134, Society of Automotive Engineers, Detroit, MI, 1975.

[87] Majcher, J. S. et al., "Analysis of Vehicle Suspensions with Static and Dynamic Computer Simulations," SAE Paper 760183, Society of Automotive Engineers, Detroit, MI, 1976.

[88] Orlandea, N. and Chace, M. A., "Simulation of a Vehicle Suspension with the ADAMS Computer Program," SAE Paper 770053, Society of Automotive Engineers, Detroit, MI, 1977.

[89] Sano, M., Fujiwara, Y., and Naka, A., "Experimental and Theoretical Analysis on Independent Rear Suspension and Body Structure to Reduce Interior Noise," SAE Paper 770177, Society of Automotive Engineers, Detroit, MI, 1977.

[90] Radaj, D., et al., "Novel Developments and Applications of Finite Element Methods at Daimler-Benz," SAE Paper 770596, Society of Automotive Engineers, Detroit, MI, 1977.

[91] Hodgetts, D. and Parkins, D. W., "Vibration Modes of an Automobile Driveline," SAE Paper 740952, Society of Automotive Engineers, Detroit, MI, 1974.

[92] Egubson, A. K., Hodgetts, D., and Ellis, J. R., "Vibration of a Rear Axle," *Vibration and Noise in Motor Vehicles*, The Institute of Mechanical Engineers, London, 1971.

[93] "Vehicle Dynamics Terminology," SAE J670e, Society of Automotive Engineers, Detroit, MI, June 1978.

[94] Plume, R. W. and McIntyre, W. C., "Shake—Complete Car Analysis with Excitation Through Road Wheels," SAE Paper 533B, Society of Automotive Engineers, Detroit, MI, 1962.

[95] Butkunas, A. A., "Random Vibration Analysis and Vehicle Shake," *Vibration and Noise in Motor Vehicles*, The Institute of Mechanical Engineers, London, 1971.

[96] Anderson, D. T. and Mills, B., "Dynamic Analysis of a Car Frame Using the Finite Element Method," *International Journal of Mechanical Science*, Vol. 14, 1972, pp. 799–808.

[97] Sisson, T., Zimmarman, R., and Martz, J., "Determination of Modal Properties of Automobile Bodies and Frames Using Transient Testing Techniques," SAE Paper 730502, Society of Automotive Engineers, Detroit, MI, 1973.

[98] George, R. J., "Determination of Natural Frequencies and Mode Shapes of Chassis Frames," SAE Paper 730504, Society of Automotive Engineers, Detroit, MI, 1973.

[99] Flanigan, D. L., "Testing of an Automotive Frame to Determine Dynamic Properties," SAE Paper 730505, Society of Automotive Engineers, Detroit, MI, 1973.

[100] Horvath, J. K., "Structural and System Models," SAE Paper 750135, Society of Automotive Engineers, Detroit, MI, 1975.

[101] Melosh, R. J., "Finite Element Analysis of Automobile Structures," *SAE Conference Proceedings P-52, International Conference on Vehicle Structural Mechanics: Finite Element Applications to Vehicle Structural Design*, Society of Automotive Engineers, Detroit, MI, 1974, pp. 26–38.

[102] Augustitus, J. A., Kamal, M. M., and Howell, L. J., "Design Through Analysis of an Experimental Automobile Structure," *SAE Conference Proceedings, P-71, Second International Conference on Vehicle Structural Mechanics; Structural Analysis in the Vehicle Design Process*, Society of Automotive Engineers, Detroit, MI, 1977, pp. 69–81.

[103] Bolton-Knight, B. L., "Engine Mounts: Analytical Methods to Reduce Noise and Vibration," *Vibration and Noise in Motor Vehicles*, The Institute of Mechanical Engineers, London, 1971, pp. 24–34.

[104] Hodgetts, D., "Vibrations of a Crankshaft," *Vibrations and Noise in Motor Vehicles*, The Institute of Mechanical Engineers, London, 1971, pp. 35–50.

[105] Sykes, G. and Wyman, H. J., "The Dynamic Characteristics of Automobile Drivelines," *Vibrations and Noise in Motor Vehicles*, The Institute of Mechanical Engineers, London, 1971, pp. 102–111.

[106] Akio, Y., et al., "Analysis on the Improvement of Vibration and Acoustic Characteristics of Automobiles," SAE Paper 740950, Society of Automotive Engineers, Detroit, MI, 1974.

[107] Sakata, T., "Analysis of the Transmission of Engine Vibration to the Body by the Mechanical Impedance Method," SAE Paper 740163, Society of Automotive Engineers, Detroit, MI, 1974.

[108] Parsons, K. C. and Griffin, M. J., "Methods for Predicting Passenger Vibration Discomfort," SAE Paper 831029, Society of Automotive Engineers, Detroit, MI, 1983.

[109] Jennequin, G., "Is the Computation of Noise Level Inside a Car Feasible?" *Vibration and Noise in Motor Vehicles*, The Institute of Mechanical Engineers, London, 1971, pp. 132–137.

[110] Jha, S. K. and Priede, T., "Origin of Low Frequency Noise in Motor Cars," *XIV International Automobile Technical Conference of FISITA*, The Institution of Mechanical Engineers, London, 1972.

[111] Joachim, C. A., Nelske, D. J., and Wolf, J. A., Jr., "Application of a Structural-Acoustic Diagnostic Technique to Reduce Boom Noise in a Passenger Vechicle," SAE Paper 810398, 1981.

[112] Chung, J. Y., Pope, J., and Feldmaier, D. A., "Application of Acoustic Intensity Measurement to Engine Noise Evaluation," SAE Paper 790502, Society of Automotive Engineers, Detroit, MI, 1979.

[113] Sung, S. H., "Automotive Application of Three-Dimensional Acoustic Finite Elements," SAE Paper 810397, Society of Automotive Engineers, Detroit, MI, 1981.

[114] Hata, S. and Takahashi, M., "Application of Acoustic Intensity Measurement to High

Frequency Interior Noise, SAE Paper 830342, Society of Automotive Engineers, Detroit, MI, 1983.

[115] Miller, D. C., *Anecdotal History of the Science of Sound*, MacMillan, New York, 1935.

[116] Robinson, D. W. and Dadson, R. S., "A Re-determination of the Equal Loudness Relations for Pure Tones," *British Journal Applied Physics*, Vol. 7, 1956, pp. 166–181.

[117] Pollack, I., "The Loudness of Bands of Noise," *Journal of the Acoustics Society of America*, Vol 24, No. 5, 1956, pp. 533–538.

[118] Fletcher, H. and Munson, W. A., "Loudness, Its Definition, Measurement and Calculation," *Journal of the Accoustic Society of America*, Vol. 5, No. 2, 1933, pp. 82–108.

[119] Stevens, S. S., "The Calculation of the Loudness of a Complex Noise," Journal of the Acoustics Society of America, Vol. 28, No. 5, 1956, pp. 807–832.

[120] Kryter, K. D., *The Effects of Noise on Man*, Academic Press, Inc., New York, 1970.

[121] Bauer, B. B., Torick, E. L., and Allen, R. G., "The Measurement of Loudness level," *Journal of the Acoustics Society of America*, Vol. 50, No. 2, 1971, pp. 405–414.

[122] Peterson, A. P. G. and Gross, E. E., Jr., *Handbook of Noise Measurement*, General Radio Corporation, Concord, MA, 1972.

[123] Wells, R. J., "A New Method of Computing the Annoyance of Steady State Noise versus Perceived Noise Level and Other Subjective Measures," *Journal of the Acoustics Society of America*, Vol. 46, No. 1, 1969, p. 85.

[124] Beranek, L. L., Marshall, J. L., Cudworth, A. L., and Peterson, A. P. G., "The Calculation and Measurement of the Loudness of Sounds," *Journal of the Acoustics Society of America*, Vol. 23, No. 3, 1951, pp. 261–269.

[125] Kryter, K. D. and Pearsons, K. S., "Some Effects of Spectral Content and Duration on Perceived Noise Level," *Journal of the Acoustics Society of America*, Vol. 35, No. 6, 1963, pp. 866–883.

[126] Hillquist, R. K., "Objective and Subjective Measurement of Truck Noise," *Sound and Vibration*, Vol. 1, No. 4, 1967, pp. 8–13.

[127] Young, R. W., "Effective Duration of an Aircraft Flyover," Reports on the 6th International Conference on Acoustics, Paper F-3-11, Tokyo, Japan, 1968, pp. 109–112.

[128] Harris, C. M. and Crede, C. C., *Shock and Vibration Handbook*, 2nd ed., McGraw-Hill Book Co., New York, 1976.

[129] International Standards Organization, *Guide for the Evaluation of Human Exposure to Whole-Body Vibrations*, ISO 2631-1974(E), Geneva, Switzerland, 1974.

[130] Miwa, T., "Evaluation Methods for Vibrational Effect," in seven parts, *Industrial Health*, Vols. 5 and 6, Japan, 1967–68.

[131] Reynolds, D. D., Stondlee, K. G., and Angevine, E. N., "Hand-Arm Vibration, Part III: Subjective Response Characteristics of Individuals to Hand-Induced Vibration," *Journal of Sound and Vibration*, Vol. 51, No. 2, 1977, pp. 267–282.

[132] Parsons, K. C. and Griffin, M. J., "The Effect of the Position of the Axis of Rotation on the Discomfort Caused by Whole-Body Roll and Pitch Vibrations of Seated Persons," *Journal of Sound and Vibration*, Vol. 58, No. 1, 1978, pp. 127–141.

[133] Scobey, R. P. and Johnson, C. A., "Displacement Thresholds for Unidirectional and Oscillatory Movement," *Vision Research*, Vol. 21, 1981, pp. 1297–1302.

[134] Griffin, M. J. and Parsons, K. C., "Vibration and Comfort IV. Application of Experimental Results," *Ergonomics*, Vol. 25, No. 8, 1982, pp. 721–739.

[135] Lee, R. A. and Pradko, F., "Analytical Analysis of Human Vibration," SAE Paper 680091, Detroit, MI, 1968.

[136] "Design Specifications for Urban Tracked Air Cushion Vehicles," U.S. Department of Transportation, Washington, DC, 1972.

[137] Butkunas, A. A., "Power Spectrum Density and Ride Evaluation," SAE Paper 660138, Society of Automotive Engineers, Detroit, MI, 1966.

[138] Smith, C. C., McGehee, D. Y., and Healey, A. J., "The Prediction of Passenger Riding Comfort from Acceleration Data," ASME Paper 77-WA/Aut-6, American Society of Mechanical Engineers, New York, 1977.

[139] Oborne, D. J. and Clarke, M. J., "The Determination of Equal Comfort Zones for Whole-Body Vibration," *Ergonomics*, Vol. 17, No. 6, 1974, pp. 769–782.

[140] Grether, W. F., "Vibration and Human Performance," *Human Factors*, Vol. 13, 1971, pp. 203–216.

[141] Harris, C. S. and Shoenberger, R. W., "Combined Effects of Noise and Vibration on Psychomotor Performance," AMRL Technical Report 70-14, AD 710959, Aerospace Medical Research Laboratory, Wright-Patterson AFB, OH, 1970.

[142] Huddleson, H. R., "Human Performance and Behavior in Vertical Sinusoidal Vibration," IAM Report 303, Institute of Aviation Medicine, Farnborough, England, 1964.

[143] Broadbent, D. E., "Effects of Noise on an Intellectual Task," *Journal of the Acoustics Society of America*, Vol. 30, 1958, pp. 824-827.

[144] Harris, C. S. and Sommer, H. C., "Combined Effects of Noise and Vibration on Mental Performance," AMRL Technical Report 70-21, Aerospace Medical Research Laboratory, Wright-Patterson AFB, OH, 1970.

[145] Leatherwood, J. D., Dempsey, T. K., and Clevenson, S. A., "A Design Tool for Estimating Passenger Ride Discomfort Within Complex Ride Environments," *Human Factors*, Vol. 22, No. 3, 1980, pp. 291-312.

[146] Ruegg, M., "Laboratory Simulation of Car Shake," SAE 275, Society of Automotive Engineers, Detroit, MI, 1954.

[147] Marshall, K. D., unpublished BFGoodrich research results, Breckville, OH, 1975.

[148] Harrison, H. R. and Bassim, A., "Wheel Hub Forces Due to Vehicle Encountering a Bump, *International Journal of Vehicle Design*, Vol. 3, No. 2, 1982, pp. 243-247.

[149] Muthukrishnan, M., "Instrumented Car Responses During Obstacle Envelopment by Rolling Tires," SAE Paper 830161, Society of Automotive Engineers, Detroit, MI, 1983.

[150] Hillquist, R. K. and Carpenter, P. C., "A Basic Study of Automobile Tire Noise," *Sound and Vibration*, Vol. 8, No. 2, 1974.

[151] Thrasher, D. B., Miller, R. F., and Bauman, R. G., "Effect of Pavement Texture on Tire/Pavement Interaction Noise," SAE 762001 in SAE Highway Tire Noise Symposium Proceedings, P-70, Detroit, MI, Nov. 1976, pp. 69-79.

[152] Heckl, M., "Tire Noise Generating Mechanisms—A Short Survey of Current Hypotheses," *Proceedings of the International Tire Noise Conference*, Stockholm, Sweden, 29-31 Aug. 1979, pp. 31-35.

[153] Heckl, M., "Tire Noise Generating Mechanisms—State-of-the-Art Report," *Proceedings of the International Tire Noise Conference*, Stockholm, Sweden, 29-31 Aug. 1979.

[154] Hayden, R. E., "Roadside Noise from the Interaction of a Rolling Tire with the Road Surface," *Proceedings of the Purdue Noise Conference*, West Lafayette, ID, 1971, pp. 62-67.

[155] Wilken, I. D., Oswald, L. J., and Hickling, R., "Research on Individual Noise Source Mechanisms of Truck tires: Aeroacoustic Sources," *SAE Highway Tire Noise Symposium Proceedings P-70*, Paper 762022, Detroit, MI, Nov. 1976, pp. 155-165.

[156] Eberhardt, A. C., "Investigation of the Truck Tire Vibration Sound Mechanism," *Proceedings of the International Tire Noise Conference*, Stockholm, Sweden, 29-31 Aug. 1979, pp. 153-165.

[157] Nilsson, N., Bennerhult, O., and Soderqvist, S., "IFM Research Report 6.371.02," IFM Akoustikbyran, Aug. 1980.

[158] Nilsson, N. and Bennerhult, O., "Tire/Road Noise Generating Mechanisms—An Experimental Study: Measurement Methods," IFM Research Report 6.084.01, IFM Akoustikbyran, Jan. 1979.

[159] Simonson, B. and Westin, L., "Prediction of External Tire/Road Noise using Tire Parameters Derived from Measurements on Non-Rolling Tires," IFM Research Report 7.374, IFM Akoustikbyran, April 1981.

[160] Nilsson, N., Soderqvist, S., and Bennerhult, O., "Air-Resonant Radiation—A Possible Mechanism for High Frequency Noise from Cross-Bar Tires," IFM Report 6.084.02, IFM Akoustikbyran, March 1979.

[161] Nilsson, N., "Air Resonant and Vibrational Radiation—Possible Mechanisms for Noise from Cross-Bar Tires," *Proceedings*, International Tire Noise Conference, Stockholm, Sweden, 29-31 Aug. 1979.

[162] Sandberg, V., "Road Texture Induced External Tire Noise," VTI Report 174A, National Road and Traffic Research Institute, Stockholm, Sweden, 1979.

[163] Sandberg, V., "Characterization of Road Surfaces with Respect to Tire Noise," *Proceedings—International Tire Noise Conference*, Stockholm, Sweden, 29-31 May 1979, pp. 169-183.

[164] Pope, J. and Reynolds, W. C., "Tire Noise Generation: The Roles of Tire and Road," *SAE Highway Tire Noise Symposium Proceedings P-70,* Paper 762023, Society of Automotive Engineers, Detroit, MI, Nov. 1976.

[165] Plotkin, K., Fuller, W., and Montroll, M., "Identification of Tire Noise Generation Mechanisms Using a Roadwheel Facility," *Proceedings*—International Tire Noise Conference, Stockholm, Sweden, 29–31 Aug. 1979, pp. 127–141.

[166] Sandberg, V. and Eismont, J. A., "Three Basic Methods for Measurement of Tire/Road Noise," *Proceedings of Internoise-84,* Noise Control Federation, New York, 1984. pp. 93–98.

[167] Bennerhult, O., "Acoustical and Mechanical Impedances of Road Surfaces and the Influence on Tire Noise," *Proceedings—International Tire Noise Conference,* Stockholm, Sweden, 29–31 Aug. 1979, pp. 185–197.

[168] Nilsson, N., "Possible Methods of Reducing External Tire Noise," *Proceedings—International Tire Noise Conference,* Stockholm, Sweden, 29–31 Aug. 1979, pp. 247–259.

[169] Walker, J. C. and Williams, A. R., "The Improvement of Noise and Traction due to Road/Tyre Interaction," *Proceedings, International Tire Noise Conference,* Stockholm, Sweden, 29–31 Aug. 1979, pp. 261–271.

[170] Chien, C. F. and Soroka, W. W., "Sound Propagation Along an Impedance Plane," *Journal of Sound and Vibration,* Vol. 69, No. 2, 1975, pp. 9–20; also Vol. 69, No. 2, 1980, pp. 340–343 (for corrections).

[171] Richards, M., "Cross Lug Tire Noise Mechanisms," Paper 762024, SAE Highway Tire Noise Symposium, *Proceedings P-70,* San Francisco, Nov. 1976, pp. 181–186.

[172] Mercusot, M., "Application of a Nearfield Measurement Technique in Tire Noise Analysis," *Proceedings, International Tire Noise Conference,* Stockholm, Sweden, 29–31 Aug. 1979, pp. 199–204.

[173] Wilken, I. D. and Hickling, R., "Measurement of Truck Noise Using a Single Wheel Trailer," *SAE Highway Tire Noise Symposium Proceedings P-70,* Paper 762014, Detroit, MI, Nov. 1976, pp. 101–108.

[174] Knudsen, V. O. and Harris, C. M., *Acoustical Designing in Architectures,* John Wiley and Sons, Inc., New York, 1950.

[175] Morris, P. M. and Ingard, K. U., "Theoretical Acoustics," McGraw-Hill Book Co., New York, 1968.

[176] Wolf, J. A., Jr., Nefske, D. J., and Howell, L. J., "Structural-Acoustic Finite Element Analysis of Automobile Passenger Compartments," SAE 760184, Society of Automotive Engineers, Detroit, MI, Feb. 1976.

[177] Nefske, D. J. and Howell, L. J., "Automobile Interior Noise Reduction Using Finite Element Methods," SAE 780365, Society of Automotive Engineers, Detroit, MI, 1978.

[178] Chao, C. F., "Modal Analysis of Interior Noise Fields," Ph.D thesis, MAE Department, Princeton University, Princeton, NJ, 1980.

[179] Richards, T. L. and Jha, S. K., "A Simplified Finite Element Method for Studying Acoustic Characteristics Inside a Car Cavity," *Journal of Sound and Vibration,* Vol. 63, 1979, pp. 61–72.

[180] Harris, C. M., *Handbook of Noise Control,* McGraw-Hill, New York, 1957, Chapter 13.

[181] Weiner, F. M., "Experimental Study of the Airborne Noise Generated by Passenger Automobile Tires," *Noise Control,* July/Aug. 1960.

[182] Ford, R. D., et al., "The Measurement of Noise Inside Cars," *Applied Acoustics,* Vol. 3, Elsevier Publishing Co. Ltd., England, 1970.

[183] Fisher, R. A., *Statistical Methods for Research Workers,* Olivier and Boyd, London, England, 1944, pp. 192–196.

[184] Underwood, J. and Solomon, L. P., "Interior Automobile Noise Measurements Under Various Operating Conditions, *Journal of the Acoustical Society of America,* Vol. 49, No. 2, Part 1, 1971.

[185] Bryan, M. E., "A Tentative Criterion for Acceptable Noise Levels in Passenger Vehicles," *Journal of Sound and Vibration,* 1976, pp. 525–535.

[186] Hillquist, R. K. and Scott, W. A., "Motor Vehicle Noise Spectra: Their Characteristics and Dependence Upon Operating Parameters," *Journal of the Acoustical Society of America,* Vol. 58, No. 1, July 1975.

[187] Curtis, C. A., "Road Testing Cars," *Ergonomics,* Vol. 22, No. 2, 1979, pp. 245–252.

[188] Lippmann, S. A. and Oblizajek, K. L., "Tire Noise Sensed in Passenger Cars; Characteristics, Sources, Strategies for Control," *Proceedings of Noise Control for the 1980's,* Vol. 1, Noise Control Federation, New York, 1980.

[189] Varterasian, J. H., "Quieting Noise Mathematically; Its Application to Snow Tires," SAE 690520, Society of Automotive Engineers, Detroit, MI, 1969.

[190] Young, J. C. and Jordan, P. G., *Road Surfacings and Noise in Salon Cars,* Transportation and Road Research Laboratory, Vol. 655, Cronthorne, Berkshire, England, 1981.

[191] Jha, S. K., "Identification of Road/Tyre Induced Noise Transmission Paths in a Vehicle," *International Journal of Vehicle Design,* Vol. 5, Nos. 1/2, 1984.

[192] Bendat, J. S. and Piersol, A. G., *Random Data: Analysis and Measurement Procedures,* Wiley-Interscience, New York, 1971.

[193] Varterasian, J. H., "On Measuring Automobile Seat Ride Comfort," SAE Paper 820309, Society of Automotive Engineers, Detroit, MI, 1982.

James E. McQuirt,[1] Elson B. Spangler,[2] and William J. Kelly[2]

Use of the Inertial Profilometer in the Ohio DOT Pavement Management System

REFERENCE: McQuirt, J. E., Spangler, E. B., and Kelly, W. J., **"Use of the Inertial Profilometer in the Ohio DOT Pavement Management System,"** *The Tire Pavement Interface, ASTM STP 929*, M. G. Pottinger and T. J. Yager, Eds., American Society for Testing and Materials, Philadelphia, 1986, pp. 288–304.

ABSTRACT: Pavement roughness and ride quality information, for the Ohio Department of Transportation (DOT) Pavement Management System, can be accurately computed directly from highway pavement profiles measured with the Ohio DOT inertial profilometer. The pavement ride quality information includes the present serviceability index (PSI) and PSI trigger values for nonroutine maintenance.

Pavement profiles measured with the Ohio DOT inertial profilometer have also been used to calibrate the Ohio DOT Mays ride meter system, to analyze the Mays Ride meter system performance, and to provide a link between that system and pavement roughness and ride quality information obtained from the Ohio DOT inertial profilometer.

KEY WORDS: pavements, profilometers, present serviceability index (PSI), pavement roughness, pavement ride quality, ride meter, Mays ride meter, ride meter calibration, ride meter performance, nonroutine pavement maintenance, pavement maintenance trigger values, inertial profilometer, pavement management systems

The inertial profilometer was developed in the early 1960s by Elson Spangler and William Kelly at the General Motors Research Laboratories in Warren, MI. The profilometer was developed as a research tool to allow measured pavement profile to be brought into the laboratory for use as input into vehicle suspension computer studies. The first presentation on the inertial profilometer was made by Spangler and Kelly [1] at the Annual Transportation Research Board meeting in Washington, DC in 1965. Through the efforts of the

[1]Research and development engineer, Ohio Department of Transportation, 25 S. Front St., P.O. Box 899, Columbus, OH 43216-0899.

[2]President and staff engineer, respectively, Surface Dynamics, Inc., Suite 220, 800 W. Long Lake Rd., Bloomfield Hills, MI 48013.

General Motors Corporation, the technology associated with the inertial profilometer was made available for use in the highway community. Early inertial profilometer implementations have been used by the states of Michigan [2], Pennsylvania, Kentucky [3], and Texas [4], and the country of Brazil as part of a World Bank project.

Since these early systems, significant improvements have been made in inertial profilometer implementations. These improvements include a noncontact displacement sensor, a high-speed digital computer, and the spatial computation of the measured pavement profile. These improvements have removed the measuring speed constraints imposed in the earlier system by the road following wheel and the time based profile computation. This improved inertial profilometer measurements for pavement profile at any speed and is designed to operate in the normal highway traffic environment. The use of a high-speed digital computer also made it possible to store measured road profile data on industry compatible magnetic tape for use as input to the newly evolving pavement management systems. This improved inertial profilometer is now in use in four states including Texas, West Virginia, Minnesota, and Ohio. These four inertial profilometer systems meet the requirements of ASTM Test Method for Measuring the Longitudinal Profile of Vehicular Traveled Surface with an Inertial Profilometer (E 950) [5].

This paper discusses the integration of a Law Model 690DNC inertial profilometer into the Ohio Department of Transportation (DOT) pavement management system and the use of pavement profile data measured with the inertial profilometer to provide pavement ride quality data for the system. In particular this paper discusses:

- calibration of the Ohio DOT Mays ride meter
- PSI from measured pavement profile
- need for nonroutine maintenance

Ohio Research Needs for Pavement Rating

As in other states and countries, budgetary pressures within the state of Ohio have established the need for objective procedures for rating the present condition of Ohio's highway inventory, identifying highway pavement repair needs, establishing priorities for nonroutine maintenance, and selecting cost-effective maintenance alternatives. Based on these needs, the Ohio Department of Transportation, in 1981, purchased a Law Model 690DNC noncontact inertial profilometer and an array of computer application programs designed to produce meaningful pavement management data. The Ohio Department of Transportation also entered into a research project with Surface Dynamics, Inc. to provide technical support for the integration of the inertial profilometer into the Ohio Department of Transportation pavement management system. This paper discusses some of the preliminary results of that research project.

Profilometer and Rating Panel Study

In the course of the Ohio DOT research project, the Ohio Department of Transportation was invited by Ketron, Inc. to participate in National Cooperative Highway research project (NCHRP) 1-23 [6]. Since the objectives of the NCHRP project were in line with the objectives of the Ohio DOT project, the invitation presented an opportunity for the Ohio DOT research project to benefit from a much larger joint research effort.

In this joint research effort, the Ohio DOT inertial profilometer was used to measure 52 Ohio pavement test sections made up of an equal number bituminous concrete, portland cement concrete, and composite surfaces representing a full range of pavement ride quality. At the same time, a 36 member Ohio rating panel was making a subjective ride quality evaluation of each of the 52 pavement test sections in accordance with an experiment design and instruction set developed by Ketron, Inc. for the NCHRP research project. The Ohio DOT Mays ride meter vehicle was also used to obtain Mays ride meter indices for the 52 pavement test sections.

In addition to providing a valuable data set for use in the National Cooperative Highway Research Program (NCHRP) Research Project 1-23, the joint effort also produced an equally valuable data set for the state of Ohio, which was specifically directed at the pavement conditions in the state of Ohio as they existed at that point in time. This data set and the processing of this data set will be treated in the next four sections of this paper.

PSI and Historical Ride Quality Data

One of the objectives of good pavement management system is to develop a long-term pavement condition data base that will allow the user to observe long-term pavement condition trends. One measure of pavement condition used by most transportation agencies is the present serviceability index (PSI). The present serviceability index concept was developed by Carey and Irick [7] at the American Association of State Highway and Transportation Officials (AASHTO) road test in the 1950s. In that work the investigators developed a mathematical transform between objective measurements made with the AASHTO profilometer and present serviceability ratings (PSR) obtained from subjective ride panel members. The present serviceability index concept has been carried forward through the years with mathematical transforms being developed for the various ride quality measuring devices that have emerged since the road test.

Carey and Irick [7] in the development of the present serviceability index concept at the AASHTO road test, defined two terms that assisted them in their development efforts. These terms are

• *Present Serviceability Rating (PSR)*—The mean of independent ratings by individuals of the present serviceability of a specific traveled surface.
• *Present Serviceability Index (PSI)*—The mathematical treatment of the physical measurement of a specific traveled surface so formulated as to predict the PSR for that surface within prescribed limits.

In the context of the Ohio DOT research project, the present serviceability rating (PSR) is mean subjective ride quality rating of the 36 member rating panel, for each of the 52 pavement test sections. The present serviceability index transform is the mathematical treatment that relates measured pavement profile to its present serviceability rating. And the present serviceability index is the quantity produced when measured pavement profile is transformed by its present serviceability index transform.

As mentioned earlier, the experimental design and instruction set used in the collection of the present serviceability rating data in Ohio was developed by Ketron, Inc. within the NCHRP Research Project 1-23 [6]. Also, within that project, the Ketron, Inc. investigators evaluated the effects of such variables as vehicle size, vehicle speed, prior training of the rating panel, and the regionality of the subjective rating panel. In their evaluation, they found that the use of a reasonable range of vehicle sizes and vehicle speeds does not influence the present serviceability rating of the pavement and suggest that these variables need not be measured in future panel ratings, although they should remain fixed within an individual panel rating experiment. Prior training of the rating panel also appears to have no effect, since both layman and experts from the same region or area subjectively rate roads the same. The NCHRP 1-23 investigators did find a small effect of panel regionality on present serviceability rating and suggest that state agencies should be aware that subjective rating panel results may be slightly different in different areas of the country. However, since the Ohio subjective ride quality ratings were made on pavements in the state of Ohio by an Ohio subjective rating panel, the regionality effect would have no bearing on the Ohio results.

The present serviceability rating of the 52 Ohio pavement test sections was performed by a 36 member Ohio rating panel in the fall of 1983. Most of the rating panel members were employees of the Ohio Department of Transportation with no prior experience in the rating of pavement ride quality. Four identical, current model, compact, Ohio DOT automobiles with drivers were used to drive the rating panel members over the test sections. All rating panel members were passengers with one passenger in the front seat and two in the rear seat.

In order to maintain continuity with the other parts of the NCHRP Research Project 1-23, Ketron, Inc. provided on-site supervision of the subjective ride quality data collection in Ohio, including the selection of the test sections, instruction to the test car drivers, and detailed instruction to the

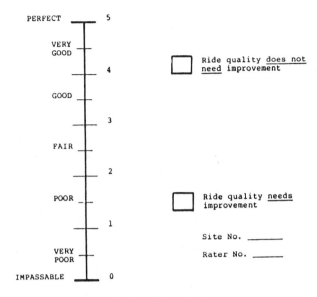

FIG. 1—*Ride quality rating form.*

rating panel members, which was personally given by a Ketron, Inc. staff member. Instruction to the rating panel members specifically addressed the pavement ride quality rating form (Fig. 1) to be used in the project, and instructed the panel members on how to convert their individual pavement ride quality evaluations to an entry on the ride quality rating form.

Calibration of the Ohio DOT Mays Ride Meter System

One of the objectives of the Ohio Department of Transportation Research Project was to develop a method for calibrating an existing Ohio DOT Mays ride meter system and to provide a link between the ride quality data obtained with that system and ride quality data obtained with the inertial profilometer.

The concurrent acquisition of mean subjective ride quality ratings (PSR), measured pavement profiles, and Ohio DOT Mays ride meter indices, for the 52 pavement test sections, provided an excellent test data set for the calibration and in-depth analysis of the performance of the Ohio DOT mays ride meter system.

The first step in the Mays ride meter performance analysis was to use the test data set to develop a calibration for the Ohio DOT mays ride meter system based on the measured pavement profiles. This calibration, shown graphically in Fig. 2, relates the actual Ohio DOT Mays ride meter index

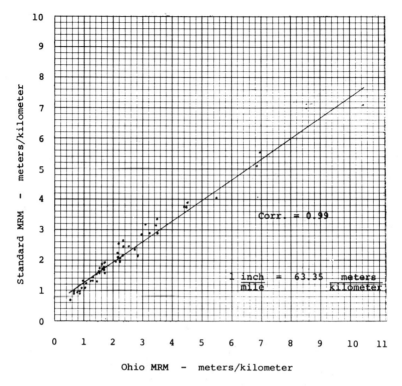

FIG. 2—*Ohio DOT Mays ride meter calibration.*

(abscissa), for each pavement test section, to the standard Mays ride meter index (ordinate) computed from the standard vehicle parameters developed by Gillespie et al. [8] in NCHRP Research Project 1-18. The high correlation ($r = 0.99$) for the actual and computed Mays ride meter indices shows that the actual mays ride meter system is linear, and that the computer simulation accurately models the mays ride meter system.

The relationship between the actual Ohio DOT Mays ride meter and the standard Mays ride meter index can be expressed by the following equation

$$\text{Standard MRM} = 0.59 + 0.68\,(\text{Ohio MRM}) \qquad (1)$$

where the Mays ride meter indices (MRM) are in units or metres per kilometer.

A point of interest and concern in the calibration transform (Fig. 2 and Eq 1) is the ordinate intercept value of 0.59. This means that the calibrated Ohio DOT Mays ride meter system would have a Mays ride meter index of 0.59

m/km for a perfect road, and all roads would have a Mays ride meter index greater than 0.59. Although this zero offset is of concern, no effort was made to find an explanation, since its effect is negated in the calibration. It does, however, highlight the need for calibration of Mays ride meter systems.

The second step in the Mays ride meter performance analysis used the mean subjective ride quality ratings (PSR) and the standard (calibrated) Ohio DOT mays ride meter indices to evaluate the ability of the Ohio DOT Mays ride meter system to measure pavement ride quality. This relationship is shown graphically in Fig. 3 where the standard Ohio DOT Mays ride meter index (abscissa) is plotted against subjective ride quality rating (PSR, ordinate) for each of the 52 pavement test sections.

A linear regression program was used to compute a least squares best-fit transform for the paired data points shown in Fig. 3. The resulting equation along with the correlation coefficient r are shown below

$$PSI = 4.00 - 0.49 \text{ (standard MRM)}$$
$$\text{correlation} = -0.75$$

where the standard MRM is in units of metres per kilometer. This transform

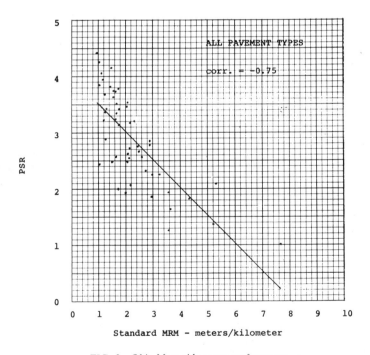

FIG. 3—*Ohio Mays ride meter performance.*

relates the Ohio DOT Mays ride meter index and the subjective ride quality rating (PSR) for all the pavement test sections made up of the three pavement types.

When the three pavement types are considered individually, the following transforms and correlation coefficients can be computed:

1. Bituminous concrete (Fig. 4):

    PSI = 4.02 −0.48 (standard MRM)
    correlation = −0.86

2. Portland cement concrete (Fig. 5):

    PSI = 4.57 −0.75 (standard MRM)
    correlation = −0.60

3. Composite (Fig. 6):

    PSI = 4.52 −0.91 (standard MRM)
    correlation = −0.63

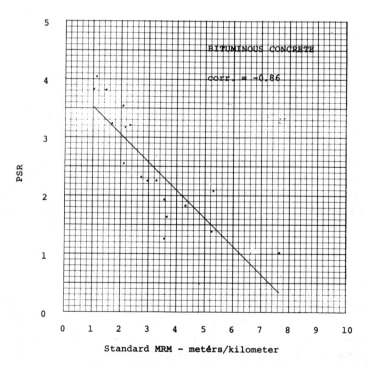

FIG. 4—*Ohio Mays ride meter performance.*

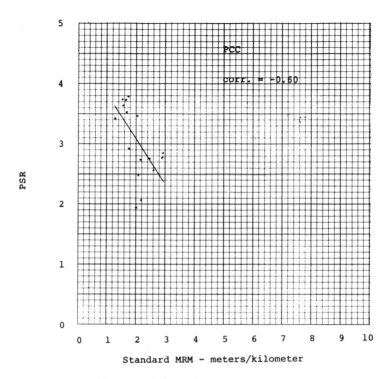

FIG. 5—*Ohio Mays ride meter performance.*

The PSI transforms for the three individual pavement types can be shown graphically on Fig. 7 as the best-fit straight line for the data points of each pavement type.

The high correlation coefficient (−0.86) for bituminous concrete shows that the Ohio DOT Mays ride meter measures the ride quality of bituminous concrete pavements more accurately than portland cement concrete and composite pavements. This finding also confirms the validity of practice in the highway community of using different transforms for different pavement types.

PSI from Measured Pavement Profile

A second objective of the Ohio Department of Transportation, in the purchase of the Law Model 69DNC inertial profilometer and the associated Ohio DOT research project, was to develop a transform between measured pavement profile and the present serviceability index (PSI) used as input to the Ohio DOT pavement management system.

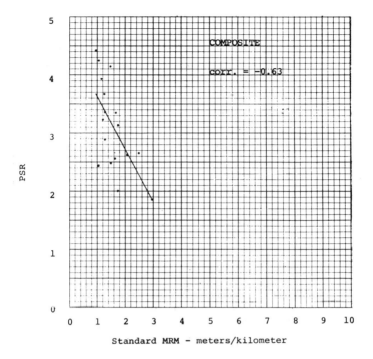

FIG. 6—*Ohio Mays ride meter performance.*

In the Ohio DOT research project, the subjective ride quality panel ratings, developed in the NCHRP Research Project 1-23 for each of the 52 pavement test sections was considered to be equivalent of the present serviceability rating (PSR) for each test section. Concurrent with the subjective ride quality rating, the profiles of the 52 pavement test sections were measured with the Ohio DOT inertial profilometer. The measured pavement profiles were stored on magnetic tape for use within the NCHRP Research Project 1-23 and by the Ohio DOT research project investigators. The 52 data pairs, consisting of present serviceability rating and measured pavement profile, then made up the ride quality data set used in the Ohio DOT research project to develop transforms between measured pavement profile and the present serviceability index.

The transform presented here treats the measured pavement profile as a continuous function of distance in the spatial domain. As a result the present serviceability index can be computed continuously in real time as the pavement profile is being measured. The transformation used in this computation is described by the following equation

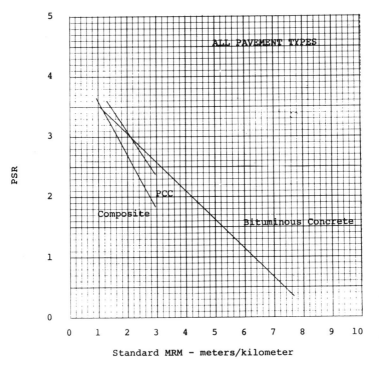

FIG. 7—*Ohio Mays ride meter performance.*

$$\text{PSI} = 4.54 - 75.2\left[\text{rms}\left[\frac{S^2}{S^2 + 2\zeta\omega S + \omega^2}\right]P\right] \tag{2}$$

where

PSI = present serviceability index,
rms = root mean square,
P = measured pavement profile, m,
S = complex operator, 1/m,
ω = spatial natural frequency = 0.33 cycles/m, and
ζ = damping ratio = 0.7.

In the PSI transform of Eq 2, the quantity inside the brackets can be expressed as the root mean square (rms) of the spatial Laplace transform of the measured pavement profile. In effect, what the transform does is to compute the present serviceability index (PSI) by taking the root mean square of the short wavelength acceleration content of the measured pavement profile.

The resulting high correlation of this transform for all the pavement types measured is illustrated graphically in Fig. 8 by plotting the transformed PSI of each of the 52 measured pavement profile data points against their corresponding present serviceability rating (PSR). A linear regression program was used to compute a least squares best-fit line for the plotted data points with a resulting correlation coefficient r of 0.91.

The high correlation of the transformed pavement profile with present serviceability rating is impressive, since the correlation is for bituminous concrete, portland cement concrete, and composite pavements over a full range of pavement roughnesses. Also from the findings of the NCHRP Research Project 1-23, the transform is valid for a reasonable range of vehicle sizes and is independent of vehicle speed.

The present serviceability index transform presented here was developed within a currently active Ohio DOT research project. Work in the develop-

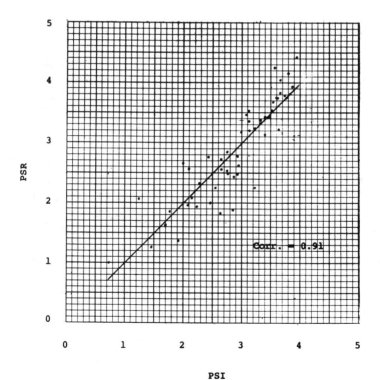

FIG. 8—*PSI transform correlation.*

ment of PSI transforms will continue in hopes of finding a transform that might have a higher correlation coefficient r than the 0.91 found to date.

Need for Nonroutine Maintenance

A third objective of Ohio DOT research project was to demonstrate the use of measured pavement profiles to establish PSI monitoring trigger values for nonroutine pavement maintenance.

Here again the ride quality data developed in the joint NCHRP 1-23 and Ohio DOT research project was available for use in this effort. One of the items on the ride quality rating form (Fig. 1), designed by Ketron, Inc. for the NCHRP Research Project 1-23, is a question on the need for ride quality improvement for the pavement test section being evaluated.

Although the answer to the question was either yes or no, the data were processed by Ketron, Inc. to produce the percentage of the 36 member Ohio

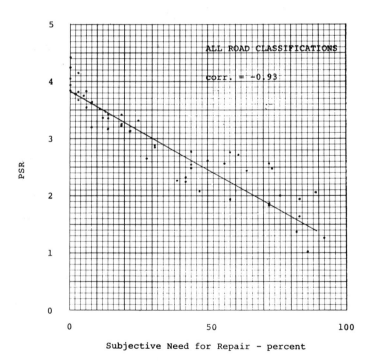

FIG. 9—*Need for nonroutine maintenance.*

rating panel who felt there was a need to improve ride quality for each of the 52 sites. This data, when plotted (Fig. 9) against the present serviceability rating (PSR) is badly scattered. Although the correlation coefficient for the least square best-fit line is high ($r = -0.93$), the data does not make much sense. However, when a linear regression program was used to compute the individual least square best-fit lines for the six Ohio DOT functional road classifications, relationships like those shown in Figs. 10 and 11 are produced. The least square best-fit lines for each of the six Ohio DOT function road classifications are shown in Fig. 12.

Since the question on need for improved ride quality could only be answered yes or no, it is felt that the subjective need for repair data is the most accurate around the 50% point. This area in Fig. 12 was, therefore, expanded in Fig. 13 for more detailed study. The PSR levels at the 50% point for the six Ohio DOT functional road classifications and their correlation coefficients are in Table 1.

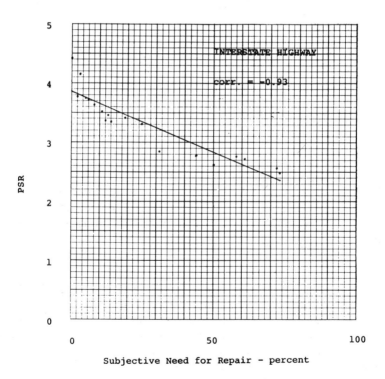

FIG. 10—*Need for nonroutine maintenance.*

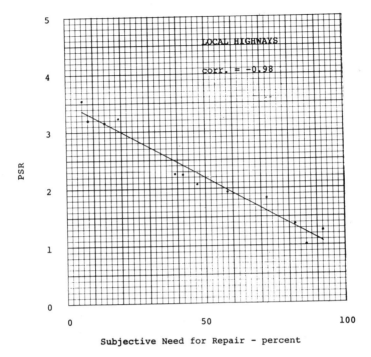

FIG. 11—*Need for nonroutine maintenance.*

The distribution of these lines and their high correlation coefficients *r* tend to indicate the traveling public is quite discerning with regard to the ride quality they expect for the various Ohio functional road classifications. The resulting PSR levels are evenly distributed over the full range of functional road classifications and are good candidates for use as trigger values for nonroutine pavement maintenance in the Ohio DOT pavement management system.

With these relationships, the Ohio DOT can measure road profile with the Ohio DOT inertial profilometer and make a rational decision on its need for nonroutine maintenance without getting involved in an extensive subjective ride quality evaluation of each of the pavements in the Ohio DOT highway inventory. Although it is expected that these trigger values will not change appreciably with time, it is suggested that the values be confirmed periodically until their time stability is confirmed.

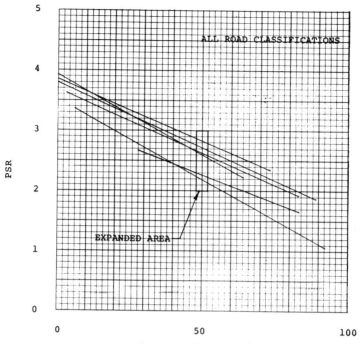

FIG. 12—*Need for nonroutine maintenance.*

TABLE 1—*PSR levels at the 50% point for the six Ohio DOT functional road classifications and their correlation coefficients.*

Functional Road Classification	Trigger Values for Nonroutine Maintenance	Correlation Coefficient r
Interstate	2.82	−0.92
Principal arterial	2.72	−0.97
Minor arterial	2.62	−0.99
Major collector	2.60	−0.96
Minor collector	2.27	−0.97
Local	2.19	−0.98

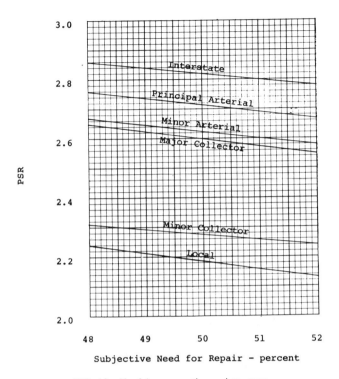

FIG. 13—*Need for nonroutine maintenance.*

References

[1] Spangler, E. B. and Kelly, W. J., "GMC Road Profilometer — A Method for Measuring Road Profile," Highway Research Record 121, Washington, DC, 1966.

[2] Darlington, J. R. and Milliman, P., "A Progress Report on the Evaluation and Application Study of the General Motors Rapid Travel Road Profilometer," Highway Research Record 214, Washington, DC, 1968, pp. 50-67.

[3] Burchett, J. L., Rizenbergs, R. L., and Moore, T. A., "Surface Dynamics Profilometer and Quarter-Car Simulator: Description, Evaluation, and Adaptation," Research Report 465, Kentucky Department of Transportation, Lexington, 1977.

[4] Hudson, W. R., "High-Speed Road Profile Equipment Evaluation," Highway Research Record 189, Washington, DC, 1967, pp. 150-163.

[5] 1985 Annual Book of ASTM Standards, Vol. 04.03, American Society for Testing and Materials, Philadelphia, 1985.

[6] Janoff, M. S., Nick, J. B., Davit, P. S., and Hayhoe, G. F., "Pavement Roughness and Ride Quality," NCHRP Report 275, Washington, DC, 1985.

[7] Carey, W. N. and Irick, P. E., "The Pavement Serviceability Performance Concept," Highway Research Board Bulletin 250, Washington, DC, 1960.

[8] Gillespie, T. D., Sayers, M. W., and Segel, L., "Calibration of Response-Type Road Roughness Measuring Systems," NCHRP Report 228, Washington, DC, 1980.

Author Index

Subject Index